# KING HENRY V

Philip Lindsay

# KING

# HENRY V

## A Chronicle

HOWARD BAKER, LONDON

Philip Lindsay
KING  HENRY  V


©   Copyright, Philip Lindsay, 1934


Originally published in Great Britain
by Ivor Nicholson and Watson, November 1934


Howard Baker Edition, 1969


Howard Baker Books are published
by Howard Baker Publishers Limited,
47 Museum Street, London W.C.1.


SBN  09  304960  9


Printed in Great Britain by
Stephen Austin & Sons Ltd.,
and bound by Wm. Brendon & Sons Ltd.,
of Tiptree, Essex

*Dedication*

*for*

HUGH ROSS WILLIAMSON

My dear Williamson,

*It is with a deep sense of pride that I write your name on this page, and, let me add, also with a certain sense of shame. As you know, the book intended for you, the book you directly inspired, I have been forced to lay aside because of one of those accidents always threatening writers of history. Another had got there before me. And now, glancing through the typed pages of what I have written, I deeply regret that accident. I feel that the other would have been a book more worthy of you. But I suppose I would think that about any book I wrote.*

*We are both lovers of English history, and by one of those lucky flukes, our periods do not conflict. Mine is the medieval-renascence, a large ground, and yours is mainly the seventeenth century—on my death-bed I will still implore you to write that most necessary life of Cromwell! In saying this, I hasten to add that I make no further comparison between our work. That would indeed be a rash act for anybody to attempt with the author of* John Hampden, *one of the greatest modern historical biographies.*

*I intended to speak here to you about this book itself,*

DEDICATION

but what can I say when the book lies before you, awaiting anxiously your praise or condemnation? It is a life of Henry V, of one of the greatest medieval Kings, a tale of heroism and of tragedy. . . . But this you know as well as I. And if the retold story does not stir you, the fault is mine—the author's, not the actor's.

One point, however, I must remark, and that is my effort to be accurate and impartial in everything. You know what a confusion of lies medieval history is, and therefore I feel a certain security in your judgment. You will not condemn me too hastily, because you will appreciate the difficulties that stood in my path. I have never ignored these difficulties, and if I have scaled some of them rather clumsily it was not for want of effort.

I have tried here to write, not a constitutional or diplomatic history, but a personal biography. If I have strayed from the path occasionally, it is because the tracks opening on every side have been too tempting to ignore. Perhaps I have written too largely on the Lollards, and yet I felt that their story must be told, or the reader would believe, seeing only Henry, that the fifteenth century was passively acquiescent under the Catholic Church, which it most certainly was not. The Reformation had already begun with John Wycliffe; how strong it grew can be seen by the ease with which Henry VIII swept the Pope aside in the sixteenth century. There was only the protest of the Pilgrimage of Grace in the north, and that was political as well as being religious. The rest of England accepted the act because it was the culmination of their own desires inherited from the fifteenth century, from the Lollards.

# DEDICATION

*I have written too much already, and with reluctance I must lay my pen aside—with reluctance, because every word I write keeps you from the awful moment when you will first begin seriously reading the book itself, and when I must await your judgment. Let me imitate my hero, King Henry V, and be brave, let me stand aside. . . .*

*But I have not explained why I feel particularly both pride and shame in placing your name before my book. Let me say that my pride is because I so deeply admire your work, and my shame is because this book is not worthy of being offered you.*

PHILIP LINDSAY.

LONDON, N.W. 8.

# CONTENTS

# CONTENTS

Agincourt, Agincourt!
Know ye not Agincourt?
Dear was the vict'ry bought
    By fifty yeomen.
Ask any English wench,
They were worth all the French,
    Rare English Bowmen!

ANON

# PROLOGUE

W E have not one contemporary statement giving the birth of the child who became King Henry V of England. So unimportant was the event considered that no man bothered to note it. In all England no pen was pressed on paper to record the fact that the future conqueror at Agincourt was wailing in the midwife's arm. And it is only recently that the date has been definitely fixed by a statement of one of Henry's chaplains, Thomas Elmham, who places the great day as September 16, 1387.

Future generations, eager for marvels, rummaging fruitlessly into the past, invented the usual stories. And a hundred or so years later a cradle was actually made—and can still be seen in the London Museum—purporting to be Henry's.

One story tells that the father was at Windsor when the boy was born, and that as he hurried across the Wye to Monmouth, the first person to tell him the news was the ferryman. This may be true. Certainly we know that Henry was born at Monmouth Castle.

Beyond that we know nothing. Another story, and a likely one, informs us that the child was sickly and that he was taken from the castle and nursed in the nearby manor of Courtfield.

The mother was young, only sixteen, but we must not forget that a girl of sixteen in those days was equivalent to a girl of about twenty in these modern times of retarded physical and mental development. The father was two years older than his wife. And you must also remember that this was not Mary de Bohun's first child. She had produced a boy at the age of twelve, although he did not live long. It does not seem that these early marriages were really very harmful. After Henry the babies appear with clocklike regularity, with barely a year between each, and they all lived to manhood or womanhood, although it is true that the mother herself died young.

In silence Henry enters history, and this silence continues for many years, apart from references to his wardrobe. Until he is crowned we watch him with a certain suspicion, unable to make up our minds about him. Only through official records can he be glimpsed fully, although his was an active youth. Much of his behaviour is still doubtful. There are the tales of early debaucheries, perpetuated for ever in Shakespeare's magnificent dramas, over which historians still squabble.

But this argument can be safely left to a later chapter. Henry is still only a baby in the arms of his nurse, Joan, his tiny limbs bound fiercely in the swaddling cloths to make them grow straight and firm.

There we must leave him for a short time while we speak of his father and mother, even of his grandfather, and take a rapid survey of England under King Richard II.

Henry's father—also Henry—was the eldest surviving son of John, Duke of Lancaster, called Gaunt, because the English of the time couldn't get their tongues round Ghent, his birthplace. Gaunt was King Richard's uncle, and when Richard's father lay on his death-bed, he placed Gaunt first amongst his executors. Gaunt kept the trust which his brother put into his hands, despite the insistence of his enemies that he failed to do so. He has suffered much from the hatred of later generations: it has been said that he strove to usurp the throne, it has even been suggested that he sold England and that he conspired against his nephew.

We do not have to dig far to discover the root of these calumnies. Although a most devout Christian, Gaunt for political reasons stood behind that great man, the reformer, John Wycliffe. That was an act which the Church found it hard to forgive. Wycliffe, with his frenzied attacks on simony and on the money that was eating purity from the Church, would perhaps have been murdered if Gaunt's iron hand had not been there to protect him. The monkish chroniclers splash ink like gall on his name; one can see the little hunched-up monks grinning as their pens scrabble over the paper, spitting insult after insult at the name of John of Gaunt.

Gaunt was no blameless man, but he was certainly not the rascal that most writers have made him appear. I confess that I too thought him far worse than he was before I began to study the period closely. Then all my sympathies went out to one who strove so patiently to withstand the irresponsible, almost lunatic, spite of young King Richard II.

For some reason, probably because of his youth, Richard has usually inspired historians with pity.

Perhaps too, it is because of Shakespeare's play where the half-poetic prince wishes to sit upon the ground and tell sad stories of the deaths of Kings. Richard was actually no poetic youth—although a patron of literature. He was undoubtedly a murderer; he had a most tremendous temper—with a stick he thrashed Arundel in Westminster Abbey while Queen Anne's burial service was taking place, because Arundel arrived late and wanted to go early—; he was spiteful, jealous, a debauchee and an extravagant dandy. We must not make too hasty a judgment, however, because Richard's upbringing had much to do with his behaviour; and he had many good points: he was a patron of art and he strove always for peace with France.

Just as I can feel pity for Gaunt trying to calm a wilful nephew, so can I feel pity for that nephew being bullied by his uncles. But Gaunt was by no means the worst of those uncles.

Gaunt had many children, but few of them lived. The eldest boy to live was Henry—father of Henry V—all the other sons died in infancy, except for those borne by his third wife, Katherine Swynford. Katherine's marriage was a rather hurried one and it scandalised the whole court. She had been in the household of Gaunt's first wife, and she remained there after her death and during Gaunt's second marriage—a purely political one—with Constance of Castile. Her husband, Sir Hugh, was also alive at the time, but this did not stop Katherine from producing four children—John, Henry, Thomas and Joan, surnamed Beaufort, and all publicly known as Gaunt's. Sir Hugh died fighting in Aquitaine in 1372, Constance died in 1394, and Gaunt married Katherine in 1396, after a liaison lasting over twenty years. When one considers the usual treatment of mistresses in those days Gaunt's act was a very noble one, and it brought much ridicule upon him. But he married for the children's sake, and King Richard declared them legitimate, although it appears that the act of marriage itself would legitimise them, according to Canon Law.

These were to be Henry V's uncles, vastly different from Richard's.

When Henry was born in Monmouth Castle, Gaunt was not in England. He was off on that superbly hopeless venture—a mixture of temporal and spiritual ambition—the conquest of Castile. I regret that we must not waste time upon this, although it is a fascinating tale of ambition and despair. We have to remain in England with the father of Henry V, Gaunt's eldest living son.

This man was the only child Gaunt left in England when he sailed for Spain, and he was the man whom Richard most wanted to get rid of. Henry, Earl of Derby, was a brave soldier, of the same age as Richard, both being born in 1367—Henry in April, Richard in January—, and they were first cousins, but they were the opposites in temperament. Henry was a patient man, far-seeing and courageous, who took his responsibilities most seriously; Richard never cared for anybody except himself, his first wife, a few men favourites and a collection of old women; least of all did he care for England. Conflict between these two men was inevitable.

B

It is impossible to cut history up into chapters headed by the names of Kings, as schoolbooks do. Each King overlaps the other, and the sins of one are the heritage of his successor. If I opened this book with the coronation of King Henry V much would be inexplicable. For the understanding of Henry's reign and of the condition of his throne it is essential that we begin with Richard. And I now find that I shall be doing Richard a great injustice if I refrain from telling the reader a little about his grandfather, King Edward III.

Edward was presumably an exceptionally handsome man with a subtle grace of manners. When a youth he had been a brave soldier and that had gained him the love of England. Always the memory of his splendid youth returned to those who were horrified by the corruption of his last years. And he had such charm that the angriest man could be soothed, no matter how strong the justice of his complaints. Being entirely unprincipled, Edward would make the most dazzling promises which he never intended to keep. It was by this gift that he held his people in control. Yet he had one attribute very necessary to a great King—he was a cunning judge of men and knew well how to choose his ministers.

He ruled for fifty years. His father had been murdered by rebellious nobles, and Edward had been trained by those same nobles. Later he was to seek revenge, and by his conquests in France it seemed at first that England had at last a perfect King. Even when no one could doubt that Edward was in decay, when his court and even the country, was ruled by his mistress, Alice Perrers, the people clung to him. His son, Edward of Woodstock—

whom later generations, for no presumable reason, were to label the Black Prince—was adored by every one. A brave man and a noble leader, there seemed nothing in Prince Edward to which one could object. Those who hated the father looked towards the son for a future of conquest and honour.

But the son died. He died before his father, and for the first time Parliament dared really show its hatred of Alice Perrers and the King's corrupt ministers. It has been said, though with small reason, that the Black Prince was fighting on the side of the reform party. At any rate his death drove that party to despair because the future then became black indeed. The Prince's eldest brother, John of Gaunt, did his best to quieten the people, but his efforts only drew their hatred upon him as well. He struggled futilely against Parliament and against the Church. It seems that at this period Gaunt was actuated by only the finest principles. He may have been with the wrong party, the court party, but it seems that he was blinded by loyalty. He was no friend of Alice Perrers, yet he stood beside her and his father because that was the right thing for him to do, because all his training, his belief in honour and chivalry, demanded that he fight for his own people, even if he knew that those people were corrupt and worthless.

The Black Prince had left one son, Richard of Bordeaux. Brought up in a palace of intrigue, a minor permitted no will of his own, the young King treasured his resentments, waiting for an opportunity for revenge. On Gaunt was concentrated his deepest hatred, because Gaunt was the strongest man in England and his eldest living uncle. By his marriage with the Lancastrian heiress Blanche—of whom Chaucer sang so sweetly—Gaunt had estates dotted all over the country, some of which took in great sweeps of England. He was as powerful as the King. Yet never once, despite the lies spread about him, do we find Gaunt really abusing this power.

As Richard had no children he decided to place his inheritance in the hands of his father's eldest living brother's children. At the age of sixteen he had married Anne, daughter of the Emperor Charles. Unlike most political marriages the couple seem to have been extremely contented together, probably because they were more comrades than lovers, and Richard was heart-broken at her death in 1394. Although he was then twenty-eight, the problem of an heir never seemed to bother him; it is likely that he had no intention of having children. Richard's sexual character is rather a problem and on many points resembles that of his great-grandfather Edward II, but of course we cannot be definite on such questions. At any rate women interested him so little—or it may have been that he reverenced the memory of Queen Anne—that he married next a child of eight, Isabel, daughter of Charles VI, the mad King of France. He seemed perfectly content to leave the throne of England to Roger, Earl of March, grandson of the Duke of Clarence, third son of Edward III. Much of Richard's recklessness, his contempt for the wishes of the people, might be put down to the fact that the throne died with him; other kings have been forced to restrain their selfishness for the sake of their sons.

Although one cannot help being angered by Richard's stupidities and extravagance, it would be unfair to damn him out of hand. We must remember that Edward III left the country in a state of almost complete exhaustion. It would have taken a genius like Edward I or Henry II to reconstruct England after such a reign, and Richard was no genius. He took the easy path and followed his grandfather, without possessing his grandfather's charm or cunning.

It had seemed when he was a boy that there was much of the Black Prince in him, for at the age of fourteen he had calmly faced the furious peasants under Wat Tyler. Henry V's father was with him at the time, and Richard showed a courage that older men might have envied. At Smithfield, with a small following, he sat his horse before the rebels and showed no wink of fear. A valet present remarked that Tyler was "the greatest thief and robber in Kent," on which the rebel drew his dagger and would have stabbed the man. The mayor of London, William Walworth, strove to arrest Tyler, and Tyler struck at him; but the mayor wore a shirt of mail beneath his gown, and the point jarred off his chest. In his turn Walworth drew his baselard—half-dagger, half-sword—and stabbed Tyler on neck and head, while a valet— or footman—struck him on the chest. The rebels strung their bows but before they could fire, young Richard rode boldly to them, spurring to their front ranks, crying, "I will be your captain; follow me!" And by his fearlessness he conquered the peasants. That was the only occasion on which he proved himself the son of the Black Prince.

After his death Richard was labelled the

"Redeless"—the Shiftless—and it is a title that suits him. Looking back on history, we see so clearly the foolish acts of men and women that we feel we can judge them with a lofty air of omnipotence, yet we have little right to judge them. We are calm in our studies or ferreting about in libraries or museums, we are not faced with calamities at every point; we may have our petty problems—domestic troubles, debts and such—but what are they to the problems that faced a medieval King?

I would rather have been the poorest of those wretched peasants who dragged his starved limbs to Smithfield than King Richard II. The peasant had a tangible enemy, he had the King to revile, the King's ministers, or the priest who took a third of his goods for tithes; but what could a King do? He was lonely in his palace, he was watched and bullied and cajoled and cheated. Richard, I feel, was almost conscious of his own foolishness. Deliberately he made himself a bad prince in rage against his uncles and against the broken heritage left him by his grandfather.

Richard passed this heritage on to Roger, Earl of March, as has been said. But in 1398 Roger was killed fighting in Ireland. He left two sons, Edmund and Roger, and to these boys would descend the crown if Richard should die childless.

Of the same age as his King, Henry Plantagenet —later called Bolingbroke, because of his birthplace—the eldest surviving son of John of Gaunt, was, it seemed, all that Richard was not. And although we have no proof of any man's emotions it is more than likely that Richard was deeply jealous of his brave cousin-german.

It was not so much the cousin who was hated as the uncle. When at last Gaunt left for that insane crusade of his in search of the crown of Castile, Richard probably felt that he was free, that he had rid himself of his most powerful master. It was not long before he was wailing for that master's return.

Richard's other uncle, the youngest, Thomas of Woodstock, Duke of Gloucester, jumped into Gaunt's place as head of the council. But Gloucester was made of different stuff from his brother. He was not content to guide the King, he wanted to be King, he wanted absolute dictatorship.

Sided with him were many of England's most powerful nobles—Warwick, Arundel, Nottingham and Henry, Earl of Derby, father of Henry V. Henry was not completely with his uncle, he was too cautious a man to pledge himself beyond the danger-point. Warwick and Arundel were probably sincere enough, hating the King's favourites more than the King, particularly Robert de Vere, Earl of Oxford, a futile creature. The last of these nobles, Thomas Mowbray, Earl of Nottingham, is the one for whom we can have least respect. He was a rascal without the sincerity of Warwick and Arundel, the ambitious strength of Gloucester or the sanity of Henry. He was out to take what he could get and was ready to be bought by either party.

The conflict reached a head when Richard made de Vere Duke of Ireland. Gloucester saw his chance, knowing how the favourite was detested by everybody, and he made a wholesale sweep of all Richard's ministers and friends. He convicted the chancellor, Michael de la Pole, Earl of Suffolk, on the flimsiest of evidence of malversation; his property was confiscated and his person locked in the Tower until he could pay a monstrous fine. With Suffolk out of the way Gloucester showed his real aim, he demanded the power of regency. This was too much for Richard. He had been bullied for years now, and he had no sooner ceased from rejoicing over Gaunt's trip to Castile than an even more abominable uncle appeared. He rebelled.

This by the way was in 1386, before the death of Queen Anne, before Richard became entirely hopeless so far as England's faith in him was concerned. He was as yet hated mainly for his desire for peace and because of his insolent favourite, de Vere. As Arundel put it in later years, the people objected to "government by boys and widows," for Richard loved elderly ladies, who probably toyed with him and gave him a girlish pleasure with their admiration and their stupid advice.

When Gloucester came forward with his preposterous demands, Richard took Suffolk out of prison and treated him with more than usual affection. He gathered his friends about him, leaving Gloucester and his council in London to argue about France and the English navy, and plotted to raise the country against his enemies. He made one foolish slip—he tried prematurely to arrest Arundel, an insolent man who said what he thought, which was usually something insulting. The barons immediately prepared for battle and were soon organised. De Vere was defeated utterly by Henry of Bolingbroke, and fled to France.

It had been Henry, Gaunt's son, who had

thrashed his most beloved friend, and Richard must have concentrated his jealous hatred on this man of his own age who seemed his strongest enemy. Gloucester was brutal and obvious in his intentions, but Henry was a soldier and a calm, secretive man. If it had been a pitched battle Henry's victory might not have been so galling; but so hated was the favourite that de Vere's men flung down their banners at Henry's command and refused to fight against him. Henry had conquered without a blow being struck. That was unforgivable.

Richard did not forget. He was waiting until he reached the age of twenty-one. After that, Gloucester would have no legal excuse for retaining the power, and as for Henry . . . Richard was probably not quite sure what he would do to Henry; he could safely leave time to give him the opportunity for revenge.

On May 3, 1389, Richard declared himself of age. It is rather curious that Gloucester had not prepared himself for this move, as it seems the obvious one for Richard to make. Perhaps Gloucester did not trouble greatly about it, relying on Richard's weakness and his lack of friends. He does not seem to have realised that himself had now probably fewer friends even than Richard, for he had been most arrogant in his rule.

Although Gloucester might have been prepared for Richard's first move, it is by no means likely that he anticipated the next—and most cunning—move. Richard demanded the recall of John of Gaunt.

Gaunt had appeared the demon in the old days,

but Richard was wiser now. He realised that he had not the strength to stand alone, and that there was only one man in England powerful enough to protect him.

Gaunt delayed his return but Richard could not wait. He insisted that he come back immediately. And Gaunt had to give in. He landed at Plymouth, November 19, 1389.

From that moment Gloucester was doomed. It was not that he and Gaunt were enemies— there is no suggestion of that—but Gloucester knew perfectly well that with his elder brother in England, himself had no power, and also he knew that the King was treacherous.

He was soon to learn how treacherous the King was, although one can scarcely blame Richard for seeking revenge. It is his method of seeking revenge with which one quarrels.

He waited his chance with extraordinary patience for so reckless a man. It was not until 1397 that he showed that he had not forgotten. He stated suddenly that his enemies were plotting treason and he named the Duke of Gloucester, the Earls of Arundel and Warwick, and the Abbot of Westminster. He acted cunningly: he invited these "traitors" to a banquet at Coldharbour, near St. Paul's. Warwick was the only one trusting enough to accept the invitation and he was immediately arrested and sent to the Tower. Arundel, having no doubt about what was intended, didn't even bother to answer Richard's request; he locked himself into his castle at Reigate. Gloucester with appalling lack of foresight pleaded that he was too ill to leave home. He could not have pleaded a more dangerous excuse. He was arrested by Richard personally, having been taken so completely by surprise that he wasn't dressed and had but a few chaplains with him. After jeering at him with boyish malice Richard sent his uncle to Calais in the charge of Mowbray, Earl of Nottingham—the rascal who had been one of Gloucester's associates in the coup of 1386 and of whom we shall hear more later.

Was there a conspiracy or did Richard invent the charge? I rather doubt if there was one. The story comes mainly from Froissart, and Richard was one of Froissart's patrons. Gloucester may have been a tactless bad-tempered bully, but he must have realised that with his brother Gaunt in control, a conspiracy would have small hope of success.

Gloucester was taken to Calais and he never came back. We have little proof but we scarcely need any to state that Gloucester was murdered by Mowbray's ruffians at Richard's command. One of Mowbray's men, John Hall, confessed after Richard's deposition that Gloucester was carried from Calais Castle to a house called Prince's Inn and was there smothered with a "feather bed." There is no reason to disbelieve this.

In Westminster, during Parliament, on September 17, Richard formally impeached Gloucester, Warwick, Arundel and the Abbot of Westminster, Arundel's brother. The captain of Calais certified that Gloucester was dead—his excuse of illness coming in handy here—but this did not stop Richard from attainting him of high treason so that he could take his lands. The abbot was banished, as also was Warwick. On Arundel fell the full penalty. He was a brave reckless man, this Arundel, and when Gaunt as seneschal questioned him, he answered only with terrible insults and jeers. He knew that he was doomed and he preferred to die fighting. It is certainly a magnificent picture that history gives us here of Arundel lounging back contemptuously and answering with scoffs and brutal contempt anything asked of him, speaking "with more passion than discretion." His accusers shouted at him, everybody seems to have lost his temper. The eight appellants actually danced on the floor with rage. "Traitor! Liar!" they bellowed. Arundel insisted that he had been pardoned in full—referring to a pardon given in 1387—but Richard had revoked that and he could not claim immunity there. "Truly thou liest," cried Arundel when told of this with the insult "traitor " added; "never was I traitor!" And when Gaunt therefore asked if he was no traitor why did he seek a pardon, "To close the mouths of mine enemies," retorted Arundel with splendid courage, "of whom thou art one. And in truth, as for treasons, thou needest pardon more than I."

He was sentenced to the usual penalty of being drawn, hanged and beheaded and quartered, and his lands confiscated; Richard commuted the worst details and Arundel died that same day.

I have wasted too large a space on this "conspiracy," but Arundel's impeachment is so colourful a scene that I could not dismiss it entirely. Besides, it reveals the new Richard, the man growing out of the wilful boy who had had all his worst qualities coaxed by the widows who so horrified Arundel. He has now a man's ability to plot and a man's patience to see that the plot is carried through to the end. For the first time Richard felt the terrible satisfaction of power and it intoxicated him. From now, his life is nothing but scheming, revenge and traitorous acts.

And his waiting proved the best policy. Shortly two others fell to him and one of these was the father of Henry V.

This episode must be dwelt on more fully, for from it begins the whole of the Lancastrian usurpation. It is from this moment that Henry of Monmouth, still a child, draws closer to the throne.

Henry, Earl of Derby, was now Duke of Hereford, but to avoid confusion it would be perhaps safest to call him Bolingbroke, as that is the name given him by most historians. You will remember that he had been involved with his uncle Gloucester in the rising against Richard, and that he had defeated de Vere. Nevertheless he was cunning enough to avoid impeachment—or perhaps the influence of his father Gaunt protected him. You will also remember that Thomas Mowbray, Duke of Norfolk—then Earl of Nottingham—had also been involved in this rising but had quickly shifted his allegiance to Richard, and at Richard's command had had Gloucester murdered in Calais.

One day in 1398, between Parliamentary sittings, these two newly created dukes were riding together from Brentford to London. It is very unfortunate that we have only one story of what took place—Bolingbroke's story; Mowbray's side of it we shall never know. At the same time there seems little reason to doubt Bolingbroke; he may have exaggerated a few points but basically his story rings true, although Mowbray's stupidity seems incredible unless we believe him to have been drunk at the time.

He talked in a panic-stricken manner about conspiracies, about Richard's cunning and spite. He said that himself was in danger, that Bolingbroke was in danger and that Gaunt also was in danger. Bolingbroke listened carefully, then told his father; his father sent him to Richard.

Secretly Richard must have smiled as Bolingbroke told of Mowbray's treachery. No King likes to have near him men who know too much, as Mowbray knew too much about Gloucester's end. He commanded Bolingbroke to impeach Mowbray at the coming Shrewsbury Parliament.

Mowbray was not present when Bolingbroke rose in his place and repeated that treasonable conversation, and a writ was issued demanding him to answer within fifteen days. Eventually it was decided that the two dukes should fight it out in the old fashion—by arms, in the lists.

It is an interesting comment on the state of armourers in England in those days that both men got their harness from abroad: Bolingbroke from Milan—the armourers' centre—and Mowbray from Bohemia.

There was enormous excitement about the outcome, Bolingbroke being favourite. The meeting was to take place at Coventry, on Monday, September 16, 1398.

Historians have spoken of Bolingbroke's act as one of treachery, but surely he cannot be blamed for seeking his revenge? He took it openly, not by any trick such as Richard would have used. Mowbray had intrigued with Bolingbroke and had then deserted for the other side; he had murdered Bolingbroke's uncle, Gloucester.

England, as a matter of fact, seemed to believe that this was a judgment on Mowbray for that act. It was God showing His hand at last. So great was the crush this morning in September that, apart from the usual palisades, a wet ditch had to be dug around the lists. Bolingbroke arrived at nine o'clock and on receiving the constable's challenge, he gave his name and swore that he had come to do his duty against that false traitor, Thomas Mowbray, Duke of Norfolk. He then took the oath that he believed in the justice of his cause, crossed himself, and rode to his seat, which was draped with the arms of St. George and was covered with cloths so that he could not be spied on. Richard came next with his friends and his guard. And after Richard, Mowbray arrived, who submitted to the same formula as Bolingbroke.

While the people were thrilled by the romantic idea of a joust, the great men of the realm watched Richard anxiously. A battle like this between such lords was not right and many had pleaded with Richard to prevent it from taking place. Richard had said nothing. He had learned the delight of secrecy, the small boy's pleasure in keeping others in suspense. Knowing himself what he intended, he probably enjoyed the sight of Gaunt's worry and of the other nobles' anxiety.

Into the lists rode Bolingbroke and Mowbray. Their lances were tested, measured and returned. Each combatant pushed his lance into its rest and gazed up through the narrow slit in the great helm which was buckled down so that it could not move. Sheathed in steel, horse and man, they waited for the signal, each at opposite ends of the list, the long barrier—the tilt—between them.

"Faitez vos devoirs!" cried the heralds. "Laissez les aller!"

Bolingbroke had actually pulled on the reins and started his horse when King Richard lifted his hand and flung down the baton.

It was for this moment that he had waited, keeping them all in painful perplexity while he savoured their agony. And even now he was not satisfied. For two long hours Bolingbroke and Mowbray stayed in their places, astride their horses, fidgeting, wondering, while the King talked apart with his councillors. For two hours he kept those men in gnawing suspense before he sent out a messenger with a parchment roll giving his decision.

When it was heard that Bolingbroke must leave England for ten years the people shouted their fury. But Mowbray's sentence soon followed: he was banished for the term of his natural life.

Richard probably congratulated himself on his cunning. Actually he should have bewailed his stupidity. On the surface this seems a very clever trick to rid himself at one blow of two men whom he feared, but every act has its repercussions. The injustice of such a sentence aroused popular feeling for Bolingbroke and eventually cleared the way for him to grasp at Richard's throne. Nobody felt sorry for Mowbray. He was Richard's assassin and deserved anything his master might do to him. Nevertheless, it was definitely treacherous for Richard to destroy a man who had merely done his bidding.

Both dukes had to leave within five days and were forbidden to get in touch with each other abroad or even to live in the same country.

On October 19 Mowbray set out for the Rhine and, as Richard had ordered, went on a pilgrimage to Jerusalem. On the way back he died of the plague in Venice. Bolingbroke went to Calais and at last to Paris.

There for a moment in their separate places we will leave our characters, except to state that Gaunt died within a few months of his son's banishment. Richard had now absolute control of England and he behaved with abandoned tyranny.

It is time for us to take up the threads of the life of the little boy called Henry of Monmouth, later to become the heroic King Henry V of England.

c

# CHAPTER ONE

## *Childhood*

AGAINST the background of Richard's last years, Henry of Monmouth passed his early days. While he grew from childhood to boyhood the great events we have just watched were taking place.

We know very little of his childhood, but he was probably reared in some of his grandfather's numerous castles. His mother died, after producing three other sons and two daughters, at the age of twenty-four, in July 1394. Henry must have been almost an orphan, for his father was very rarely home, even before his banishment.

Bolingbroke's had been a roving life, somewhat like an early errant-knight's, and if he did not succour distressed damsels from dragons, he certainly cast a pretty eye on one young damsel, although her dragon was a kindly old gentleman, her husband, Duke John IV of Brittany. But this was much later, after the real errant days, just before his descent upon England.

In 1390 he had taken part in a grand tournament on the plain of St. Ingelbert, near Calais; Richard had been with him, but few noticed Richard. Bolingbroke drew all praise by his courage and his skill at fighting. With three hundred English knights he followed the Duke of Bourbon to the siege of Tripoli; he fought with the Germans on the shores of the Baltic and in the Gulf of Danzig; in 1392 he set sail on a pil-

grimage to Jerusalem but had to turn back, to
his everlasting regret; four years later we find him
in command of a thousand English lances at the
battle of Nicopolis, from which slaughter he
escaped by getting aboard a Venetian galley,
with the King of Hungary as a fellow-passenger.
It will therefore be understood why little Henry
so rarely had his father at home.

Our meagre knowledge of Henry's childhood
comes mainly from private accounts. Here we
learn of a demigown for him in 1388, of kirtles
and of satin and tartyn gowns in scarlet and
white, and of twenty-eight pairs of russet shoes
for him and his brother Thomas. Of more interest
is the record of February 1396—"4s. for seven
books of grammar bought at London for the young
lord Henry," and in the following years, "8d. by
the hand of Adam Gastron for harpstrings for the
harp of the young lord Henry." Psychologists
might be interested to hear that at this early age
Henry evidently showed a fondness for war. In
1397 we learn that 12d. has been paid for a new
scabbard and "1s. 6d. for three-quarters of an
ounce of tissue of black silk for the sword of the
young lord Henry."

Of still greater interest is the discovery that the
tales of his weak childhood are not purely apocry-
phal, for Thomas Pye gets "6s. 8d. for a horse
hired at London on 18 March 1395 to go with all
speed to Leicester on account of the illness of my
lord Henry."

One of the strongest traditions about Henry is that
at one time he studied at Oxford in the charge of his
uncle, Henry Beaufort, the son of John of Gaunt

and Katherine Swynford, born before marriage but made legitimate by Richard II. There is no authority for this belief, although the chamber over the Queen's College gateway, opposite St. Edmund Hall, once bore a Latin inscription stating in charming verse that Henry lived there. Both inscription and gate have long since gone, although they existed in the eighteenth century. The verse ran:

> *"Imperator Britanniae*
> *Triumphator Galliae*
> *Hostium rector et sui*
> *Henricus Quintus, hujus collegii*
> *Olim magnus incola."**

There may be truth in this story, as Beaufort was chancellor in 1398, when Henry was eleven. And in later life Henry was always interested in Oxford. Beyond that we know nothing.

We do know, however, that the boy witnessed a tournament in Pleshy in March 1397, for a horse was sent to him there from Tutbury, with black silk for his spurs and black housings for his saddle.

It appears that King Richard was genuinely fond of young Henry, for he gave him an income of £500 a year, no miserly sum in those days. And one story tells us that Richard liked to repeat an ancient prophecy foretelling that a prince called

---

*As Englished by my brother, Jack Lindsay:
> *Henry the Fifth, all Britain's Lord,*
> *who conquered France beneath his sword,*
> *mastering his foes and his own soul,*
> *was entered on this college-roll,*
> *and here a little room had span*
> *enough to house the mighty man.*

Henry "will be born in England who, through the nobility of his character and the splendid greatness of his achievements, will illumine the whole world with the rays of his glory."

Often Richard would add, glancing at the boy, "And verily do I believe that this young Henry here will be he."

After the banishment of Bolingbroke, King Richard did an insanely reckless thing. He went to Ireland. Before this, however, he did an even more insane thing. One would almost believe that he deliberately dragged his doom upon himself.

John of Gaunt died in February 1399 at the age of fifty-nine, not old in modern terms but old for those days when men lived fully, squandering the hours, and were considered grown up at fourteen: Gaunt had entered France with his father's army in 1355, and had witnessed his first battle—a naval engagement with the Castilians, and a very bloody one—at the age of ten. Doubtless his son's banishment hastened his death; and with his passing Richard was utterly free. He had now the opportunity to show England what sort of a King he was.

His first act was the insane one just mentioned: he seized all Bolingbroke's lands, just as he had seized Gloucester's. Having thereby driven the exile to the end of his patience and revealed to the world the injustice of his banishment, Richard sailed for Ireland, leaving the country open to any conqueror. He took young Henry with him, probably as a hostage, or perhaps merely because he liked the boy.

For ten days the considerate winds struggled

to hold him in England, but at last he beat his way out of Milford Haven and set sail. Besides young Henry, Richard had his cousin with him, Humphrey, son of the murdered Duke of Gloucester.

Although Richard was one of the very few English Kings—apart from the Yorkists—who were loved in Ireland, with his usual tactlessness he had managed to rouse the country. He took from a chief called Art MacMurrogh the lands dowered from his wife, and he gave them to a friend. The chief immediately rebelled, and that was Richard's purpose in sailing, he wished to stop the trouble. Yet even after landing he seems to have done very little until he chased his enemies into a wood, an act that no sane general would ever permit. Pioneers forced a path through the trees, but the English had no hope. They were sniped off by the Irish, and at last famine and despair made them fall back to Dublin.

The whole episode would not be worth our discussing if it did not bring young Henry before us. So certain had Richard been of defeating MacMurrogh that before his descent into the woods he had a clearing made and his standard erected. And in that clearing the "fair young handsome bachelor," little Henry of Monmouth, nearly twelve years of age, was knighted by his King.

As the chronicler Jean Creton—who was in Richard's service—tells us, the King called the boy to him "out of pure and entire affection. . . . And so dubbed him knight, saying: 'My fair cousin, be henceforth gallant and brave, for little bravery wilt thou have unless thou dost conquer.' And the more to honour and encourage him by adding to his happiness and pleasure, he made yet other knights, eight or ten; but indeed," adds Creton, "I know not their names."

Bolingbroke had not been idle. He acted so quickly and in such secrecy that even now we cannot follow his movements in detail until he sets sail from Boulogne, having with him a very small force of about fifteen lances and forty to sixty men-at-arms.

After touching at various ports he eventually landed at the now vanished port of Ravenspur, near Bridlington, the same spot from whence Edward IV was later to begin his reconquest of England. Bolingbroke was in no hurry. He knew that the country, particularly the north, was on his side, and that Richard was safe in Ireland fussing about a chief he had robbed.

Pickering, a royal castle, was Bolingbroke's first objective. The gates were opened to him without an arrow being flown. Knaresborough came next; the gates were not so quickly opened here, but eventually Bolingbroke was permitted to enter. Pontefract followed, then Doncaster. London suggested that he might come south. Friends were riding to his standard, and some of them were highly influential nobles—the Earls of Northumberland and Westmoreland were particularly satisfying allies.

As Edmund Mortimer, the six-year-old heir-apparent, was alive, Bolingbroke could not demand the throne openly. He merely said that he had returned to claim his inheritance, the lands Richard had stolen, and to reform the government.

He swore to this on his oath.

Even now, with his enemy stealing his kingdom from him, Richard idled precious hours away in Ireland. He posted the Earl of Salisbury to England, but himself seems to have done nothing for about three weeks, except to reproach his hostage, little Henry of Monmouth.

He called the lad to him in Dublin.

"Henry, my boy," he said, "see what thy father hath done to me! He hath invaded my land and put my subjects to death without mercy. Certes, am I sorry for thee, since through these unhappy doings thou wilt perchance lose thine inheritance."

Henry answered his master boldly. "In truth, my gracious lord and king," he is reported to have replied, " I am greatly grieved at these rumours. But I believe your lordship understands that I am innocent of my father's deeds."

"Yes," said Richard, "I know that thou hast no part in thy father's crime and therefore I hold thee excused of it."

When Richard left at last for England, he placed little Henry and Humphrey in the castle of Trim, in Meath. He apparently did not attempt to use them seriously as hostages.

If Richard had kept his courage he might have defeated his cousin. But he behaved in a childish manner and seemed incapable of making up his mind about anything. His failure was his own fault. His own vacillating actions lost him the help of his people. He dared not venture into England, and relied on the Welsh, and eventually fled from them, disguised as a priest, to where Salisbury was collecting a large army near Conway. But Salisbury's men were tired of waiting for a leader who did not appear, and by the time the wretched King turned up, most of them had deserted. His treasure was seized by Albemarle and Worcester, who did not get far with it, themselves being soon robbed by the Welsh.

In despair Richard decided to negotiate with his enemy, and sent the two Holland brothers, Surrey and Exeter, to see what could be done. Himself, still in his priest's hood, ran frenziedly to Beaumaris, where he found nothing but straw to sleep on. He spent the hours, we are told, in pleading with the Blessed Virgin, reviling Bolingbroke and weeping like a girl.

He certainly had a great many reasons for prayers and tears. His own cowardly behaviour had lost him his troops. And even worse than the desertion of the soldiers, some of his most powerful friends sided with Bolingbroke.

Richard's uncle, Edmund of Langley, Duke of York, who had been regent during the King's absence, not only permitted Bolingbroke to enter and run through England without a blow being struck, but now openly wore his badge. From that moment Richard was definitely doomed, for York's change of colours gave an air of legality to Bolingbroke's pretensions.

Richard had to give in but even now, in this desperate corner, it seems that he relied on his cunning for success. Evidently "cunning" had come to be a joy for its own sake, instead of being an underhand means to an end. He is reported to have said when agreeing to speak with Bolingbroke: "But in truth, whatever agreement or peace he may make with me, if I can get him into my

power I will cause him to be foully put to death."
This, by the way, was spoken immediately before
going to Mass, at which Richard was most devout.

But cunning could not conquer Bolingbroke.
The cousins met at Flint on Tuesday 19, 1399.
After dinner Richard and Bolingbroke faced each
other in the courtyard. The slight handsome King,
still dressed in the dirty priest's garb, his feminine
face strained and peaked with his privations and
despair, faced the armed man who was his conqueror. Bolingbroke was dressed in steel but
was unhelmed, and he bowed twice before his
captive.

Richard took off his hood and said in his quick,
slightly stuttering speech, "Hail, fair cousin of
Lancaster."

For a third time Bolingbroke bowed and, perhaps embarrassed, briefly said that he had come
only to help Richard govern England better than
he had done. Richard, still with the determination
of a "cunning" man, kept his self-possession and
answered courteously, "Fair cousin of Lancaster,
if ye be pleased so are we."

From now on Richard was a prisoner, and, to
make him realise the fact, Bolingbroke appointed
as his governors the two sons of his greatest
enemies, sons of the two men he had killed—one
with a feather-bed, the other with "justice"—the
Earls of Gloucester and Arundel.

In their charge Richard was carried to Chester.

Now Parliament must be called. Writs were
sealed in the King's name and posted off. Then,
with the captive Richard, Bolingbroke rode to
London.

Once Richard tried to escape. He climbed out of his window in the night but was quickly caught. After that he was forced to suffer the humiliation of never sleeping alone. Two guards were always in his chamber.

On reaching London Bolingbroke rode to St. Paul's to offer thanks to God; Richard went to the Tower.

The suggestion had been that Richard would be taken before Parliament. Probably Richard himself trusted to that. If he did, he was a far less cunning man than his captor. It would have been a most dangerous act to place a deposed King before Parliament where a sudden reminder of the royal rights, of the people's oaths and allegiance, might have aroused the spirit of the commons. Bolingbroke had no intention of running this risk, and as Parliament had been summoned for September 30, he was determined to extract from Richard a formal abdication before that date. We do not know what methods he employed but we do know that on September 29, the very last day remaining to Bolingbroke, Richard gave in.

But he refused to sign until he saw again his enemy face to face. Bolingbroke had wished to avoid this more than awkward situation but there seemed no other course for him to take. He had to meet his cousin. It would indeed be interesting to know what those two said when Richard drew Bolingbroke apart in his chamber in the Tower. The Archbishop of Canterbury was present too. We can only guess at what passed but I do not think it is too difficult a guess. Bolingbroke very likely promised Richard anything if he would only abdicate, and, most peculiarly, Richard must have believed him, for he appeared to be quite merry and read the whole statement aloud. He said that he wanted his cousin to succeed him and actually gave Bolingbroke his signet-ring, with his own hand placing it on the usurper's finger.

This statement, signed by Richard, should have been enough. In it he absolved all his. subjects, lay and ecclesiastical, from homage and obedience; he renounced his kingship and everything that went with it, and declared that himself had been "naught worth to govern," being useless and insufficient; lastly, he swore that he would never impugn the validity of this document. He appointed the Archbishop of York and the Bishop of Hereford to lay his abdication before Parliament.

One would have thought that so definite a statement would be sufficient, but Bolingbroke and his friends were afraid—and rightly so—that it might be thought that they had extracted it from Richard by torture or menaces. They decided to impeach the King and thus throw the weight of the usurpation on to the people as well as on to the usurper and his friends.

On Tuesday, September 30, 1399, Parliament met at Westminster. The Hall was crowded, not only with Bolingbroke's friends but also with Richard's. At the lower end it was a miracle the people were not stifled. The throne was empty, draped with cloth-of-gold, its very emptiness accentuating its presence. Bolingbroke, taking his father's chair and wearing a tall fur cap, sat next to the Bishop of Carlisle.

The Archbishop of York, Richard Scrope, read

aloud, in both English and Latin, King Richard's renunciation of the throne. Then began the voting. Not a single "No" was heard. Everybody said "Aye" to Richard's abdication.

Then were read aloud the very carefully prepared articles of accusation. There were thirty-three of them and it would be both tedious and irrelevant to quote them here. Sufficient to state that they were accepted immediately. After that began the real drama—Bolingbroke's pretensions to that vacant throne.

He stood up and solemnly crossed himself on forehead and breast, then said in English so that all could understand: "In the name of the Father, Son, and Holy Ghost, I, Henry of Lancaster, challenge this realm of England with all the members and appurtances thereto, I that am descended by right line of the blood coming from the good King Henry III, and through that right that God of His grace hath sent me, with the help of my kin and of my friends, to recover it; the which realm was in point to be undone for default of governance and undoing of the good laws."

You will note that Bolingbroke was never very definite, for his claim was a shadowy one. It is said that in his impatience he had at first intended to demand England by right of conquest, but his advisers overrode such rashness. In the above statement he suggests the three claims summed up by Chaucer:

> *O conqueror of Brute's Albion,*
> *Which that by line and free election,*
> *Been verray King.*

Nobody could deny that first claim of "conquest,"

Bolingbroke had conquered without doubt. The second claim of "lineage" was more indefinite, he based it on descent from Richard Crouchback, and it must not be forgotten that the real heir-apparent, little Edmund Mortimer, was still alive, although a minor. The third claim of Parliamentary "election" was a most important one, although no one present probably realised its importance. For the first time the real power of Parliament was expressed. After this day no King could reign without the sanction of his people. Therefore Richard, who more than any other King—except Edward II, whom he closely resembled in many ways—had striven to break from the people and to live by divine right alone, indirectly placed the real power in the hands of Parliament. His reign was worth suffering to earn such a triumph.

Again, there was heard no shout but "Aye" as Bolingbroke showed Richard's signet-ring on his finger. Then the Archbishop, Thomas Arundel—who had been banished by Richard and who had returned with Bolingbroke—took him by the right hand and led him to the throne.

After the shouting had died down, Arundel preached a short sermon, and Bolingbroke then stood to his feet again and spoke:

"Sirs," he said, "I thank God and you spirituals and temporals and all the estates of the land, and I do you to wit [to know] that it is naught my will that no man think that by way of conquest I would disinherit any man of his heritage, franchise or other rights that he ought to have, nor put him out of that he hath and hath had by the good laws and customs of this realm, except them that hath

been against the good purpose and the common
profit of the realm."

A new Parliament was summoned to meet on
October 6. At such short notice it was naturally
impossible to have a Parliament elected, and the
members then present were asked to attend.
Bolingbroke however was very careful to explain
that he wished to create no precedent, and that
only the urgency of affairs made him disregard the
usual course.

We find Henry of Monmouth at this new Parliament, with his brother Thomas. Henry had
reached England at the end of September, although
Creton tells us that he had come to England with
Richard—or at any rate shortly after Richard.
This is obviously a mistake. When Bolingbroke
was at Chester he arranged with one, Henry
Dryhurst of West Chester, for a ship in which to
carry his son from Dublin. This is according to an
entry of payment in the royal accounts, far more
dependable evidence than Creton's statement.

Henry's fellow-prisoner, Gloucester's son, died
of fever, evidently during the voyage.

Young Henry took the chief place amongst the
temporal peers at this Parliament. On October 12
we again meet his name, this time heading the
list, with his three brothers, of the forty-five new
knights created by the King in honour of his
coronation.

He was introduced into an entirely new order,
created by his father, now King Henry IV. This
new order may have been a deliberate attempt to
rival Edward III's Order of the Garter, which

was beginning to fall into decadence. If that was the intention it was rather purposeless.

There has been much mystery built up around Edward's order but it has always seemed to me that the garter was used merely as a symbol for the Round Table. Froissart more or less suggests this, but he rather confuses his dates, placing the founding of the order in the same paragraph as the building of the Round Tower at Windsor, which apparently had been begun some years before. This might have been deliberate, for Edward built the Round Tower—a great feat: 722 men built it in ten months—to house his Round Table, in imitation of Arthur. The much disputed words, *Hony soyt quy mal y pense*, probably have no dark meaning whatever. They are typical of the sometimes quite irrelevant and jesting mottoes of chivalry, and might have been a quip on the jealous questions of wives about what their men did at the Round Table, similar to our modern jokes about Masons. The story of Edward III picking up the Countess of Salisbury's garter at a dance is, of course, a sheer fable with no authority in the least, except for a pretty story in Froissart. In this story Edward makes hopeless advances to the countess in her castle while her husband is away. Beyond this the myth has no authority, and Froissart certainly does not mention anything so carnal as a garter; the episode is treated by him in the chaste fashion of a medieval fairy-tale, and very probably is a sheer romantic invention. According to the dates he gives it could not have taken place.

Bolingbroke's new order had no queer symbol. Its members were called the Knights Companions of the Bath, because one's feet were always washed before any great religious ceremony; and while Edward's Garter had been restricted to twenty-six members, Bolingbroke's was unlimited. Its emblem was three crowns, with the words *Tria juncto in uno.*

The King with his newly created knights walked from the Tower to Westminster to his coronation, the knights being dressed in priest-like cloaks of green. And again young Henry is prominent. He bore the pointless sword of State.

On the 15th he was created Prince of Wales, Duke of Cornwall and Earl of Chester, his father with his own hands placing a pearl-studded gold coronet on the boy's head, a ring on his finger, and in his hand he put a golden rod. Then the King kissed his son, and the Duke of York conducted the lad to his seat in Parliament, where the commons swore allegiance to him as their Prince.

There were still further honours for young Henry: he was created Duke of Aquitaine, also Duke of Lancaster.

# CHAPTER TWO

## *King Henry IV*

HENRY BOLINGBROKE was now King Henry IV of England. He had Richard locked safely away, and himself had been elected by Parliament. One would have thought he could have rested satisfied, having all this power in his hands, being King of so small and yet so great an island; and Henry would have been content if only he could have had peace. His reign is a pathetic one. There was little cruelty in the man, little of anything magnificent or contemptible; he was not brilliant nor was he dull. He was a sane and honest ruler who held his position shakily against numerous enemies. As the years passed from that triumphant day in Westminster Abbey when the Archbishop placed the crown upon his head, Henry must often have gripped that crown in both his hands and longed to hurl it from him. Afflicted by continual debts, with enemies on every shore and border of his kingdom, then tortured by the act of God—by a disease supposed to be leprosy and by a tumour under his nose—he must indeed have gazed despairingly about him and even have envied that pettish boy who had once been King Richard II, but who himself had so soon become only the sad story of the death of a King.

It was not long before King Richard died. After signing his abdication he was taken from the Tower to some secret place in the country. At a sitting of the House of Lords on October 23 it had been decided quietly, on the motion of Northumberland, that Richard should be imprisoned for the term of his natural life. After that he disappears from history. None of his followers were permitted to visit him; he was hidden away somewhere in England. His friends eventually destroyed him, as we shall see. By rising to rescue him, they forced Henry's hand; they made the killing of Richard a necessity.

No thought of the future darkened that coronation ceremony on October 13, 1399.

It followed the usual formula, except for the introduction of the oil given by the Blessed Virgin to St. Thomas Becket, Archbishop of Canterbury, when he prayed one night at the church of St. Colombe at Sens. Mary had presented this oil particularly for those future Kings of England who should recover Normandy and Aquitaine and who should slaughter all the pagans in the Holy Land. She had told Becket to hide it in the quire of the church of St. Gregory at Poitiers. The oil itself was in a crystal phial, the phial being enclosed in a golden eagle. It had been unearthed during Edward III's reign, being discovered in a leaden vessel containing the story of its presentation, written in St. Thomas's own hand. The phial was brought to England by the Duke of Lancaster and was placed in the Tower where Richard II found it.

Now for the first time this precious oil of Mary's was sprinkled on the russet head of Henry IV.

After the coronation came the banquet in Westminster Hall, and while the King ate with his bishops and lords, the King's champion, Sir Thomas Dymock, clad in full steel, rode in and offered to defend Henry's title against any challenger. The answer was rather typical of Henry.

"If need be, Sir Thomas," he said, "I would in mine own person ease thee of this duty."

Celebrations over, Parliament resumed its sitting, and after various discussions, up came the most important question of succession. Edmund Mortimer was still alive, being kept safe at Windsor, but Henry had not taken Richard's throne to give to somebody else, and he had no intention of becoming a mere regent. Henry's son—our Henry, who for convenience sake we will call the Prince until his coronation—was recognised as heir-apparent, being made Prince of Wales, as already stated.

Henry needed all his tact in the furious days that followed in Parliament. I have no intention here of repeating all the laws passed, as this is no constitutional history, but one must be mentioned —the abolition of liveries. The wearing of liveries— of a lord's badge—had been violently abused during Richard's reign. Great nobles gathered around them armies of ruffians, all of whom were protected by their livery-badges. Richard himself had had a mob of scoundrels called the White Harts. The lord's protection was used in the most villainous ways, not only in the simple method of assault and murder, but in legal cases. False litigants, backed by their master's power and money, could destroy the weak by taking them to law, and many a man lost property and goods because he was too penniless to defend them. There were armies of these livery-men; they roved the countryside, murdering, stealing, ravishing at their will. People dared not go abroad except when well guarded; merchants were afraid to hold those fairs so necessary to medieval trade lest a band of ruffians descend on them and rob every booth. When a noble came to Parliament he came like the invader of a foreign country, surrounded by steel-clad troops.

The abuse was too terrible to last, too crippling to trade, and Henry's first Parliament tried vainly to sweep it aside. It forbade any subject either to give or to wear a livery-badge. The King alone could grant this right, and the badges were to be worn only in his presence or when abroad or during wartime. Like most medieval enactments, this was ignored.

The act was aimed directly at Richard's late friends, the appellants—the Dukes of Albemarle, Surrey and Exeter, the Marquis of Dorset, and the Earl of Gloucester. These five men had quickly deserted Richard's cause, but they were never really with Henry. They felt degraded at bowing to a King who had so recently been no better than themselves.

Henry was tactful, too tactful. If he had behaved with greater cruelty, executing these men who nobody doubted were his enemies, his throne would have been more secure and his reign more popular, for these men were hated by the commons. But Henry wished to conciliate everybody, and therefore he pleased but few.

This first Parliament became one prolonged uproar. The commons started it by asking Henry to impeach every one of Richard's councillors who had been involved in particular misdeeds of

Richard's—namely: the banishment of Henry himself and of Archbishop Arundel, the murder of Gloucester, the execution of the Earl of Arundel, Richard Fitzalan, and the giving of Parliamentary powers to a committee.

For Henry to impeach the evil councillors of all these acts would have been too sweeping, and he shied from it. It would have meant the immediate arrest of Albemarle, Surrey, Exeter, Dorset and Gloucester, all very powerful nobles. He permitted, however, the arrest of Sir William Bagot, one of the lesser rascals and one of the best hated in the land.

Bagot put all the blame for his crimes on Richard and on Albemarle. Albemarle leaped up and challenged his accuser, hurling his hood at him. Fitzwalter then challenged Albemarle, openly accusing him of murdering Gloucester; others hurled gages at him, hoods and gloves. It was said that from twenty to thirty gages were flung at Albemarle amidst jeers and shouts of defiance, until Henry managed to quell the uproar. Bagot then put all the blame upon one John Hall, at that time in Newgate prison.

Day after day the fight continued. Hall confessed, and he, too, accused Albemarle. He was afterwards dragged by horses to Tyburn, and while he was still alive—or supposed to be alive— his bowels were cut out and burnt in front of him, the usual treatment given traitors. He was then beheaded and quartered.

Hall might thus be got rid of easily, but Albemarle was too powerful a man to drag down just yet. At last, on November 3, Chief Justice Thirning announced the verdict of King and peers upon him and upon others of Richard's friends. Albemarle, Surrey and Exeter were deprived of their ducal titles, becoming again the Earls of Rutland, Kent and Huntingdon, the Marquis of Dorset becoming Earl of Salisbury, and the Earl of Gloucester the Lord Despenser. And they were to forfeit all estates acquired since 1397, besides, of course, giving up their liveries and disbanding their armies. Salisbury for some reason was not even condemned to these extra small penances, he was placed in the Tower for a short while and then released on bail.

Both parties were infuriated by the verdict—the nobles because they had had to suffer at all; the anti-Ricardians because they wanted their enemies at least to be banished from the realm. Henry found an anonymous letter in his closet suggesting that he had been bribed, and threatening a revolt unless the nobles were immediately executed.

Henry's troubles were not all internal ones. The Pope, Boniface IX, with Spain, Portugal, Germany, Brittany, Hainault and Gulders, recognised his kingship. But France was definitely Ricardian. Here Henry was rather lucky. The King, Charles VI, was an old man at thirty after a youth of violent debauchery, and he had to be locked up now and again during outbursts of lunacy. His realm was split into factions, and Charles's three uncles squabbled for power. These were the Dukes of Anjou, Berri and Burgundy. While Charles was horrified at the news of Henry's conquest he was too afraid to make any direct attack while his daughter, Richard's widow, was in English hands.

His only method of taking revenge was to try to steal parts of Aquitaine, but the Gascons remained firmly English.

Henry had an even worse enemy than France to face—Scotland. Here, too, the King, Robert III, was almost politically useless, and his son, the Duke of Rothesay, was Guardian of the Realm. For many years England and Scotland had been at peace, and the Scots were tiring of their in-activity. The memory of their crushing defeat at Otterbourne was fading and they gazed over the Border with envious eyes at the rich pasture-land.

As the important northern earls were in London, the Scots swarmed down and burned the castle of Wark, carrying back with them Thomas Grey, who had been captain of the castle, with his children and tenants, and property worth two thousand marks. For ransom they demanded £1000.

When he heard of this, Henry swore that he himself would take an army to the north, but his council restrained him, pointing out the dangers of leaving London unprotected. Instead of fighting, he was forced to dissemble, to write pleasantly to King Robert and to send the Earl of Westmoreland to keep order.

There was danger nearer at hand. Richard's friends were gathering together, they called them-selves King Richard's Nurselings, and, despite the recent prohibition, openly stuck his White Hart in their caps or wore it on their arms.

And there was a conspiracy. Amongst the con-spirators was a priest called Richard Maudeleyn. This man had been one of Richard's friends and was physically almost his double. His part was to ape Richard when Henry was captured and before Richard himself could be rescued. As there was to be a tournament at Windsor there would be little difficulty in taking armour there, and the rebels were to ride in carts while friends inside the castle were to murder the guards and open the gates. The rising was planned for January 4; the conspirators were to meet at Kingston that night and ride direct on Windsor.

We are not quite certain who played the traitor but the evidence points to Edward, Earl of Rutland—he who so recently had been Duke of Albemarle and who had stood at bay amongst the furious men in Parliament. At any rate, whoever the traitor was, he delayed telling the King until the very night of the rising. With the Prince and his other sons Henry had been spending a melancholy Christmas at Windsor, and he had been heard to remark that he did wish Richard would die. This throne of England was not the easy seat he had expected; he was not very popular, and his advisers were inexperienced. It was a sad Christmas he spent in those draughty halls. The whole family was ill, King and Prince included, and many suspected poison. Outside, there was the threat of menace, of the plotting of King Richard's Nurselings.

Then came the traitor with his news. Henry wasted not a minute. It would be dangerous to be cut off at Windsor. His throne was not secure enough for him to rely on help without his presence to encourage the troops. He called for horses, and in the late afternoon galloped with his sons and two attendants for London. His road carried him straight through the rebel lines, but somehow he managed to pass and was in London by nine that Sunday night. The conspirators reached Windsor scarcely twelve hours after he had fled.

Although Henry had escaped their vengeance, the conspirators still felt assured of victory. The castle let them enter with barely a protest, and they had many friends and sympathisers on whom they could depend for help. So sure of victory was the Earl of Kent that he rode to Sonning, near Reading, to visit Queen Isabel. He tore Henry's badge from her servants and proclaimed that Richard would soon again be King of England.

The rebels gathered at Colnbrook and were preparing to descend on London when Rutland appeared. He assured them that to fight was hopeless; Henry was marching on them, he said, with a great army.

And all the fight went out of the rebels. They ran, making for Wales.

It was true that Henry had his army and was marching out of London. The Prince of Wales was not with him. With his brothers he remained in the safe-keeping of the mayor and aldermen. Henry rode hard to intercept his enemies, and he caught up with them at Maidenhead. Although none of the leaders were killed in the ensuing battle the army was routed, the conspiracy broken. Kent alone put up a spirited resistance. While his baggage was being carried to safety he held the bridge against Henry's army, and himself managed to escape.

It was not long before the leaders were caught. Most of them reached Cirencester, only to be attacked by the townsfolk. They surrendered on condition that their lives be spared until they met Henry. Kent, Salisbury and Lord Lumley were instantly murdered; the rest were handed over to that rogue of a Rutland who accounted for twenty-six or twenty-seven of them. Huntingdon, who had stayed in London, was killed by a mob as he tried to fly; Despenser was murdered at Bristol. Bishop Merks, Robert Walden, Maudeleyn (Richard's double) and others were tried in London. Merks was imprisoned, Walden was acquitted, and Maudeleyn was executed at Tyburn.

The rebellion was over. It had been a gigantic failure, and it doomed Richard. After this, Henry could no longer permit him to live. He had warned the nobles that after any rising he would execute Richard. We do not know how Richard died; we are unsure whether he starved himself to death or whether Henry had him starved. It is more than probable that he was murdered in some way. Coming so soon after the rising his death is most suspicious, to say the least. The popular story, however, about Sir Peter Exton with seven men fighting Richard who was armed only with a battle-axe, and how Richard killed four of them until Sir Peter jumped on a chair and hit him on the head twice with an axe, is definitely disproved by the condition of Richard's skull, which was examined towards the end of last century. Mr. Edward King examined the skull in Westminster Abbey and stated that "there did not appear any such marks of a blow, or wound, upon it, as could at all warrant the commonly received history of this wretched King's unhappy end."

*59*

On February 17, £80 was paid from the exchequer to carry Richard's corpse from Pontefract to London, so that England could be certain that its late King was now dead. The emaciated body was gazed on by the curious, it was soldered in lead, and all that could be seen of the poor deposed King was but a little of his face, "from the brow to the throat."

For two days Richard lay in St. Paul's, where Henry himself attended the service for the dead, and gave twenty shillings in offerings to the poor. Eventually the body came to the Friars Preachers at Langley, Hertfordshire, and a thousand Masses were arranged to be said in various churches. The marble tomb in which the body was laid had been arranged for by Richard himself long before his death. It showed copper effigies of Richard and Queen Anne, and here we discover that he had a tiny forked beard although he is usually depicted as clean-shaven. We also find this beard in the miniatures illustrating Creton.

Richard was dead and Henry of Bolingbroke was King. There was no rival now—save the minor Earl of March—who could spring suddenly from prison with an army at his back. The throne was Henry's at last, it was his in which to loll at ease, the exchequer was his into which he could dip his hands. But he found this throne of England no comfortable chair, and his hands could not dig far into an empty exchequer. He had no chance of merriment, none of the luxury of power—the unemptying cup, the laughter and the wenches to come at the crooking of a finger. The crown was heavy on his head, he was crushed by it. Alone, he stayed in his great palaces, wifeless, almost friend-less, with only his three sons and his daughters to give him courage to face the perils that raced upon him from every side, that were prepared to sail from every shore.

Scotland came first. With an army, Henry marched on Scotland and fought his way over the Border. There is little to interest us in this campaign, except for Henry's extraordinary humanity. He did not burn every village he came to, or destroy the countryside, or murder his prisoners, and he left unharmed any town or castle that surrendered at the call of his herald.

No sooner did the tired King return from Scotland than there was fighting in Wales. And here we must pause.

From now on, that other Henry, the Prince of Wales, begins to enter the stage. We must start another chapter.

# CHAPTER THREE

## *Henry, Prince of Wales*

WALES was not then a part of England, no Welshman rode to London to represent his country at
Parliament. It was a principality and its overlord
was the King. It was cut off from England by
mountain-ranges that were dotted with castles.
Here on the fringe of the untamed country the lords
marcher held command. Each was almost a king
in his little world—he taxed his people, he waged
war. Hated by those they governed, considered
foreigners—which they were—the lords marcher
used a mailed fist in all their dealings with the
conquered. Their overlord was the Prince of
Wales. It was essential for them to have such great
powers because theirs was a difficult task. They
must keep the Welsh in subjection, and the Welsh
were a violent hardy courageous people, who did
not rest in chains. But often the lord's powers were
too great. This was the breeding-spot for insurrec-
tion. These lords-marcher, if banded together,
could destroy the King of England himself; and
counties like Cheshire were considered such abomi-
nations, such outlawed communities, that few
Englishmen dared enter them without an army.

The trouble this time in Wales was a luckless,
silly affair which should have been easily avoided.
Living on his estates was a man of Welsh descent called Owen Glendower—or Glyn Dŵr or
Glyndyfrdwy, if you wish. This Owen was

English in every way and had been trained as a lawyer at London and probably at Oxford. He had been with Richard II in the Scottish campaign of 1385 and had been an esquire to the Earl of Arundel and, it appears, to Henry Bolingbroke during some of Henry's errant adventures abroad. He was a brave, generous man who kept open house, and was at this time forty-one years of age. Later Welsh singers were to build gaudy tales about Owen's descent but his lineage was not essentially great. He had married Margaret, the daughter of one of Richard's justices of the King's bench; of his children we cannot be certain. He had daughters and at least one son.

One of the strongest of the lords-marcher was Reginald, Lord Grey of Ruthin, and Owen and he quarrelled over some lands claimed by Owen. Owen took the trouble to court, while Grey did the fighting, leading his men again and again in expeditions of plunder and murder in true border style.

Then came the Scottish expedition, and Henry, when summoning Owen to follow him, sent the message through Grey, who was the chief marcher of north Wales. Grey, of course, failed to send the message on in time, and when Owen tried to explain his failure to appear, Grey accused him of lying. On top of this, one of Owen's neighbours, Gruffydd ap Dafydd ap Gruffydd, "the strongest thief in Wales," called on Grey for a pardon for past crimes, and he only escaped by the luck of having a friend who could warn him of his intended fate. He fled to his castle in the hills and wrote indignant letters to Grey, who retorted by promising him "a rope, a ladder and ring high on gallows for to hang. And thus shall be your ending."

This had nothing to do with Owen, but soon—we are not certain why—Owen was in rebellion. North Wales rose with him and marched over the border, flooding into Shrewsbury, burning, plundering, murdering, ravishing. Henry could not ignore this. With the Prince he led his men to battle and he struck into Wales itself. But he could find none to attack. Here in this mountainous country it was impossible to get at grips with an evasive enemy; besides, Henry preferred peace if possible. There were more pardons than hangings before he drew back, leaving the Prince of Wales behind him in Chester. Here a proclamation was given out that all rebels who would surrender to the Prince before the meeting of next Parliament would be forgiven.

We must not jump to the conclusion that because the Prince was ostensibly in command at Wales that he was actually. He was guided by his council, and the strongest man on this council was Henry Percy, the famous Hotspur. Hotspur was a courageous man, but he was no strategist or tactician. He was a soldier more than a leader, but by his strength and courage he was the ideal tutor for a boy like Henry of Monmouth. We must dismiss the stupid Shakespearean story of rivalry between the two. There is no reason to believe such a thing—far from it. Hotspur was a grown man and the Prince was only thirteen years of age at the time.

The situation in Wales was far more serious than the King realised. In Owen the Welsh had found the long-sought leader, and the old sporadic border-fighting began to crystallise into a genuine

war. Henry confiscated Owen's estates and—later
—Owen retorted by calling himself Prince of
Wales. Men were flocking to his standard. Welsh
students at the universities deserted their books,
Welsh labourers left plough and axe and fled from
England. The bards fingered their harps and
trolled their songs, twining about the figure of
Owen imaginary ancestors, singing of marvellous
portents that had scared the heavens at his birth,
of horses in the stables sweating blood.

While this was taking place in Wales, in England
things were beginning to quieten a little. Henry at
last was gaining control. There was trouble with
France at first about Queen Isabel, but even that
was nearing a settlement. Henry had wanted to
marry her to the Prince but the French would
not consider it. They demanded her immediate
return with her dowry. The dowry was the
problem, and negotiations dragged on wearily,
each country trying to cheat the other.

Then rebellion again flared in Wales. Owen had
drawn strong armies to him. The situation there
could no longer be ignored. William ap Tudor
captured Conway Castle. This was no glorious
victory, as the garrison at the time consisted of
only fifteen men-at-arms and sixty lances under
John Massey of Puddington. Ap Tudor attacked
on Good Friday while the soldiers were in chapel,
and the gates were opened to him by a Welsh
comrade disguised as a carpenter, "who feigned to
come in to do his work."

Hotspur and the Prince rushed to the rescue,
on Hotspur's money, but they could do little. The
town was loyal but the castle was a strong one
and was well provisioned. The one hope of the

E

English was to starve ap Tudor out, and as this was a laborious procedure, Percy and the Prince drew off, leaving a force behind to continue the siege. Soon there was trouble inside the castle, and ap Tudor was only too eager to negotiate. Pardon was offered on condition that nine of the worst rebels surrendered. This was easily arranged. The nine poor wretches were seized while sleeping and were handed over to the English.

But Conway was only one of the many thorns that made poor Henry's situation desperate. Owen still lived, and his name was magic to the Welsh. He swore to stamp out English speech and to free all the Welsh and Scots tied to England.

Henry called for men and marched again on Wales, only again to turn back. It was unimportant, he explained, and the Welsh "were but people of small account."

Very shortly these people of small account made him ride a third time to the border, only to be defeated by bad weather and the hopelessness of fighting a nation that took to the mountains the minute an armed force drew near. A cunning Welshman offered to betray Owen, and led the English for many a weary mile before he boasted that he was cheating them, and was instantly drawn, hanged, beheaded and quartered. Hotspur, weary of the whole business, had resigned his position on the council, for it was a very expensive one, and the Welsh therefore had a freer hand. Owen by amazing luck managed to get hold of some of the Prince of Wales's baggage.

With Hotspur gone, the Earl of Rutland was made Lieutenant of North Wales, and Thomas Percy, Earl of Worcester, was entrusted with the less difficult task of South Wales. The Prince, of course, remained still the head of the council—in theory at any rate. Worcester was appointed his tutor in place of Hotspur. And now we find the Prince associated with a man who was to remain with him for many years, and from whose memory arose the myth of Falstaff, Sir John Oldcastle. There was nothing whatever Falstaffian about Oldcastle. Later events will reveal him as a man of most courageous moral purpose, honest and, until pressed too far, loyal to his King.

We next glimpse the Prince far from Wales, in London, on May 8, 1402, agreeing to marry Katherine, sister of King Eric of Denmark, and witnessing a betrothal agreement between his sister Philippa and that same Eric.

Soon he was back in Wales where affairs were rapidly becoming uncontrollable. Owen was in touch with France and Scotland, and—even worse than this—was intriguing with the disappointed English. By great good luck he caught his old enemy, Lord Grey of Ruthin (he had him ransomed at so vast a sum that Grey was crippled for life), and then surprised Sir Edmund Mortimer at Bryn-glas, near Knighton, and defeated him utterly, capturing Mortimer himself. Later the English were to suggest that Mortimer permitted his army to be beaten. This Mortimer was a most important person; he was not only in command of the marches, but he was the younger brother of that Earl of March to whom Richard had bequeathed his crown, and therefore the uncle of little Edmund Mortimer who was in Henry's grip, being kept at Berkhampstead.

It is difficult to be certain about Mortimer's treachery at this point. Personally I doubt it. The battle was a brutal one, scarcely the kind that a man would arrange to deceive anybody. He had been caught in a narrow valley with little hope of success. Many of his soldiers openly joined Owen—or, rather, Owen's lieutenant, Rhys Gethin, for Owen himself was not in command—but these deserters were themselves Welsh. It is said that over a thousand men died in that narrow way, and that after the battle the Welsh women wandered amongst the dead and wounded, mutilating them in revolting fashion.

Mortimer was carried with all honours to the mountains of Carnarvon.

This was too definite a defeat to be ignored and King Henry started gathering yet another army to quell these "small account" people. He divided his forces in three—one was to be at Hereford under the Earls of Arundel, Stafford and Warwick; one at Shrewsbury under Henry himself; and a third at Chester under the Prince of Wales.

But before the great campaign could begin further tragic news came to Henry. The Scots were preparing to attack, although England had for hostage the Scottish Prince James who had been caught at sea in 1406. The boy was now King of Scotland, and was well bolted within the Tower of London. This, however, did not stop the Scottish lords from riding over the Border.

The Welsh were of more importance for the moment. The three armies set out, some reinforcements being posted north, but the weather defeated them, Henry himself being nearly killed by his tent falling on top of him, and probably would have been killed had he not been in armour. Men died of the cold and the wet, and it was said that Owen Glendower was a wizard who could conjure storms into the sky and that he could walk where he wished, invisible.

The great English army had to turn back.

But in Scotland Henry had good fortune. At Homildon Hill the two Percies, father and son, met the Scots and defeated them. This was scarcely an act of loyalty. It must be remembered that the north was the Percy-country, and they were only protecting their personal property. Great as this victory was, it was to usher in calamity. King Henry, probably afraid that the Percies—already the most powerful nobles in England—would become too powerful if he did not interfere, demanded that they send all their prisoners to London before ransoming them. This was a stupid act, for soldiers mainly fought in the hope of gaining ransom, and fortunes could often be made by men lucky enough to net an important knight. Hotspur refused to obey. He agreed at last to let the Earl of Douglas go to Henry if Henry would ransom Sir Edmund Mortimer from Owen. Henry, very suspicious of Mortimer, would not do this. And soon his suspicious were verified: Mortimer married Owen's daughter, Katherine.

Henry must have realised that the Percies were playing with treason, but what could he do? There were no men he could trust outside his young family. The people had not yet accepted him fully, and one night when he went to bed he discovered a poisoned caltrap twined in the sheets.

A caltrap was a great spiked metal ball usually thrown on to battlefields to rip open the horses' hoofs. Without the poison it would have been sufficient to finish Henry if he had lain on it.

His only hope was in the Prince, and him he made his Lieutenant of Wales.

From now we may accept young Henry as being actually in command. Before this he had always been under the tuition of either Hotspur or Worcester, now he was definitely a soldier, a leader, although Worcester retained his position as tutor.

The Prince took command on April 1, and was ordered to continue the war, with authority either to punish or to pardon. His headquarters were at Shrewsbury. Carrying out his policy of keeping the power as much as possible in his own family, King Henry sent his second son, Thomas, to Ireland.

Then came the news of Mortimer's revolt. We must not forget that Mortimer's nephew's claim to the throne was far stronger than Henry's, and now—whether seduced by Owen or infuriated with Henry for not paying his ransom—he issued a circular to his friends and tenants in Radnorshire stating that Richard was to be remade King, if he lived; if dead, the rightful Earl of March would have the throne.

Hotspur, inspired by his victory at Homildon, angered by his King's demand for his prisoners, heard from Mortimer, his brother-in-law, and gave him his mailed fist in friendship.

He was a powerful lord, this Hotspur. On gaining the throne, Henry had made Hotspur's father, Henry Percy, Earl of Northumberland, Constable of England for life. This was a most important position, the most important in the realm next to the King himself. He had control of the army, seeing if the right quota of men was sent by the military tenants, and he could judge and sentence those tenants in his own court. Apart from this purely royal appointment the Percies were exceptionally wealthy, owning vast tracts of the north and, by careful marriages, large portions of land all over England.

The father, Northumberland, had been banished by Richard for refusing to appear at court when his son was charged with treasonable language. It was for this reason that he had sided with Henry, not for any love of the man; actually he had been an enemy of Gaunt, Henry's father.

The son had all his father's violence. He was a reckless man, with little knowledge of strategy but with ambitious courage. Now he threw in his lot with Mortimer; and Henry had thereby against him both Wales and the north of England.

To withstand the shock of this gigantic rebellion, there stood, beside himself, only the lad, Henry, Prince of Wales, not yet fifteen.

The Prince had shown that he was no weakling. Although not a man in years he had revealed courage and quickness of mind, presaging the magnificent soldier he was to become. We have his dispatches and they are straightforward documents, giving direct facts with no frills or exaggerations.

On May 15, 1402, we find him writing thus to his father: "We have been lately informed that Oweyn de Glendordy caused to assemble his force of other rebels and of his adherents, a great number, proposing to override, and also to fight, if the

English people should resist his purpose, and thus he boasted to his people; whereupon we took our people and went to a place of the said Oweyn, well built, which was his principal mansion called Saghern, where we supposed that we should have found him if he had been willing to have fought in manner as he said; but upon our arrival there we found no one; hence we caused the whole place and many other houses of his tenants in the neighbourhood to be burnt, and then went direct to his other place of Glendourdy to seek for him there. We caused a fine lodge in his park to be burnt, and all the country thereabout, and we lodged there at rest all that night; and some of our people went thence into the country and took a great gentleman who was one of the chieftains of the said Oweyn, who offered five hundred pounds for his ransom to save his life, and to have paid the said sum within two weeks; however, this was not accepted and he was put to death, as were several other of his companions who were taken on the same day; and then we went into the Commote of Dedirnyon in [the county] of Merioneth, and there we caused a fine well-inhabited country to be burnt; and then we went into Powis and [being] in want of food for the horses, we made our people carry oats for them, and we lodged for —— days."

There are only six of these dispatches, written in French. The next dispatch, dated May 30, 1402, is mainly a complaint for money. The soldiers were threatening to rebel unless they got their pay, and the Welsh were aware of this. Henry did not want to retreat but what else was he to do? "Without a body of men we can do no more than any other man could of lower estate; and at present we have very great expenses, and have made all the pawning we are able of our little jewels to defray them, for two of our castles, Hardelagh [now Harlech] and Lamadern, are besieged and have been for a long time, and we must rescue and provision them within ten days; and besides defend the march around us with the third body against the entry of the rebels."

Despite the lack of money both castles managed to hold out a further two years, although eventually they were taken by the rebels.

Now came the blow of Hotspur's treachery. He rode down from the north, gathering men as he came. A famous hermit joined his ranks. This man had prophesied King Richard's death and now he was prophesying King Henry's. At Lichfield the inevitable proclamation was issued. It was of no use for Hotspur to pretend that Richard was still alive—although there was a false Richard, the "mummet," lurking in Scotland — so he announced that the Earl of March was the rightful heir, as he most certainly was. The Earls of Northumberland and Worcester and Hotspur all renounced their allegiance to King Henry, charging him with perjury, with lying, because he had stated on his first arrival that he had come to claim, not the throne, but his own inheritance; notwithstanding this he had imprisoned and murdered King Richard and had had himself crowned; he had promised and had failed to carry out his promise, not to tax the clergy or people without the advice of Parliament; he had not permitted free Parliamentary election; and he had refused to ransom Mortimer from Owen Glendower.

Having relieved themselves of these weighty grievances and given an honourable air to the whole rebellion, they rode to join Glendower, who had promised to meet them. The next morning Hotspur was at Shrewsbury, having covered the almost incredible distance of forty-five miles, and was demanding his admittance into the Castle Doregate. But the standard of King Henry did not flutter down from its pole at Hotspur's shout, and as Henry was riding hard to the rescue, Hotspur drew back sullenly for a little over three miles towards Whitchurch, until he reached a small hill by the road suitable for defence. His men he drew up in an open field known as Hayteley. Before them stretched a field of peas and a few ponds. It is difficult to estimate numbers in a medieval army; one chronicler tells us that Hotspur had 24,000 archers and 2000 lances, and another drops to 14,000 all told. The latter figure is the more probable. We do not know how many soldiers Henry had.

King Henry and the Prince rode out of Shrewsbury hoping to forestall Hotspur. Early on the morning of Saturday, July 21, 1403, King Henry distributed his army in the customary three battles, the van being under the command of the Earl of Stafford, himself and his son commanding the other two. Even now he hoped to avert a definite conflict and sent Thomas Prestbury, Abbot of Shrewsbury, offering terms. But Hotspur would not listen. He sent the Earl of Worcester to insult Henry. This was particularly galling, as Worcester —like Hotspur himself—had been the Prince's tutor, and his desertion was inexplicable.

"You rob the country every year," he is now

reported to have told Henry, "and always say that you have nothing, that your treasurer has nothing, you make no payments, keep no house, you are not the rightful heir!"

Henry tried to calm him. He said that he was chosen King and that he taxed only for the government of the country, not for his private pouch, and he promised favour if only they would not fight.

"We cannot trust you," was the answer.

"Then on you must rest the blood shed this day," said Henry, "and not on me. . . . Forward banner!"

Hotspur did not have his sword with him. It was his favourite weapon and when told that it had been left last night in the village of Berwick, he grew pale and cried: "We have ploughed our last furrow, for a wizard in mine own country foretold that I should die at Berwick."

He had no time for despair. Even before King Henry cried *"En avant baner!"*—"Forward banner!"—the Prince's men on the left had led the advance. "St. George!" they cried, "St. George upon them!" And, "Esperance Percy!" cried the rebels, "Esperance Percy!"

The rebels had the better archers, and into this winged hail, steel-tipped, the Prince led his soldiers. An arrow sliced his cheek, and his tutors strove to make him retire and have it tended. One chronicler tells us that young Henry swore that he would not leave, saying that he would rather stand and die than stain his knightly honour by flight; another states that he feared that his men might lose heart if their leader drew back.

It was his first battle. And must the hot barb of

an arrow rob him of its joy? He led his men, his face red with the running blood.

King Henry charged to his aid, trying to circle round the ponds. The Prince needed little aid. He brought his shouting troop up the hill, swept the rebels' right aside and folded it up against its own left, towards his King and father. There, so muddled was the battle, so restricted the space, that you could not tell friend from foe, and each fought with the man in front of him, striking out with axe or sword or mace, furiously, in a sweltering stumbling mass of soldiers.

Hotspur was seeking King Henry, breaking his way through the ranks seeking that one man whom now he hated. His prisoner, Douglas, was with him. They had sworn to touch no lesser men, to fight with none " save only with the King." With thirty followers behind them, they cut their way through rank after rank, heroically, madly. So determined, so furious was that little band of angry men, that they reached even the royal standard and tore it from its staff. Knight after knight they killed, notwithstanding their oath, but Henry they could not find. Great men died about the trampled standard of their King but Hotspur was not satisfied. In all the confusion of battle he thought of nothing except the King he hated. That little band seemed protected by some magic created by its own lunatic courage. Striking through the quick sea of steel and flesh they fought their way from point to point, seeking always King Henry of England.

Then Hotspur died. We do not know what hand struck down that courageous soldier. Somewhere in the press of battle, as he pushed his way through, a stranger lifted his mace or his axe, or some one strung an arrow, and Hotspur was no more. His soldiers did not see him fall but they missed his familiar presence. "Henry Percy King!" they wailed, seeking to glimpse him. Then King Henry saw his chance. He rushed to the front ranks and cried, "Henry Percy dead!" And the two cries mingled, "Henry Percy King!" and "Henry Percy dead!" until the rebels realised that their great leader was gone, and without his presence it was as if they were stripped of their armour, as if they were unprotected by the absence of a god.

They did not give in, but the gusto was gone. It was only despair that made them keep their ranks until after sunset. Then Henry was the conqueror, the field was his, the rebels had mainly fled. Yet so confused was everything in the gloom that many fell where they were and slept till dawn, friend and foe side by side, neither quite sure who had won.

They lay "in mixed heaps, weary, and beaten, and bleeding."

Thus ended one of the bloodiest battles England had then known—"one of the worst battles that ever came to England, and unkindest."

Shakespeare tells us that the Prince struck down Hotspur with his own hand but there is no truth in this. It was but dramatic licence on his part.

The lad's wound was presumably too serious to permit him to travel, and when King Henry returned to London, the Prince remained at Shrewsbury, with power either to pardon or to execute the rebels.

This was Henry of Monmouth's first battle. And it was no unworthy one.

# CHAPTER FOUR

## *The End of Owen*

THE victory was not complete. Hotspur was dead, but in a way his death did King Henry harm, although it was essential that he die. But he had been a popular hero and the people mourned his going. So strong was the resentment at his death that only a few days after the battle the King was forced to send messages through England warning his subjects not to speak ill of the government. Poor Henry! One cannot help feeling sorry for him. He had taken the crown from the head of an irresponsible weakling and, himself wishing to govern wisely, was hated nearly as much as Richard had been hated.

Almost immediately after Shrewsbury he had to ride north to treat with Northumberland, Hotspur's father, whom he pardoned. Worcester was executed, with others, as he well deserved, and the Earl of Douglas was now Henry's prisoner.

We have kept so close to the Prince that we have rather ignored the father, and I feel that it is now necessary to retrace our steps for a few paragraphs to give some idea of affairs in England.

Queen Isabel had at last been sent back to France. The negotiations about her return had dragged on and on ever since Henry's usurpation. At first he had hoped to marry her to the Prince of Wales but the French would not hear of that.

They wanted her back and the remainder of her dowry with her. This dowry had been 500,000 francs, given on condition that 200,000 francs should be refunded if there were no children at Richard's death. Besides this large sum, Henry had to return all her jewellery and treasures. As a counterblast to this demand, Henry resurrected the old question of King John's ransom which had never been paid in full by the French. The matter more or less rested there, and Isabel returned to her country, to her lunatic father and debauched mother.

Then there was that false "mummet" in Scotland, an imitation Richard, on whom Henry could not lay his hands, but whom the Scots naturally treated with great respect.

King Henry now married. I remarked that on his way to England he had stopped at the court of Duke John IV of Brittany. John had married as his first wife the Princess Mary, sister of John of Gaunt, and was therefore Henry's uncle by marriage. When Mary died, John, evidently being fully satisfied with English women, married a second one, Joan Holland. Like the first, she died childless, so Duke John tried a different nationality, a mixture of French and Spanish, Joan, daughter of Charles II, King of Navarre. By her he succeeded splendidly. This second Joan had six children, although her husband was old enough to be her grandfather.

Then came Henry of Bolingbroke riding on his way to embark for Ravenspur, and he never forgot the beautiful young wife of the old duke. When her husband died, Joan secretly procured a dispensation from Pope Benedict XIII giving her permission to marry whom she pleased. The man to please her was Henry, and they were wedded by proxy on April 3, 1402.

We most now return to Wales where the battle of Shrewsbury had by no means settled the question of mastery. Owen Glendower was still at large and, as Prince of Wales, was signing treaties with King Charles of France. England's navy was at this period her weakest spot. It was the merchant-navy that guarded shipping, and a man-of-war then was not a man-of-war in any modern sense; it was a merchant-ship with extra armoury. The privateersmen were our real sailors. It was the privateer—a kind of legal pirate—who fought to uphold English power on the narrow seas, and his was not a strictly royal ship. This question was later to worry King Henry V and to be studied deeply by him and partly rectified; in King Henry IV's time it was beyond hope. The Welsh coast was completely unprotected, and France could send as many soldiers as she pleased to swell Owen's troops.

The Prince evidently did not long remain at Shrewsbury after the battle, probably only staying until his wound was more or less healed, for we next find him in London in November, being cheered as he rides beside his father.

"Welcome to our noble King Henry!" cried the people. "God bless the lord Prince his son!"

In 1404 the Prince of Wales appears again at the forefront in Wales, arriving at Shrewsbury in April. We are now fortunate in having more of his dispatches. On June 26 he writes to his father that he has "removed with my little household to the town of Worcester, and at my request there is come to me in very good heart my very dear and well-beloved cousin [used very loosely in the Middle Ages and even later as a general term of affection] the Earl of Warwick, with a fine company of his people, at his very great expense, for which he is well worthy to be well thanked by you for his good will at all times.* And as for news of the Welsh, whether they are true, and what measures I have taken upon my march, of which you desire to be ascertained, may it please your highness to learn that before my march, and while on the way, I was lately certified that the Welsh had descended into the county of Hereford, burning and destroying the said county in very great force, and were provisioned for fifteen days, and it is to be seen that they have burnt and made great destruction in the borders of the said county, but since my arrival in the county I hear of no injury which they are doing, thank God; but I am certainly informed that they are assembled with all the force which they can raise, and hold themselves together for a great purpose, and according to what is said, to burn the said county, and therefore I am sending to my very dear and well-beloved cousins, my Lords Richard of York, and the Earl Marshal, and other most sufficient people of the county from this March with me at Worcester on Thursday after the date of these [presents] to inform me fully of the governance of their territories, and how many

*Warwick did splendid work at Campstone Hill near Grosmont. We know very little of the fight, but it seems that Owen himself was nearly killed and that his banner was captured. Later, at Craig-y-dorth he again brought Owen to bay, but the battle was indecisive, Warwick having rather the worst of it.

F

people they can raise if there be means, and to show me their advice touching that which seems to them the best course for the safe defence of the above-mentioned parts; and with their advice I will raise all that is possible for me in resistance of the rebels and salvation of the English territories to the very best of my small power according as God shall give me grace, always trusting in your very high lordship that you will be pleased to remember my poor estate and that it is not in my power to continue here unless something different be ordered for my stay, and that these expenses are intolerable for me to bear; and be pleased so to order for me in haste, so that I may be able to do service here for your honour, and save my small estate. My most Redoubtable and most Sovereign Lord and Father, may the Almighty Lord of Heaven and Earth grant you very gracious and long life and very good prosperity for your pleasure."

Four days later his debts were still more pressing, his men were clamouring for money, and he had little to give them. In haste the Prince wrote to both his father and the council, sending the messages by a particular man, his esquire, Raulyn de Brayllesford. Unfortunately the letter to his father seems to be no longer extant, but we have the one to the council. It implores them to "move our said most Redoubtable Lord and Father" to send him more money and troops.

This time he evidently did get some help, for at the end of August, when King and council met, the gentlemen of Hereford begged that the Prince be thanked for his protection of their county, and it was decided that he should be given three thousand marks within three years to help him guard the castles of north Wales. He was also promised five hundred marks with which to pay his troops and was ordered to muster five hundred men-at-arms and two thousand archers.

His next dispatch is dated March 11, 1404–5, and is written to his father. He states that on " Wednesday, the 11th day of this present month of March, your rebels of the parts of Glamorgan, Morganuoli, Usk, Netherwent and Overwent, were assembled to the number of 8000 people by their own account, and went the same Wednesday in the morning and burnt part of your town of Grosmont within your lordship of Monmouth, and went forth immediately my most dear cousin le sire de Talbot and my small body of my household, and to them assembled your faithful and valiant knights, William Newport and Johan Greindre, who were but a very small force in all; but it is well to be seen that victory is not in the multitude of people, and this was well shown there, but in the power of God; and there, by the aid of the Blessed Trinity, your people held the field and conquered all the said rebels, and killed of them according to loyal account in the field up to the time of their return of the pursuit, some say eight hundred, some say a thousand, at the peril of their lives; whether it be the one or the other in number, I will not contend. And in order to inform you fully of all that is done, I send you a man of credibility in this case, my loyal servant the bearer of these [presents] who was at the feast and did his service most faithfully as he has done on all occasions. And such amends has God granted to you for the burning of your houses in your above-mentioned town. And of prisoners there was taken only one, and he was lately a great chieftain among them, and whom I would have sent but that he is not yet able to ride at his ease. And touching the government which I propose to effect after these [events], may it please your highness to vouchsafe full credit to the bearer of these presents in that which he will show to your same highness on my part. And I pray to God that He may preserve you always in joy and honour, and grant to me that I may [be able to] solace you speedily with other good news. Written at Hereford, the said Wednesday in the night."

This was the real turn of the tide. This letter with its restrained triumph actually announces the first real forward sweep of the English. It had begun at Shrewsbury when the magnificent Hotspur died; with this victory behind him to inspire the courage of his men our Prince Henry was proving the strength of his mettle.

He was but seventeen years and a few months old at the time, and was now preparing with fresh commissions to strike boldly into north Wales. King Henry left Windsor in April to join his son but by the time he had reached Worcester further news awaited him to prove his presence unnecessary. The Prince had met the rebels at Usk, had defeated them utterly, killing (it is said) Owen's brother, Tudor, and taking prisoner Owen's son, Gruffydd. France came to Owen's help, King Henry rode to Wales, but little was done beyond skirmishing. Owen drew back to the south.

There was trouble in the north. Northumberland had revolted again, and now had with him Thomas, Lord Bardolph, and Thomas Mowbray, the Earl

Marshal, and the Archbishop of York, Richard le
Scrope. Before the Prince could attack, the rebellion
collapsed—Mowbray and the Archbishop surrendered to the King. Nevertheless it is possible
that young Henry stayed near Scotland. According
to the chroniclers he led an invasion over the
border some time in his early career. If the story
is true it must have happened now.

We find him back in Wales by August but the
dangers here were lessening, and it is very likely
that he spent much of his time in London. Then
Northumberland and Bardolph, who had fled to
Scotland, managed to sneak into Wales and join
Owen, and it seems that at this time the famous
Tripartite Indenture, the division of England,
must have been drawn up—if it ever was drawn
up. According to this agreement Owen was to
have all Wales and its marches to a line drawn
northward from Worcester to the source of the
Mersey; Northumberland was to get the twelve
northern counties down to Warwick, Northampton
and Norfolk; and the rest was to belong to Mortimer.

Although it appears that the Prince remained in
London near his father all through 1406, the
victories continued in Wales. He had driven in
the wedge, he had frightened the Welsh—the bare
mention of his name on the marches, it is said,
drove the rebels frantic—and his soldiers were
inspired by him even when he was not personally
there to lead them. There is nothing that gives
courage to an army like the name of a great leader.
We see this again and again in history—Eugène,
Gustavus Adolphus, Charles XII, Napoleon,
Nelson, King Henry V. . . . It is not the army, it

is the man who conquers, it is his spirit that spurs his men to victory. And already Prince Henry's name had come to mean all this.

On St. George's Day his men won such a battle that both Northumberland and Bardolph fled to Brittany, and soon all south Wales and the marches were at peace; only the mountainous north remained defiant. Prince Henry led his troops against the castle of Aberystwyth. But the castle was impregnable. Those great cannon shipped specially from Bristol could not even dent the rocky walls. To attack was useless. The only hope was to starve the besieged out; and this young Henry quietly settled himself down to perform. In a very short time the famished garrison under Rhys ap Gruffydd swore "on the Lord's Body" that if the English were not chased away by Owen "between the 24th of October next coming and the Feast of All Saints, they will restore the castle."

Owen might not be able to chase the English away but he did manage to reinforce the garrison and to denounce the treaty. The siege continued through one of the coldest winters known, although the King and Prince were not there to overseer it.

The whole affair ends in rather a mist but it does seem that the castle surrendered either in late summer or early autumn.

This is the real climax to the Welsh rebellion. The war had been a tedious and unexciting campaign, being mainly efforts to catch the rebels in formation. It was guerilla fighting, but it trained the Prince as a soldier, it taught him patience and the necessity of being thorough, and for that reason it is of importance. Without this schooling in his youth it is doubtful if Henry would have become the conqueror at Agincourt and the man who broke the walls of Rouen.

So as not to interrupt the narrative later let us finish now with Owen Glendower. He continued his guerilla warfare amongst the mountains for many years, but there were no more decisive battles. Soon he lost Harlech, that most important castle, and with Harlech he lost things more precious  his wife, his daughter, wife of Mortimer, and his four grandchildren.

We cannot follow his actions. He roved about the mountains, an outlaw, chased by the English, hidden by the Welsh. In after years the English said that he was starved to death, but they were probably thinking of Richard. The Welsh insisted that he died of old age in the pleasant company of English sons-in-law at Ewyas and Monington, in Hereford. Neither of these stories appear to be true. On July 5, 1415, Gilbert Talbot had instructions to treat with him but Owen did not take advantage of the offer. It seems that he was too ill at the time, too close to death to bother about earthly pardons. His privations and sorrows had sapped his strength; yet he was no longer young and must have been over sixty. In the early months of 1416 he died and was buried hurriedly at night. Later he was dug up again and carried to some secret spot that never was divulged.

We must return to our Prince, who is coming now definitely into the foreground. He had served his apprenticeship at soldiering; he was to begin his apprenticeship as a diplomat.

In both areas he proved that seemingly England had at last a future King capable, heroic, patient and far-seeing.

# CHAPTER FIVE

## The Council-chamber

HENRY IV was a very sick man. He had presumably a bad tumour under his nose, and it was said that he was dying of leprosy. Like Dr. Wylie, I doubt the charge of leprosy. Medieval people had a natural horror of this disease, a horror that amounted sometimes almost to mania, in which lepers were known to have been burnt; laws were passed banning lepers to their lazar-houses, damning them to a life of horrible isolation. They were not permitted within the walls of cities, and must never stand to the windward of a healthy person. The poor wretches lived on charity, having an "attorney" to beg for them. Even a King, I feel, would have been segregated if he suffered from real leprosy, and Henry was never segregated. To the last we find him conducting affairs of State. Also it must be understood that "leprosy" in the Middle Ages comprised every form of skin disease; perhaps the King suffered from eczema in a serious way, and eczema can be a revolting sight. Henry without doubt was disfigured by disease, although in the usual medieval manner these disfigurements were probably grossly exaggerated. The Parisians said that his toes and fingers were eaten off, and the Scots believed that his body had shrunk to the size of a twelve-year-old child. These examples will give some idea of the high-pitched imagination of medieval men and women, which makes the task of medical diagnosis well-nigh impossible. As Dr. Wylie remarks, it seems "as hard to diagnose a medieval disease as to make sense of a medieval battle."

When we come nearer home and study the English writers, much of the exaggeration goes, but the confusion remains. Hardying tells us that Henry's face was "so foul that leprous doth appear," which is quite consistent with advanced eczema. Other chroniclers are satisfied with a brief reference to leprosy, and within a very few years after his death it was said that both his mother and father had also died of it, for which I can discover no substantiation in their lives. Gaunt seems to have died normally. Blanche—the mother—died of plague, and Chaucer's lovely descriptions of her are scarcely consistent with a scorbutic woman.

The recently discovered portion of Usk's *Chronicle* says that for five years Henry's flesh had been rotting, and that his death had been prophesied at his coronation when his hair was found to be thick with lice. Usk was a contemporary and was evidently present at this coronation, and therefore he cannot be dismissed lightly. At the same time, any one who has studied medieval writings will learn to view such remarks with suspicion, for people then had a passion for the wonderful; the more incredible a thing was, the more likely they were to believe it. Also, Usk was a Welshman, a friend of Owen's, and can scarcely be trusted.

The eczema theory seems to have been borne out by Henry's own youth. When he was twenty it is noted that he had twice suffered from pox— any kind of sore, pimple, boil, but usually measles— and he was continually ill. There is also—if the

Parisians are right in saying that his fingers and toes dropped off—a strong possibility that Henry may have died from peripheral dry-gangrene due to eating rye-bread infected with ergot. This suggestion, made to me by Dr. Philip Nelson, is more than plausible. Rye-bread was most popular in the Middle-Ages, and much of the "leprosy" might be explained on this theory. "This disease, characterised by dry-gangrene of the extremities," wrote Dr. Nelson in *The Antiquaries Journal*, July 1934, "and variously called St. Anthony's Fire, Ignis infernalis or Ignis sacer, was in early times not infrequently mistaken for erysipelas." The actual disease was first noted, *circa* 858, at Xanten in Germany, and was caused by the fungus *claviceps purpurea*. In his collection, Dr. Nelson has a gold signet-ring, *circa* 1500, which was worn as a protection against ergotism. On the bezil is a running hart about which is a scroll with the letters, OS: MOUNO. On each shoulder is a Tau cross. This cross—shaped like the letter T—probably, suggests Dr. Nelson, was symbolic of a crutch. It was the usual sign of St. Anthony.

Such a question as Henry's disease cannot possibly be settled, and I have wasted too large a space over it already, as it is entirely irrelevant to our main theme. Whatever disease he suffered from he was certainly a sick man, and it was therefore necessary that his eldest son be always close to him, lest he die suddenly.

During the brief periods of his leave from Wales, young Henry always sat at his father's council-table. Now that the fighting was more or less over, he took his place permanently there.

It has been said that between father and son grew an intense rivalry, but this is a problem which we can safely leave to later pages, where we will discuss all the tales about the prince's early life, about his alleged debaucheries, his thefts and drunkenness. It is only necessary to remark here that this rivalry cannot be completely put aside. When the King was ill, the Prince was ruler; when the King recovered, the Prince gave up his power. This see-saw existence, this passing of the sceptre from hand to hand, was enough to breed resentment in the most affectionate breasts, particularly when the two men's policies did not coincide, and the task of one was often to undo the work of the other.

When young Henry took his seat at the council-table, events were shaping towards peace. England held the King of Scotland a prisoner; France was broken by internal fighting between Orléans and Burgundy; and even the Great Schism which had wrenched all Christendom in halves showed signs of healing. Henry could plan towards domestic security.

The French problem had at first appeared so pressing that the King himself decided to lead an army oversea. Fortunately, by a brutal accident, this was found unnecessary.

The King of France, Charles VI, had to be locked up occasionally. He was often quite insane and refused to wash. His lean body was rotten with sores and dripping with vermin, and the only way to wash him was for about a dozen retainers to rush in, disguised, and try to terrify him, strip him naked and plunge him, despite frenzied protests, into a bath. Another form of his mania was the belief that he sometimes turned into glass, and he would shudder with fear when any one approached lest they knock him over and break him; and sometimes he would insist mournfully that he had no wife and children and would say that his name was not Charles but George.

Orléans and Burgundy fought for power, each tormenting the King to make him exclude the other, each trying to stir the people to his side with popular catch-cries—such as the invasion of England. The two pretended to clasp hands in friendship, united against England; Orléans, who was probably the more popular of the pair, set out to conquer Guienne, Burgundy marched on Calais. It was this war that had frightened King Henry into the determination to lead his troops to France. Nothing came of it all, however, and the scare soon passed. The winter set in and shortly both captains were back in Paris, boasting of what they intended doing when the sun showed its face again. The war continued slowly, in spasms. The English won a fight at sea, but Orléans was wearying of the expensive task of having to besiege Bourg. He returned to Paris to receive great honours— evidently for having done nothing except waste men and money—and to be decorated with the empty title of Duke of Aquitaine.

It was very distressing to England but not really dangerous. At the same time, it kept the council alert, ready for action if affairs should become serious. Then chance took a hand, *via* the assassin's dagger, and relieved the strain. On the night of Wednesday, November 23, 1407, Orléans had been to see the Queen. This was rumoured to be no innocent visit, and Orléans and the Queen were both rather notorious. The duke was suddenly called away by a false message and carelessly rode through the dark streets of Paris with but five attendants and with two linkmen to light the way. It was very dark, being winter, but the duke was in a gay mood. Slapping his glove against his open palm, he rode with hood pushed back, head bare, singing a lusty song, when suddenly seven or eight masked men rushed from an empty house and slashed him with daggers. They tore him from his mule, hacked off his left hand which still gripped the saddle-bow, and struck their daggers into his face and body. Then they ran, shouting, "All shut, varlets! blow out your candles!", pretending to be the watch. And as they ran they threw great pointed caltraps on to the cobbles to rip open the feet of any that followed.

Nobody doubted who had inspired the murder. The Duke of Burgundy hurriedly fled to Bapaume. The Parisians dared not follow him. They were too afraid that the duke might side with England and attack France. Soon he was back in Paris, being cheered as if he were the Pope or a deliverer.

Thus the weight of fear was lifted from England—but this was before Aberystwyth, before Prince Henry's real advent on the council.

The next trumpet-call of danger came again from the north. Northumberland and Bardolph were back in Scotland, but with extraordinary stupidity they decided to invade England in the winter. And of all winters they chose one of the worst ever known. Neither the King or the Prince were at this battle. Yorkshire men alone, without any famous soldier to lead them, charged the rebels through deep drifts of snow. Northumberland was killed, and Bardolph was captured only to die that night of wounds.

On every side it seemed that there was peace— in Scotland, France and Wales. It was time that domestic problems were settled finally. Yet the records are curiously silent: there are no Parliaments, there are few council-meetings. The King was desperately ill, in the hands of an Italian Jew, Dr. David di Nigarelli of Lucca, and listening to the consolation of his chancellor, Archbishop Arundel. So ill did he become that his son, Thomas, was recalled from Ireland to see his father before he died, and the King made his will. This is an astonishingly simple will, written in English, and deals mainly with personal debts, the Prince of Wales being made executor.

But soon the King recovered. The fear of death left him, and with it the tormenting memory of King Richard II. He was not perfectly well, but he was well enough to destroy whatever hopes the young Prince for the moment had of reigning.

The most interesting problem at this date is the question of the Lollards. The Archbishop of Canterbury, Thomas Arundel, King Henry IV's chancellor, was a powerful heresy-hunter and he was no friend of the Prince. Historians have dwelt much on the court factions, the Arundel and the Beaufort, and from this derive the antagonism between the King and the Prince, but these factions never really became dangerous. It is true that the Prince was with the Beauforts, and the King was behind Arundel, although there was no real conflict on a large scale.

In January 1409 Archbishop Arundel published various constitutions in an effort to stamp out Lollardy in the universities. Oxford has always been the centre of spiritual rebellion; to-day the Catholic revival springs from it; in the days of Catholicism the first germs of Protestantism came from it.

Oxford was forced to bow to the chancellor's proclamations and to hear Wycliffe's doctrines being formally condemned, but it did not forget the insult. Richard Courtenay, a friend of the Prince, was the man who most deeply resented Arundel's act, and it was undoubtedly through his influence that on December 21, 1409, Arundel surrendered the great seal to the King and resigned from his position.

Again we come across the name of Sir John Oldcastle of whom we will hear much more later on. He had fought with the Prince in Wales and was now, because of his recent marriage with Joan, heiress of Lord Cobham, summoned to attend Parliament in 1409. Cobham died shortly after the marriage and his son-in-law therefore assumed the title.

Oldcastle is a most peculiar character, courageous and cowardly, strong yet weak; he shifts in spasms of conscience from point to point, yet on one point he never gives way—he was a Lollard. While being a most devout and charitable Christian he was an enemy of the Pope and at the same time a friend of the Prince of Wales. Prince Henry was to be a staunch Catholic, and it is difficult to reconcile this with his friendship for a man who read the Bible openly and who was to correspond with John Hus of Bohemia. As history comes to us mainly through the pens of the religious we must be careful when considering a man like Oldcastle. Yet his enemies, even when reviling him with every insult possible, cannot deny that he was courageous, honest and charitable. How bitter have been the attacks on him can be recognised in Falstaff, that masterpiece of characterisation built on a shameful parody of Oldcastle.

No one can possibly hope to understand the fifteenth century without some knowledge of Lollardy, and I feel that we must pause for a brief excursus on it here. The origin of the name is rather a mystery, but appears to have been given first as an insult to one who lollers or mumbles. Like the titles Huguenot, Roundhead, Puritan, Quaker, it was accepted by the people as honourable, and it was said that if you met two men on any road in England in those days, one was sure to be a Lollard, while in large cities like London the Church party was definitely in the minority. It was a powerful fighting minority, however, which few could withstand. Like all reactionaries the Lollards exaggerated the simple virtues in an effort to shame the worldliness of the Church. You will recall that the Host in *The Canterbury Tales* smells a Lollard in the wind when the Poor Parson objects to oaths. There have always been these reactionaries, and less than one hundred years after St. Francis, his followers were burnt if they endeavoured to live the life of purity and simplicity he laid down. Even in the early days we find this reaction, this effort to recover strict puritanism. There is a curious story given in the chronicle of

Ralph, Abbot of Coggeshall (1187–1224). He tells us that this was a tale repeated to him by an archbishop. One of the archbishop's clerks noticed in Rheims an extremely pretty girl and on trying to seduce her was repulsed, the maiden saying, "Nay, good youth, God forbid that I should ever be thy leman or any man's; for if I were once thus defiled, and lost my virginity, I should doubtless suffer eternal damnation beyond all help." At this heretical belief, the clerk fled and reported her to the authorities. She was burnt alive.

In the fifteenth century heresy had a very strong grip, and this is really the age of the birth of the Reformation; it is from the seed of Lollardy that England prepared itself for Cromwell's sweep through the land. The reasons for its uprush at this date are not difficult to find. Many of the causes were rooted in the gigantic wealth of the Church, by plurality of benefices, by absentee bishops—the Pope would often give his friends wealthy scraps of England which they never even visited, until Edward III put a stop to it—and by the obvious decay of the old ideals of asceticism, chastity and poverty. What gave strength to the movement was the Great Schism, the fight between two rival Popes, one at Avignon, the other at Rome. In this European warfare it was said that over two hundred thousand Christians had slaughtered each other. When a man was liable to be damned as a heretic for believing in the wrong Pope people began to believe in neither of them, and for a while the French decided that sweet Jesus would be their Pope, Mary the sweet Virgin being elected as acting Popess.

In England the rising tide of rebellion found a

G

leader in John Wycliffe. He preached mainly against pluralities of benefices, image-worship, the sale of pardons and against the conception that the bread of the Eucharist became actually the body of Christ after consecration. This last was the most serious of his heresies. The satirical writers had for long shouted at the corruption of the Church, and it was well used to that. The doctrine of transubstantiation, however, was its strongest rock and that it would not give up.

Few scenes in history inspire me like the picture of John Wycliffe arraigned before the Bishop of London's court in February 1377. Although nothing really happened to the reformer, his mere placidity has something heroic in it, something of the splendid courage of Cranmer thrusting first into the flames around him the hand that had written his recantation, the hand that had sinned, and of Latimer's cry at the stake—"Play the man, Master Ridley! we shall this day light a candle by God's grace, as I trust shall never be put out!"

Wycliffe had for protectors Gaunt and Percy, the father of Hotspur. Otherwise it is doubtful if he would have left St. Paul's alive that day. He had to battle a path through the mob to reach the court, Percy slashing at the crowd until the Bishop of London commanded him to stop. Gaunt shouted back that Percy was marshal and would act as marshal whatever the bishop said. It is a lunatic scene, almost a nightmare, and amidst the roaring and fighting Wycliffe stands alone, curiously serene, the courageous little scholar protected by the iron fists of Gaunt and Percy. It ended in a general fight when Gaunt threatened to drag the bishop into the street by his hair.

Henry IV's reign has the dubious honour of starting the "burning death" in England. The Church boasted that it never condemned any one, not even a heretic. Its trick was simple. It handed the poor wretch over to the secular arm, which was told to do its duty. The secular arm therefore received the blame, for it was in its court that the sentence was passed.

The first burning, it appears, that the Church effected in England was signed on February 26, 1401. William Chatrys, a parish priest, was brought before convocation on the usual charges, the main one being that he had said "that after the words of consecration in the Eucharist, the bread remains bread, and nothing more." I will not go into details about the trial. It is a pathetic scene, and one can only admire the heretic's courage. While trying to squirm out of the lesser charges, he cannot recant from the terrible one that attacks transubstantiation. In his distress he mumbles, "I don't know," "I do not understand." On February 26 he was publicly degraded in St. Paul's, his vestments being stripped from him.

This is the point at which, officially, the Church's power ended. It is here that the Catholic apologists stop and shrug their shoulders. The mother had merely thrown the child out of the flock. What the outraged seculars did afterwards was not the Church's affair. It was most definitely the Church's affair and by no amount of quibbling can one escape the fact that, indirectly, it was by the command of the Church that heretics were burned alive.

To continue with Chatrys. The Archbishop of Canterbury applied to King Henry for an order to the mayor and sheriffs of London telling them that the Church had proved Chatrys's heresies and that it now demanded that the secular power burn the man publicly within the city of London. There was no Parliamentary sanction for this. It was a deliberate, illegal act of the archbishop's, with the King's authority behind him. The secular power, of course, did the burning. The Church merely told it what to do and therefore cannot be blamed in the least: thus argue the apologists of the Catholic Truth Society.

Undeterred by the threat of armies of Lollards marching to the rescue, the archbishop soon had his victim burnt alive. Chatrys would not give in. Chained to the stake, around his feet the heaped-up faggots smeared with brimstone, he shouted denunciations in the name of God. He died horribly in Smithfield.

After that there were a great many more recantations, for few Lollards had the backbone to stick to their beliefs with the ghastly memory of the flames at Chatrys's feet. And recantations were what the Church desired far more than burnings. In triumph it arranged for Henry to pass as law the first English Statute against Heretics, *De heretico comburendo*.

Fire could not kill the zeal of the Lollards. Despite the recantations the heresies spread, they became stronger, clearing the path for the Reformation.

We must return to the most famous of fifteenth-century Lollards, John Oldcastle, now Lord Cobham, the friend of the Prince of Wales. His effect on this Parliament was quickly felt. A petition was offered to the King requesting that those arrested under the Statute of Heretics might not be imprisoned while being examined or tried. This Parliament was distinctly Lollard and many of the knights present argued that if the Church's money could be seized, enormous amount of good could be done with it. Besides supporting the soldiers who had to fight and help their King at great expense— while churchmen waxed fat at home—it would be sufficient to build a poorhouse for every town.

Now we see the Prince's attitude definitely. Although this statute was backed by one of his old campaigners, Oldcastle, he took his stand beside the Church, and the statute failed.

Arundel was pushing the Lollards hard. Sir Thomas Beaufort was now chancellor in his place, and as a powerful churchman he had time for nothing but heresy-hunts. He called together a synod and enacted that no one within his province could preach in church or churchyard without the bishop's authority, no one was to argue about Mass, Marriage, Confession or any Sacrament or article of faith, school-teachers were forbidden to let their pupils discuss theology, nothing written by Wycliffe was to remain at Oxford or Cambridge, no one was to translate a line of the Scriptures into English, and so on.

There was an immediate outcry, particularly at Oxford, the censors appointed by Arundel were not obeyed and even themselves often quibbled over the letter of the new stricter laws.

Arundel was determined. Next he pounced on a certain John Badby of Evesham, a tailor, and tried him for heresy. For fourteen months Badby had been imprisoned because he remarked that at consecration the bread was not metamorphosed into Christ's actual body, that a priest had no more magical power than a raker, a street-sweeper, and that when Jesus ate the Last Supper He could hardly have eaten His own flesh.

He was now arraigned before Convocation but he would not recant. The long imprisonment had only strengthened his faith. He was pronounced a heretic and handed over to the secular arm as usual. This time, however, the archbishop particularly requested that he might be spared. This sounds rather peculiar coming from so persistent a heresy-hunter as Arundel, but he was a strange man with much human weakness. His strong faith blinded him until he was faced with the actual effect of his behaviour, then he weakened. Stubbs suggests that this plea for mercy was a "piece of mockery," but I do not think so. There is something pitiful in Arundel that pushed its way through the cruel exterior occasionally. His plea at any rate had no effect. That very afternoon John Badby was dragged to Smithfield and placed on the tun ready for burning.

The Prince of Wales was present, and the man's plight so moved him that he thought he had signalled, meaning that he was prepared to recant. The Prince ordered the faggots to be pulled aside, and Badby was unchained. As the heretic lay upon the ground Prince Henry besought him to abjure his beliefs. It is said that he offered him threepence a day if he would only accept the Church's infallibility. Badby refused, and the Prince stood calmly aside while the poor wretch "burnt was unto ashen dry."

Hoccleve might speak with admiration of this noble Prince whose "great tenderness thirsted sore" for Badby's salvation, but our admiration to-day goes far more towards the unfortunate tailor who had the courage to undergo the Church's "burning death" rather than abjure his faith. His was the first burning in England since Chatrys, it seems; at least, it was the first of which we know.

From now on we cannot doubt for one moment Prince Henry's convictions.

Officially Prince Henry was still lieutenant of Wales, warden of the Cinque Ports and captain of Calais; actually, although not by name, he was president of the King's council. The King was drifting further and further out of politics, being struck down heavily by disease, and his capable son was guiding England.

Arundel was still trying to stamp out heresy. But every stamp he made only hardened the Lollards. He stiffened the opposition by his furious onslaught. Now he charged again on Oxford and quarrelled furiously with the Prince's friend, Richard Courtenay, chancellor of the university.

Courtenay refused to let the archbishop enter when he came upon a visitation—that is, on a kind of ecclesiastical circuit during which religious sinners were tried and condemned to various penances. Arundel retorted by placing St. Mary's Church, Oxford, under an interdict; but two Oriel fellows, who had killed a fellow-student, insulted their provost and broken the chancellor's oak, stole the church keys, rang the bells and opened the doors, refusing to bow to the archbishop's interdict. When the archbishop threatened excommunication the students only laughed and jeered at his lack of learning. The whole affair was referred to King Henry. This time we find the Prince against the Church, but this was not so much a question of Lollardy as of the archbishop's rights over the university; and personal considerations— liking for Courtenay, dislike of the archbishop— might have affected young Henry. The King was furious with Oxford and, but for the Prince's interference, his revenge might have been more drastic. As it was the chancellor was deposed and some of the students were flogged.

The Prince's town-house was the Coldharbour, in Thames Street, "counted a right fair and stately house," according to Stow, which had reverted to King Henry through the forfeiture of the Earl of Huntingdon. The King gave it to the Prince in 1410.

It is at this date, I feel, that we must place the Prince's alleged debaucheries, the tavern-haunting and waylaying of servants, for, according to *The Chronicle of London*, his brothers, Thomas and John, were now quarrelling in the streets, creating riots. This problem, as already mentioned, had better be left until the next chapter, where we can discuss the whole question without the interference of the affairs of England.

Apart from the burnings and the stamping out of the Lollards the most important problem now facing the council was the conflict in France.

The murder of Orléans had stopped all questions of war for the moment. Burgundy had supreme control, for the King was a child in any strong man's hands. But Burgundy had many enemies, chief amongst them being the dead man's widow, who always kept her husband's dog at her side as a reminder of his assassination. Then when she died, Burgundy—who, by the by, was nicknamed John the Fearless, a title that ill suits him, as he was a dilatory creature—felt that there was none to withstand him; Orléans's sons came and gave him the kiss of peace in the cathedral of Chartres.

Then young Orléans married the daughter of the powerful Count of Armagnac, and a strong alliance was made with the Dukes of Berri, Bourbon and Brittany. This party was called the Armagnacs, and they proved too strong for John the Fearless. John turned traitor in self-defence. He got in touch with England, offering Gravelines, Dunkirk, Dixmuiden and Sluys in return for support, and promising to help Henry reconquer Normandy, while giving his daughter Anne as wife to the Prince of Wales.

Here was an opportunity too good to be missed, and sick man though he was, King Henry decided to lead the troops himself. But first he sent ambassadors to ask about that most important question—the dowry; and also, besides giving Normandy, would John the Fearless help England to hold Guienne? would he fight against his own King if necessary? and would he see to provisions and quarters for the English army?

Men were impressed for the fleet, rope was forwarded from London, work was started in the docks; and after all this fuss, while the soldiers were waiting, the ships new-rigged and afloat, King Henry decided not to go. Undoubtedly a sudden attack of his disease weakened his resolve;

and those men who had refurbished their harness for fighting abroad, reluctantly put aside helmets and steel-plates and dropped their swords and pole-axes.

The council—or many of the council—suggested that the King abdicate in favour of his son.

When Bishop Beaufort mentioned this to the King, Henry glared at him and swore that while he had breath inside him he would rule.

The whole episode is unfortunately very vague, but it must be connected with the Prince's subsequent retirement from the council and, very likely, with the strange arrest of Sir Robert Leche, steward of the Prince's household, with five other knights.

After Parliament was over this year, 1412, changes took place in the King's council. But first, on November 30, 1411, the Prince, and Bishop Beaufort, the Earls of Arundel, Warwick and Westmoreland, with others, knelt to the King and were thanked for the manner in which they had controlled State affairs.

Following quickly on this came the changes in the council. Instead of Thomas Beaufort, Archbishop Arundel the heretic-hunter, became for the fifth time the chancellor of England. And the Prince of Wales disappears from history for a time.

Things had changed again in France. It was fortunate that King Henry did not start with that expedition. The Armagnacs bought Gascon and German mercenaries and flooded northern France. These paid soldiers behaved with all the barbarism of men fighting for money alone, and not for honour or love of country. They burnt down houses, murdering all who came within reach of their swords, and letting no woman of presentable age or appearance pass unravished. They tortured their captives in the revolting manner common to most wars, and resistance was useless.

In panic, the council wailed for the return of John the Fearless. He hurried back to Paris as quickly as he could, but many of his soldiers were scarcely any better than the Armagnac mercenaries and he was having difficulties keeping order amongst his Flemings and Picards. With him rode three hundred English from Calais under the command of William Bardolph, brother of the dead traitor, Thomas. Later he was joined by a larger force under the Earl of Arundel and others, including the Lollard, Oldcastle, Lord Cobham.

These English did fine work in the ensuing assault on St. Cloud, where the Armagnacs were slaughtered by the hundreds. And again at Etampes and at Dourdan the English proved their mettle. In this last battle the English distinguished themselves indeed in a quite unusual fashion: the French wanted to butcher their prisoners but to this the English strongly objected. Before applauding their humane gesture, it must be understood that it was not love of life that prompted them, it was the lust for gold. Prisoners produced ransom. After their captives had been given them, the English sat back perfectly content, and let the French do all the butchering they wanted; which was truly English—and French.

After these crushing defeats, the Armagnacs decided that they too would get help from England.

They promised King Henry the whole of Aquitaine and any one of their daughters or relations the Prince of Wales might prefer for a wife.

The news leaked out in Paris. Some of the Armagnac envoys were captured and the contents of a leather bag were examined by the King and his council. King Charles wept when he read such awful treason. The Dauphin and the lords knelt before him, pleading for permission to fight the Armagnacs immediately. John the Fearless, like a wise rascal, pleaded as loudly as any of the others and spoke with abhorrence about such treason.

The Armagnac envoys were welcomed in England even more than Burgundy's had been. They gave better bribes—their offers covered all Poitou and Angouleme. The Prince of Wales and the Queen were Burgundians, but their efforts were useless; besides, the Prince was evidently not popular at the moment.

Again Henry swore that himself would lead the troops, and again, after the preparations, he decided to stay at home. This was the chance that should have been young Henry's. He had proved himself a capable soldier and a cunning leader in Wales. Instead, the command was given to his young brother, Thomas, who was created Duke of Clarence and named lieutenant for the King in Aquitaine.

I have not written greatly about the Prince's retirement from the council and his apparent disfavour because we have so very few facts on the subject. It is impossible now to say what caused the trouble between father and son but that there was trouble it is impossible to doubt. Hardyng writes, without explanation:

*"The King discharged the Prince from his counsail,*
    *And set my lord Sir Thomas in his stead,*
*Chief of the council for the King's more avail;*
    *For which the Prince, of wrath and wilful head,*
    *Again him made debate and froward tread,*
*With whom the King took part and held the field,*
*To time the Prince unto the King him yield."*

And that is really all we know. There may have been some rift in the council between the two parties, the Arundel and the Beaufort, for the Prince and Henry Beaufort retired from the council at the same time, and Arundel was made chancellor in place of Beaufort. Also, Thomas, now Duke of Clarence, had recently married Margaret, the widow of John Beaufort; but her brother-in-law, the Bishop of Winchester, refused to give Thomas the share of her late husband's property which he demanded. The Prince was with the Beauforts; Thomas then sided with Arundel against them and his brother.

The Prince's enemies did not content themselves with talk, they also tried to murder him. A spaniel barking in the night awoke his attendants while the Prince himself was sleeping in the Green Room at Westminster. Behind the hangings an assassin was found. After being tortured before Arundel he deposed that Bishop Beaufort had hired him to kill the Prince—an obvious lie. The assassin was knotted in a sack and hurled into the Thames, probably before he could tell the truth.

This sudden hatred of young Henry must have been based in jealousy. And Arundel, being so friendly with the King, could easily fan the resentment of a father who sees his son becoming too powerful.

The Prince decided to brave his enemies. He rode to London and appeared at Bishop Langley's Inn—"Inn" then did not have its modern meaning, it meant a house, as the word still survives in Inns of Court. On July 11 after confessing and partaking of the sacrament, he dressed himself in his State robes and in a most peculiar costume that has given rise to much speculation. He wore a gown of blue satin or damask, basted with eyelets and dangling silken needles; on his arm he wound the Lancastrian livery-badge of SS worked in gold (it is believed that this SS stood for *Sovereign*). Because of this dress it has been decided that Henry must have been to Oxford and that this was his student's gown. Miss Agnes Strickland, with her usual wonderful imagination, gives quite a profound dissertation on this subject with most insufficient authorities. It is certainly a peculiar dress, and its significance really escapes me.

At any rate, dressed in some such garb, with many friends, young Henry walked through Westminster to the Hall. There he commanded his followers not to pass beyond the fire in the centre of the floor, and alone he walked into the palace. His father was very ill and had to be carried in on a litter to greet his repentant son, who knelt before him very humbly and offered the King his dagger, crying on him to kill him with it immediately if he doubted his loyalty or honour. Then in retort to the charges of his enemies that he had misappropriated public funds, he gave two rolls proving that the money had been spent in wages for the Calais garrison. The King, faced by his son, was unable to say anything, he could only suggest that he appear before the next Parliament and defy his accusers, who would be punished if they deserved punishment.

On September 23, the Prince, again with an army of attendants, came before the King's council at Westminster and repeated what he had told his father, demanding that his enemies be either punished or made to prove the libels.

He never did appear in Parliament, which is a pity, as we should then have understood more fully what the trouble was. Before Parliament sat, King Henry IV was dead and the Prince, as King Henry V, was on the throne of England.

Meanwhile Thomas, Duke of Clarence, had set sail for France, and without opposition plundered Normandy and entered Maine. His allies were in no mood for fighting. Both parties lusted for peace and neither relished the sight of a foreign army ravaging their country. Actually, before Thomas had landed in France there was peace; Burgundian and Armagnac embraced and swore that there would be no more fighting.

The great problem was what to do with these Englishmen who were making merry with French women and robbing French towns? The country was exhausted by internal dissension, and it was decided that as Orléans had asked the invaders over he would have to pay to get rid of them.

Money was quickly raked up, and in desperation the French even dragged the magnificent golden cross from the chapel of Bruges and gave it to Clarence, with another of great value. This Bruges cross contained an actual nail that had pierced either the hand or foot of Our Lord, and was rich with gems.

The episode was to prove fatal to France for it showed the English how simple it would be to conquer a nation that was prepared to pay even more than gold to avoid a war.

The English sailed back to their island, their ships heavy with booty, with bribes and hostages. And their eyes must have turned hungrily towards that shore as it disappeared into the skyline, while the white green-streaked cliffs of Dover drew near at their backs. On that receding shore, plunder and women, conquest and honour and good fighting could be had.

They were soon to return and to have their fill, at least, of fighting.

But before Clarence had left France, while he was still ravaging Bordeaux, King Henry died.

He had been dying for years, and England waited with a certain impatience for the end, and with a certain dread, for there was still a party who believed the Earl of March the rightful heir.

King Henry stayed often with his chancellor Archbishop Arundel during these last months, and he had always near him his confessor, a Dominican, Dr. John Tille. He was too ill now even to sit astride his horse, and often he was overheard praying for the end. He was repulsive to look upon, his face pitted with sores. But he would not give in; to the last he tried to manage affairs.

Suddenly, during Lent, while he was making offerings at the shrine of St. Edward, he was seen to stagger and fall. His attendants carried him through the cloisters to the Abbot's Palace, and laid him before the fire in the chamber called the Bethlehem or Jerusalem Chamber. Father Tille was beside him, ready for the end, and the crown —as was the custom—was placed on a cushion of cloth-of-gold beside the King. Slowly coldness crept over his body, and it seemed to those who watched that he no longer breathed, so they covered his diseased face with a silken towel.

The Prince was told and he came to that quiet room where the still body of his father lay cold before the fire. The Prince lifted the crown from its cushion and carried it off with him. Then the King sighed suddenly, and when the attendants had taken the towel from his face, he gazed around him and asked where the crown of England had gone. The Prince explained that he had carried it away for safety, being the eldest son; and the King said, "What right have you to it, my son, seeing that I had none?"

"Sire," answered young Henry, "as you have held and kept it by the sword, so will I hold and keep it while my life shall last."

"Do as you will," said his father. "I commend me to God, and pray that He may have mercy upon me."

Then he struggled up on his pallet while Father Tille administered the last sacrament, telling the King at the same time to repent for the death of King Richard and for his usurpation. But Henry answered that he had performed the penance given him by the Pope, and as for the usurpation— what could he do, for his sons would never surrender the crown? He stretched out his hands to

H

his son's embrace, and begged him to pay his debts, to reward his friends, to take wise confessors, to scorn laziness and to stand always by duty.

And thus King Henry IV died on March 20, 1413.

The above scene pleases me greatly, but I feel that I should give one note of warning. The words used, King Henry's confession that he had no right to the crown, come from a most doubtful source— from France—and need by no means be believed.

Otherwise the scene rings true, and the Prince cannot be blamed for taking away the crown. Brutal as that act appears, indecent in its haste, it was necessary. The Lancastrian throne was not yet secure ; the Earl of March lived, and there were men ready to steal the crown for him. And the actual crown, that jewelled piece of gold, the obvious emblem of kingship, was a most essential factor in medieval rule.

That crown now definitely belonged to Henry of Monmouth. And none were to take it from him while he lived.

# CHAPTER SIX

## *Prince Henry and "Prince Hal"*

I FEEL that this is the moment to pause in our
narrative and to examine the facts for and against
the Shakespearean Prince Hal, the reckless
drunken lad, comrade of Falstaff and other
cowardly rascals, the robber and the cuffer of the
ears of Justice. This question continues to perplex
historians and is still open to argument. Like so
many other historical problems, such as the alleged
murder of the Princes in the Tower and the killing
of William Rufus, it will probably never be
answered definitely. We can only follow the weight
of evidence, and the evidence here is mainly on
the side of the stories' truth.

Henry's defenders argue that these tales of a
riotous youth are mere Tudor slanders and that
his days were too busy to be wasted in debauchery.
This last argument seems to me particularly
puerile. It is often that great commanders away
from the stress of fighting throw themselves into
nights of hard drinking. Alexander is the example
that springs immediately to mind; there are
others. The great Marlborough's youth was not
exactly beautiful, nor was the even greater Prince
Eugène's, while in later and almost modern times
we have that heavy drunkard, General Grant.
The harder the upbringing, the more violent
the reaction, the coarser the release for nerves
strained beyond endurance. The Shakespearean

tale must of course be discounted, but not in its entirety.

This early manhood of Henry's, forced on him by the rush of events, must have demanded a release. And often the more intelligent a man the more violent the reaction. Henry most certainly was intelligent; he could read a little Latin, and could write well in the two languages necessary to a medieval baron—French and English, his English being particularly pure. Both father and mother were musical. The records for the Duchy of Lancaster show that the elder Henry played on the ricordo, a kind of flageolet, and that his wife sang to the guitar. From the same records we discover that the Prince could play the cithera, the gittern, and later we find mention of a harp. He also read considerably and seized the library of any town he captured, an unusual trait in a medieval prince. His taste was catholic, ranging from books on hunting and chronicles to a study of the decretals and ancient history. And we still possess a copy of Chaucer's *Troilus and Criseyde* stamped with his arms when Prince of Wales. Not only did he read books but he was patron to Hoccleve—who dedicated to him his version of *De Regimine Principum*, which runs to about 5500 verses — and to Lydgate, whom he inspired to write his finest poem *The Life of Our Lady* and to translate Guys' *Troy Book*.

At first he appeared open-minded. He was friend to such courageous thinkers as Oldcastle, Roger Acton, John Greindor and Thomas Clanvowe—believed to be the poet, author of that very lovely *Cuckoo and the Nightingale*—but in time the faith took control of him and wiped all tolerance from his thoughts.

In appearance Henry was handsome. His face was oval, with broad forehead, straight nose and fresh complexion. His teeth were white and regular, the hair thick and brown, the chin cleft, and the eyes large and of a bright hazel, eyes that could be as quiet as a dove's or as raging as a lion's. Although, being a good churchman, he was not fond of tournaments or jousts—which the faith banned as deadly sins—he loved fishing, hawking and hunting, and was a splendid jumper. In running he could almost equal a hare, for it is recorded that often he would start a deer, himself chase it and—with the help of two others—catch it without dogs.

Surely in every way there seemed no nobler prince than this Henry of Monmouth?

Loyal to his friends, speaking little, a fine soldier, zealous in duty and jealous of his own honour, that is the Henry who so far appears to us. It is true that he quarrelled with his father, yet we can find no actual disloyalty in his conduct. The quarrel was nothing by which his enemies could destroy him; he was not plotting to steal the throne.

And against these historical qualities we have little more than the rumours that were to be immortalised in Shakespeare's magnificent plays.

There is truth in the tales. That cannot be denied. But I do not see that they are anything of which Henry need have been ashamed; they are but the high spirits of youth finding a vent. And commonly the lad who rids himself of his violent emotions becomes the steadier man because of that.

He was heavily in debt towards the end of his father's reign. We have the receipts for his household accounts dating from October 1410 to March 1413, and they amount to £17,253. His debts however were far in advance of this, totalling a further £6856. His actual income was derived chiefly from estates in Cornwall and amounted to about £3000 a year.

In considering these debts, we must not too quickly accuse Henry of extravagance. We know that in Wales the soldiers' pay often came out of his own pouch, and he was forced to pawn his lesser jewels; when accused of misappropriation of funds he offered to prove that the money had gone to the Calais garrison.

In her reckless manner Miss Strickland damns Henry heavily on this count, and produces inaccurate evidence to bolster her accusations. Actually he does not seem by any means to have been extravagant, considering his expenses.

We will take the stories one by one.

There is that very popular one about his robbing his own servants. I quote it here, from Stowe, the Elizabethan:

"He lived somewhat insolently, insomuch that while his father lived, being accompanied with some of his young lords and gentlemen, he would wait in disguised array for his own receivers and distress them of their money, and sometimes at such enterprises both he and his companions were sorely beaten, and when his receivers made to him their complaints how they were robbed in their coming to him, he would give them their discharge of so much money as they had lost, and besides, that they should not depart from him without great rewards for their trouble and vexation, especially they should be rewarded that best had resisted him and his company and of whom he had received the greatest and most strokes."

For many years this tale was laughed out of court as being a mere Elizabethan invention; then it was taken with sudden seriousness when the late Mr. C. L. Kingsford published and edited *The First English Life of King Henry the Fifth*, which did not appear until 1911. This book is not contemporary, being written between 1513-14, and was used by Stowe and Holingshed. The tale I have just quoted is Stowe's version of *The First Life* tale, and it follows the original more or less closely; here the story is given on the authority of an Earl of Ormonde. On very insufficient evidence, Mr. Kingsford jumped to the conclusion that this must refer to the fourth earl, born 1392, died 1452. When reading Mr. Kingsford's splendid introduction to *The First Life* I was puzzled by his definite belief that this was the fourth earl, and that the author of the book must have copied from a work no longer extant. My doubts I kept to myself in cowardice, believing that a scholar of the greatness of Mr. Kingsford must have some other information, and that, at any rate, on any historical question it would have been impertinent of me to argue with him. My cowardice was further strengthened by the fact that nobody seemed to question his statement.

Now, however, Professor William T. Waugh has revived these doubts and has—to my mind—proved conclusively what I before only felt, that the Earl of Ormonde referred to in *The First Life* was not the fourth but the seventh earl, Thomas Butler, and therefore the claim of contemporary evidence cannot be made for this book. At the same time, though it is the seventh earl, the stories have a measure of authenticity. The fourth earl was his father, as both his brothers had the title before him, his father did not die until Thomas Butler was thirty. That is only one generation out, and I feel that although Professor Waugh has disproved Mr. Kingsford's contention he has not really impugned the validity of *The First Life*. If the son repeated these stories he must have heard them from his father; they are perhaps almost as safe to accept as if they were definitely contemporary.

We may therefore assume that, if not exactly true in all details, the tale of young Henry robbing his receivers is based on fact. With the backing of Ormonde I feel that we must accept it, although it may have been greatly twisted in the process of passing from mouth to mouth.

We had better continue at once to the most popular Shakespearean tale of all—the insulting of a King's Justice, who by a process of elimination we find must have been Judge Gascoigne. I will not quote this in full, because it is far too long and really not worth the trouble, for it has little or no authority behind it.

We first discover it in Sir Thomas Elyot's *The Governour*, published in 1531. Elyot was a lawyer,

son of a lawyer, and because of this, some historians
—like Lord Campbell—have decided that there
must be truth in the tale. That is the only fact with
which they have to bolster it. Here is an abbrevi-
ated description of what is said to have happened,
taken from Elyot:

During his father's lifetime Prince Henry was
"noted to be fierce and of a wanton courage. It
happened that one of his servants whom he
favoured well was for felony by him committed,
arraigned at the King's Bench—whereof the
Prince being advertised and incensed by light
persons about him, in furious rage came hastily
to the bar where his servant stood as a prisoner
and commanded him to be ungyved and set at
liberty." All were horrified, except the Chief
Justice, "who humbly exhorted the Prince to be
contented." Far from being contented, Henry tried
to drag his servant out of the court, and the Justice
commanded him to stop. "With which command-
ment the Prince being set all in a fury, all chafed
and in a terrible manner, came up to the place of
judgment, men thinking that he would have slain
the judge or have done to him some damage."
He was committed instantly to the King's Bench,
by "which words being abashed and also wondering at the marvellous gravity of that worshipful
judge, the noble Prince, laying his weapon apart,
doing reverence, departed and went to the King's
Bench as he was commanded." To conclude the
moral tale, Elyot tells us that the King on being
informed of what had happened, first sat silent, then
"as a man all ravished, with gladness holding his
eyen and hands up towards heaven," cried in a
loud voice—"O, merciful God, how am I above

all other men bound to Your infinite goodness specially that Ye have given me a judge who feareth not to minister justice, and also a son who can suffer semblably and obey justice."

The story grew rapidly. Hall makes the Prince "strike the Chief Justice with his fist on the face."

The only comment that can be made on all this is that the tale is credible but unproved. The argument of the defence that there is no record of the occurrence in the Plea Rolls of the court has been ably answered by the late Mr. Vernon Harcourt. He points out that over one-third of the Controlment Rolls for this period are missing and that no record would have been made on any roll unless the Prince was actually tried: a note would probably have been scribbled out and placed in the Baga de Secretis, or Privy Bag.

The problem is insoluble. The story does not appear in print until over a hundred years after Henry was dead; no contemporary chronicler mentions it.

Mr. Vernon Harcourt, however, has offered us a new problem in his paper, *The Two Sir John Falstolfs*, read before the Royal Historical Society on March 17, 1910. It is an interesting problem he gives but actually it does not help either side.

You must understand that Shakespeare only refurbished an old play, and that he changed the name of the comic character in that play from Sir John Oldcastle to Sir John Falstaff. It would not have been safe for him to parody a martyr on the Protestant stage, and some change was essential.

While retaining that feeble pun, "my old lad of the Castle," Shakespeare definitely stated that he did not mean to jeer at a very great man. In the epilogue to the second part of *Henry IV* he writes: "One word more, I beseech you. If you be not too much cloyed with fat meat, our humble author will continue the story, with Sir John in it, and make you merry with fair Katharine of France: where, for any thing I know, Falstaff shall die of a sweat, unless he be killed with your hard opinions; for Oldcastle died a martyr, and this is not the man."

We do not need this statement to prove Oldcastle "not the man." Very shortly we will follow the life of the real Oldcastle, and you can judge of that yourself.

Mr. Vernon Harcourt, however, suggests that while altering the name of Oldcastle to Falstaff, Shakespeare may have had a reason for the change, that one of the real Prince's rowdy companions was probably a Falstaff. As proof of this, he stated that he had discovered in the Close Roll for 3 Richard II the following record: "Hugh Falstolf and John Organ, citizens of London, acknowledge that they owe to John de Cobham, lord Cobham, 800 marks, to be paid to him at the feast of Pentecost next." The tale of this debt continues in the Coram Rege Roll for Hilary, 4 Henry IV, when after Hugh Falstolf's death his son John was arraigned by Cobham to discover whether he "held the manors of Bradwell, Olton and Kyrkele with their appurtenances in the county aforesaid, which belonged to the aforesaid Hugh." The case was respited "owing to the default of the jurors"— in other words, because Falstolf started a fight and threw some of the jurors out of the court. He was committed and bound over to be "henceforth of good behaviour towards the lord King and all his people, and especially towards twelve jurors impanelled.

Unfortunately the tale ends here, but Mr. Harcourt found it a strange coincidence that these two names—Cobham and Falstolf—should be linked together in a case of contempt. I fear that it is only a coincidence and does not carry us far.

The above Falstolf is not the one put forward by another school who find a further pun in the "old man of the Castle," believing it to refer to the "old man of the Caister," as there was a Falstolf of Caister near Yarmouth. This Falstolf was probably a Lollard, lived his youth in the household of Thomas Mowbray, Duke of Norfolk, and actually did own a Boar's Head Tavern, although not in Eastcheap, in Southwark. But he would have been too young a man to have been the original of Shakespeare's Falstaff.

Now, this Falstolf of Mr. Harcourt's is not too young a man; he would fit the part.

This has been an amusing amble around the battlefield of historians, but it has not brought us at all nearer to the point. Neither of these Falstolfs was Sir John Falstaff, and the coincidence certainly does not help to prove the Chief Justice story. We remain exactly where we started from.

Did Henry of Monmouth insult a Chief Justice of Henry IV? As I said, by a process of elimination—if the tale is true—the judge must have been William Gascoigne. According to the Shakespeare version, Henry on ascending the throne turned off all his old friends—that is correct, on the authority of Ormonde—and reinstated Gascoigne.

The opposite of this is the truth. Gascoigne received
his summons to Parliament as Chief Justice but
within a week afterwards he was discharged. This
certainly does give a colour of reality to the tale.
At the death of a sovereign all judicial appoint-
ments—among others—were made vacant but
it was the common procedure to reappoint whoever had held them in the previous reign. Henry's
defenders plead that Gascoigne was an old man
and would soon have had to retire; this is not
quite true. Gascoigne was only about sixty-three
and his life after his retirement was active enough.
He became a justice of the peace for some of the
northern counties and sat on a great many
important commissions. He died on December 17,
1419. He therefore could not by any means have
been in senile decay when Henry of Monmouth
was crowned; his dismissal cannot be explained
in this manner, as he lived actively for four years
afterwards. It is true that in the year following his
dismissal Henry granted to his "dear and well-
beloved William Gascoigne four bucks and does
out of the Forest of Pontefract annually for the
term of his natural life," but Sir James Ramsay
suggests that these gifts smack of an *eirenikon*, and
it seems that Sir James was right, for all the other
judges were reappointed.

There is another point that seems to throw a
little light into the darkness. Towards the close of
Edward I's reign, a Chief Justice was insulted by
William de Breosa. When giving judgment in this
case the Court of King's Bench referred to an act
of contempt committed by Edward II, then Prince
of Wales, towards a judge.

It has been suggested that this is the germ of the

story that Edward II was the Prince who insulted
the judge, about eighty years before Henry of
Monmouth was born, and that in some peculiar
manner Elyot got the Princes' names mixed. I fear
that we can scarcely accept that, however; it
appears to be merely a coincidence. If the Prince
had been another Henry it might have been
acceptable.

Now that we have examined all the evidence,
what is the verdict? I must leave that answer to
you, merely remarking that my personal opinion
is that the story is more than probable.

We know definitely that Henry's youth was not
one of extreme purity, but there our knowledge
ends. We have no details of his reckless actions;
apart from Ormonde's tales there is no episode
that can really be claimed as authentic. That his
brothers were wild we have proof in *The Chronicle
of London*, which tells us that in 1410, the King's
sons Thomas and John were mixed up in a riot
against the Londoners in Eastcheap. The Prince
could not have been involved in this or he would
have been mentioned.

Other contemporaries and near-contemporaries
assure us that Henry of Monmouth was no godly
lad. *The First Life* tells us—probably on the
authority of Ormonde—that he dismissed his old
rowdy friends when his father died. The author
of an *English Chronicle* states that "in his youth
he had been wild, reckless, and spared nothing
of his lusts nor desires, but accomplished them
after his liking; but as soon as he was crowned,
anointed and sacred, anon suddenly he changed
into a new man."

This chronicler was not strictly contemporary but the charge is echoed by many others who were. Historians of his own time, men who knew Henry, repeat the same tale, and Hoccleve wrote an impassioned plea beseeching him to be a just Prince. There is also Elmham—for Hoccleve cannot be accepted, his work might have been the usual poetic flight—and Elmham adored Henry and was one of his chaplains. According to him, "the Prince was in his youth an assiduous cultor of lasciviousness, and addicted exceedingly to instruments of music. Passing the bounds of modesty, he was the servant of Venus as well as of Mars; youthlike, he was fired with her torches, and in the midst of the worthy works of war found leisure for the excesses common to ungoverned age."

Elmham cannot be set aside, nor can Thomas Walsingham who flourished *circa* 1422. Walsingham also tells of sudden conversion: "As soon as he was made King he was changed suddenly into another man, zealous for honesty, modesty and gravity; there being no sort of virtue that he was not anxious to display."

Titus Livius de Frulovisiis (*circa* 1440) states that Henry "exercised meanly the feats of Venus and Mars and other pastimes of youth for so long as the King his father lived."

With this concurrence of contemporary and near-contemporary evidence it is useless to deny that Henry of Monmouth was not a school-story boy hero. And that is where we must leave the vexed question.

He was presumably a wild lad, a lover of wine,

women and music; he mixed with Lollards and probably he did sally out occasionally on drunken expeditions. The tale of Judge Gascoigne, however, has little basis in fact although it need not be rejected: it is more than possible.

We must rest content with the knowledge that from a wencher and a musician Henry changed abruptly into a fiery Christian—that after his coronation he touched no woman . except his wife, we have on the authority of Elmham— and that the change came about immediately his father's jewelled crown, the crown of England, was taken from its leather box in the treasury and placed upon his thick dark hair.

# CHAPTER SEVEN

## King Henry V and the Lollards

HENRY OF MONMOUTH was twenty-five when his father died. The sudden responsibilities thereby placed on his shoulders stopped whatever recklessness and amours there had been in his youth. From now on he is the righteous prince, the enemy of the Lollards, a man just, courageous and strictly continent, one of the most beloved and greatest of our English Kings.

The night after his father's death he spent with a holy recluse in Westminster, shedding himself of past sins and preparing for his new authority as father of his people.

The following day he was proclaimed King and issued the usual commands. Parliament had already been summoned and therefore many of his more important subjects were in London. They hurried to Kennington where Henry then was, an dswore the oath of allegiance to him, at the same time explaining that they did not wish to create a precedent by behaving in such an unconventional way before coronation.

The coronation soon followed. On Passion Sunday, April 9, 1413, in the Abbey of Westminster, Henry of Monmouth was formally crowned King of England and France and Lord of Ireland. He was escorted by the fifty knights he had the day before created and by the great men of his kingdom, passing through heavy snow down

I

Chepe to Westminster Palace. Between the high altar and the quire in the abbey a scaffolding had been built and was draped with cloth-of-gold. On that scaffolding, so that all might see, the august ceremony took place.

After the coronation there was feasting in the Great Hall, but it was noted that King Henry did not eat. Course after course of food soaked in herbs and spices and sauces was carried in by the retainers, some riding horses, some on foot; but none could tempt the King. Great custards—pies—with golden coffins lifted to show a mess of meat swimming in eggs and saffron and every kind of herb, stews, and wondrously cooked fishes, sweet-confections moulded into figures spouting words from their mouths . . . none of these passed the King's lips.

Outside the window snow was falling—such a blizzard as had not been seen for years. It was whispered that this was a bad omen; others said that it was a good omen, portending that all the evil of the past would dissolve. The minstrels in their long bright gowns played in the gallery above the screens. There was chatter and laughter as the cup went round.

John Dymock entered on his great horse and challenged any to stand forth and contest King Henry's right to England. And no one stirred. Yet there were many who thought that the Earl of March should have had the throne; and there were others afraid that the old rivalry between Henry and his brother Thomas—now at Bordeaux—might stir the country into civil war.

At last the feasting was over. The minstrels left first, blowing into their flutes and trumpets, clapping their hands on drums or plucking lutes; then the ladies and lords followed, and last of all came the King.

He had not taken one bite of food, men said, nor did he taste anything for three days afterwards. He entered on his kingship as a man in search of heaven who would purge all the past from his body as well as from his mind.

Throughout the following day the snow continued, covering England. Men, beasts and houses were buried; and some died in that awful blizzard. All Europe suffered, most countries far worse than England. Paris bolted every door, Parlement had to go home, men dared not stir into the streets, and some went deaf. Little could he heard in Paris except curses, shouts and the blowing of noses.

In such weather King Henry V began his reign, a reign that was to live through England's annals as one of the most splendid and the most inspiring of any King's.

There were changes in the council. Archbishop Arundel was taken from his chancellorship, and Bishop Henry Beaufort was put in his place. Although Henry might rid himself of a man he disliked he had no intention of becoming a party-king, and he balanced the Beauforts by making the Earl of Arundel treasurer.

On May 14, in the Painted Chamber at Westminster, King Henry attended his first Parliament. It was a wholly amiable Parliament and Henry agreed to consider almost everything placed before him. Amongst these requests is the complaint made against officials in the bishops' courts who charged anything up to £100 as fee for probate of a will when the legal fee was only two shillings and sixpence. Another complaint against the same court was that the fine for lechery or adultery was preposterously high at £2: the sinners would have preferred a flogging. A third complaint was a very serious one and related to the old law of deodand. According to this law, if an animal or inanimate object caused anybody's death that animal or object became the property of the King or the feudal lord. This became iniquitous when men died accidentally at sea, for it resulted in the whole ship being seized as a deodand. Henry promised to consider these matters but little seems to have been done to remedy them—at least, for a time.

Money was voted to the King, including a special £10,000 for his household, and Henry with extreme generosity pardoned all his prisoners except a few vitally important and politically dangerous ones. He released the Earl of March, his rival. This was Edmund Mortimer, the heir proclaimed by Richard II. At this time he was just twenty-two years of age, and Henry was not to regret the kind act. The Earl, except for one dubious episode, became his loyal subject, fought well for Henry in France and governed excellently in Ireland. He had never been technically a prisoner, but Henry IV had been careful to see that he had no opportunities of wandering abroad and of being used by discontented nobles. Now Henry V freed him from all constraint.

There were still dangers to the kingdom. The false mummet, the second Richard II, was in Scotland, and men were prepared to take their

oath that they had seen him with their own eyes
and that he was Richard without doubt.

Henry's conversion was no hypocritical one.
It showed many facets but few were so praise-
worthy as his efforts to rebuild the crumbling
church of St. Peter in Westminster Abbey ; the
Lollards were now to feel what it was like to
struggle against a stern determined man. For his
confessor, Henry had chosen a Yorkshireman, Dr.
Stephen Patrington, of the Carmelite Order, as
fierce a hater of Lollardy as Archbishop Arundel.
Patrington and another Carmelite, Friar Thomas
Walden, were to mould the young King's spiritual
ambitions. Under the sway of their words, Henry
shed every particle of Lollardy that might have
clung to him from his early friendship with Oldcastle and others. These two men stilled for ever the
lusts that beat in his young heart, they trained him
into the conqueror he became, into a man who
was cold to everything but love of God and his
country, and intolerant of every form of laxity—
sexual, bibulous or religious. This King who had
wenched and drunk in his youth was to change
into the soldier who cut down the vines in France
and who attempted to stop drinking in England.
His household became as stern as one of the old
monastic orders: pious and free with charity to all
who came. No one dared to whisper in his chapel.
In churches in those days men and women talked
and spat as they wished, they brought their hawks
with them to innure the birds to crowds, and often
their dogs too. Nothing of this nature ever occurred
in King Henry's chapel, where he kept priests and
singers, and twenty-four bedesmen to pray for

him at the cost of twopence each a day. His old turned-off companions must certainly have wondered at the change, and a great deal of it can perhaps be put down to the persuasion of Patrington and later of Walden.

Patrington was an Oxford man yet a great hater of Wycliffe's doctrines; Walden on the other hand came of very simple stock. His father was a netter, a maker of nets, at Saffron Walden. An enormous, almost ungovernable, detestation of Wycliffe drove the young friar to preaching to the people. He was one of those splendid self-denying fanatics who spring into being now and again, driven on by one purpose and never flinching from the paths that purpose drags them into. Perhaps he was not quite sane. His description of the unfortunate Badby's trial has a touch of madness about it, for he tells of a spider running over the heretic's face; afterwards, this spider became a great creature that hopped from the roof and which had to be held back by main force from squeezing down Badby's mouth.

Into this man's hands Henry V was to place his spiritual dreams. He was brought to the King's notice by a sermon preached at Paul's Cross, in which Walden accused Henry of being backward in stamping out the Lollards.

Convocation met when Parliament met. This was the clergy's Parliament, for in those days state and church were separate, and the religious taxed themselves. This was one of the grievances of the layman, for the religious not only taxed themselves but tried themselves as well, with the result that a clerk could often get away with murder, the spiritual judgments never being very heavy, consisting mainly of penances. Archbishop Arundel was to the fore again, publicly burning two books in front of the cross in Paul's Churchyard; but he had to leave towards the end of the sitting of Convocation. Nevertheless a determined effort was now to be made to combat the growing heresies and in particular to stop the preaching of any one not licensed by his bishop, and to drag down the great men of England who stood as bucklers to the lesser folk.

Chief amongst these great men was Sir John Oldcastle, Lord Cobham. A book he had ordered was examined at a limner's and was found to contain the most diabolic heresies. But for once Archbishop Arundel suggested caution. Perhaps the loss of his chancellorship had frightened him a little, and knowing that Henry and Oldcastle had been friends he thought to please the King. He evidently was not aware of the depth of Henry's conversion.

Passages from this book were read aloud to Oldcastle before the King, and Henry was horrified to think that such things could be written; he asked Oldcastle if he did not agree that such a book should be condemned. Oldcastle agreed immediately. He had scarcely glanced at it, he explained.

Convocation was not satisfied. It knew perfectly well that even if Oldcastle might refute this particular book he was touched by Wycliffe's doctrines, and it was determined to drag down some important man preparatory to an assault on all Lollards. Again the clergy approached the King. There was still kindliness in Henry; he could still remember the fighting in Wales and his old friendship for this heretic. He promised the bishops that he would speak to Oldcastle apart and would try to wean him from his beliefs. If he failed, he said, he would surrender the man; he would give him to the Church to do what it liked with.

But Henry could not wean Oldcastle from his faith. From that moment, after talking with the King, Oldcastle knew that he was doomed. He fled to his castle at Cooling. Henry then surrendered him to the bishops; they could now treat him according to the Church's law.

This was the bishops' opportunity. A proclamation on August 21, 1413, was given out authorising all sheriffs to arrest any priest or chaplain who was teaching Lollardy; and Archbishop Arundel marched on Cooling. The archbishop himself was refused admittance but an usher of the King's chamber who accompanied him, one John Butler, was allowed to enter. He told Oldcastle that either he must let the archbishop's sumner come to him or himself must step outside to the sumner and receive the writ. Oldcastle refused to do either, so the archbishop nailed the writ to the door of Rochester Cathedral, demanding Oldcastle's appearance at the castle at Leeds within five days.

Again Oldcastle preferred to stay at home, and the archbishop cursed him and warned him that if he did not appear by September 23 he would be pronounced a heretic and passed on to the secular arm—in other words he would be burnt.

Henry now took a hand in the business. He arrested Oldcastle, who submitted quietly, and had him locked into the Tower of London.

Oldcastle was brought to trial in St. Paul's

Chapter-house on Saturday, September 23. His trial was particularly fair, although we find Walden amongst the court. Archbishop Arundel seems again and again to have tried to bring Oldcastle to reason; but like Badby, Oldcastle could not, even when faced with a ghastly death, renounce the principles on which he had built his life and faith. Arundel offered to forgive him if he would only bow to the Church's rulings; Oldcastle refused the offer. He had brought with him, he said, his profession of faith, which he begged permission to read. The permission was graciously given and Oldcastle read aloud the following four articles:

The first article stated that the sacrament "was Christ's body in the form of bread"; in the second he said that he fully believed in penance; thirdly, he stated that he did not consider images a matter of faith but merely "calendars to lewd [ignorant] men to bring to mind the passion of Christ and the martyrdom and good living of other saints"; fourthly, he could not believe that pilgrimages alone would bring a man to heaven; he stated that many a good man who stayed at home was often worthier than those who travelled to Rome or Canterbury and yet remained sinful.

After a consultation the archbishop agreed that these articles contained much Catholic truth, but there were further details on which he desired enlightenment. Then followed the test questions: Did the accused believe that the material bread remained after consecration? and that confession to a priest was necessary in the sacrament of penance?

Oldcastle hedged at these. He referred Arundel to the bill he had just read out.

It is evident that the court did not wish to condemn Oldcastle. They wanted him to recant, for a recantation was a far more powerful weapon than a burning. Martyrs were often the most dangerous enemies of all. Arundel did his best to convert Oldcastle, and quoted many Holy Fathers. But Oldcastle was not impressed. It may be true, he said, but he could not allow Popes, cardinals and bishops the power to settle such knotty problems.

After that the court adjourned so that it could draw up, in English, an explicit statement of the Church's official attitude to these questions; and Oldcastle went back to the Tower.

On Monday the court reassembled but Oldcastle had not altered his faith. He told the archbishop that the material bread did remain after consecration, but that it veiled the spirit of Christ; to the second question he replied that confession was not essential to true penitence.

Both these statements were black heresies, two of the blackest of all. Oldcastle continued speaking; and when he stated that the adoration should be for Christ alone and not for the wood on which He hung, he was asked what honour he would pay a crucifix. To this he answered that he would wipe it and keep it clean. He swung round to face the people, the laymen, and shouted, "These men who are bent on damning me mislead themselves and you, and will drag you down to hell! Therefore beware of them!"

Even after this outburst the court would not surrender its hope of a recantation, and Arundel actually wept as he exhorted Oldcastle to believe in the Roman tenets. It was quite useless. Oldcastle would scarcely listen and was condemned as a heretic and passed on to the secular arm, to the "burning death."

In all this the Church stands in a kindly light—wishing the power of a recantation rather than a martyrdom—and Oldcastle does not show at his best. His sudden almost hysterical cry loses him a certain dignity. At the same time I am following Dr. Wylie in taking these facts entirely from the contemporary—and therefore Catholic—statement and am ignoring the later Protestant one, which is an obvious effort to make the Church appear a murderous lusting horde of wolves and Oldcastle the meek lamb. This later version is usually followed by English historians, and even if neither is very trustworthy I certainly prefer the contemporary and more sober account.

Oldcastle was fighting for his faith and he had before him the memory of John Badby writhing on the tun with the faggots and brimstone at his heels; he knew that if he did not recant he would die horribly. In such a position it is impossible for us to demand his remaining placid and heroically dignified. Consciously he was going to martyrdom —although he later proved he had no desire to die— and to such a man his faith is of far more importance than his own life. We cannot expect a Latimer every day. And even Cranmer, after he tore his recantation to pieces, fled through the rain in a frenzy to reach the stake, afraid that the weak flesh might drag him once again to cowardice. To say that Oldcastle was not afraid would be to deny that he was human. Nevertheless the Church shows in a most gentle colour, and Archbishop

Arundel wins our sympathy by his tears and his efforts to make Oldcastle recant; to a man like the archbishop, with unfaltering faith, it must have been inexplicable why anybody could believe seriously such things as Oldcastle believed. Oldcastle's determination must have seemed to him obstinacy, his beliefs a wilful and stupid blindness.

Arundel would not give up hope. He obtained from Henry the customary remand of forty days for Oldcastle before execution, and then arranged to have all the bishops in his province read to their flock, in English, the details of the heretic's condemnation as a warning to possible backsliders.

Continually, as he paced his cell in the Tower, Oldcastle was plagued with visitors entreating him to repent. He never did repent although a spurious confession was later published.

Then he escaped. How he escaped we do not know. It has been suggested that Henry helped him but I doubt it, although the peculiar laxity of the guard does point to some great man's connivance. The keeper of the Tower, Robert Morley, had been relieved of his position some time before October 10, and Oldcastle was condemned on September 25; no other official was placed in Morley's position until October 28, and Oldcastle escaped on October 19. It does therefore appear that Morley was relieved to make way for the prisoner's flight, and although Morley was arrested, he was released within three weeks, and some of his men were used in attempts to recapture Oldcastle. Therefore Morley can be exonerated.

Oldcastle's escape proves how deeply Lollardy

had bitten into England. We know the names of two of his friends—Richard Wrothe and a parchment-maker called William Fisher—but there must have been many others in the plot, many inside the Tower itself. Oldcastle was hidden safely in Fisher's house in Turnmill Street.

Altogether the whole episode is very suspicious but I cannot believe that Henry helped Oldcastle's escape. Such an action is inconsistent with his beliefs, with his love of justice that often took harsh forms; Henry prided himself on his impartiality and he once remarked that if his brother deserved death he would sentence him. This was no idle boast. Like all just men he rarely used mercy; and we are not actually certain if he had any strong affection for Oldcastle. As a matter of fact the stronger that affection the more likely Henry was to be stern. I cannot conceive him helping any one to escape who he really believed had been sentenced justly.

All the same he did very little after Oldcastle's flight, and it was not until October 28 that a proclamation was issued forbidding any intercourse with the fugitive. The Lollards did not remain so quiet. Bills were fixed to London church doors stating that 100,000 men were preparing to revolt, and messages were sent to sympathisers all over England damning the King as the Priests' Prince and calling for a rising, with the promise of 50,000 apprentices and servants ready to revolt in London itself.

Protestant writers for generations have insisted that there was no real plot afoot, but this cannot be denied. The spiritual revolt had become a political one but it is doubtful if the Lollards intended to take the throne from Henry, although they certainly did intend to take Henry from the priests. The anger was not against the King but against the Church. If this revolt had succeeded we might have had the Reformation a hundred or so years before its time; that it did not succeed must be placed to the credit of Henry who, by courage and swiftness, crushed the rising before it had fully started.

The Lollards had now a name, the name of Oldcastle, to inspire them but they lacked a leader. If they could only have found a man to equal Henry there would have been civil war, but Oldcastle was incapable of organising his mob of artisans, apprentices, labourers and merchants. He was no Jack Cade, he was a scholar, a gentle-man-soldier with little knowledge of generalship. The Lollards were a rabble, and Henry had two organised forces behind him in the State and the Church. The majority of Englishmen might be Lollards but they could not coalesce into an army. They were a disorganised mob of dreamers.

It was the evening of January 9, 1414, that the rebels began to gather in the fields near St. Giles outside the city walls. There seems to have been no attempt at a set plan, they merely gathered there. It is this haphazardness that has emboldened later Protestant writers to insist that it was a kind of prayer-meeting, that these Lollards were only meeting to worship after their fashion. This idea is untenable. The Lollards were preparing to march against their King, and their choice of position—right under the city walls—shows how greatly they relied on the sympathy of London, how powerful the movement was emotionally.

Henry was at Eltham arranging with his three brothers—Thomas was home again—for Christmas. He knew that a rising was intended for there were the inevitable traitors in the plot, and some obviously would-be assassins were found in the palace grounds and imprisoned; then news arrived of the mob in St. Giles. Instantly Henry rode with his brothers, Archbishop Arundel and a gathering of lords and friends straight for Westminster. Seeing the people moving towards the city he could not doubt the truth of the report, and sent messengers to call out the watch and to have the city gates shut and barred. Then he made for St. Giles itself.

Suddenly a meteor swept across the dark winter sky, dragging its dissolving tail of light for the length of a bow-shot. Both parties seized this as the material finger of God—to the Lollards it proclaimed that they must blaze England with the new faith, to the Church it meant that it must smite with lightning.

As the Lollards trooped from the country they were captured by the King's men stationed on the roads. In St. Giles' Field the gathering was large— we cannot be sure of the exact numbers—and the King was counselled to wait until dawn for reinforcements. But Henry knew the risks of seeming to be weak and frightened; only by courage and recklessness can a leader hope to succeed. To fall back now would hearten the rebels and dishearten his own men; the city gates were shut and the expected London help could not join the Lollards, while Henry's guards were holding any one who came from the country.

He stood his ground, and his mere presence

was enough to terrify that leaderless mob. It fled.

We cannot be certain whether Oldcastle was in St. Giles' Field that night, but he probably was. At any rate he was not captured there. Four pairs of new-made gallows were erected on the high-road near St. Giles and were called the "Lollers' Gallows." Thirty-seven condemned men were dragged there and hanged; some of them had fires lighted under their toes so that they could go straight to hell *via* both the King's and the Church's justice. A proclamation was sent to the sheriffs of every county commanding the arrest of Lollards; and further rebels paid the penalty (of their numbers we are not certain, but there must have been many). Then Henry, having shown his power and his allegiance to the Church, with great tact pardoned all but a few of the leaders.

This second proclamation proves that the Lollard doctrines were no longer accepted by the majority of the ruling classes; they had become the beliefs of the merchants and artisans. Perhaps for this reason the nobles had lost interest, object-ing to a movement that was becoming a matter of class, for the Church was distinctly aristocratic, excluding from its monasteries any one not of good birth or unable to afford heavy entrance fees. Also most of the nobles had relations in the Church, while the poor people were excluded; therefore the poor actually supported the wealthy and that explains much of the revolt. It was a socialist movement almost; a revolt not against religion but against wealth. In those days, unless a man made his will in the presence of a clerk, the will was void, and at any one's death the Church took thirty per cent. of the deceased's goods on the plea that these were tithes that had never been paid in full; the tithes themselves were exceptionally heavy, being ten per cent. on all earnings, and from this ten per cent. you could not deduct cost of materials or labour. During Parliament, as we have seen, Henry had promised to redress many of these grievances, particularly the price of the probate of wills and the excessive fines for immorality, but he had no intention of interfering with his friends, and it was not until some time later that he brought the probate price down a little, making a fixed rate. In every way from now on Henry showed himself a most strict Catholic; and a true Catholic in the Middle Ages was a man who never questioned a single doctrine and who believed the utterances of each new Pope to be utterly infallible, even when they directly contradicted the edicts of the previous Pope. We might sum the whole question up by saying that the Catholic faith was—not did you believe in Christ but did you believe in the Pope.

Nevertheless the Lollards had been allowed to grow with little interference, and it was not until the movement became political that action was really taken. All the same the political side of Lollardy was forced on them; they had to revolt if they wanted freedom, the pressure was too heavy, and none doubted that the fall of Oldcastle was but a prelude to a wholesale burning.

From now, Richard II becomes associated with the movement. Why this should be it is difficult to understand, for Richard had never been lax with the Lollards. I suppose that they had to

K

choose some symbol, and as the Earl of March was apparently loyal, there was only the false mummet in Scotland to turn to.

Oldcastle had escaped, making for Wales, and Henry offered 1000 marks from his own privy purse as a bribe to any one to catch him; while any town or village that would surrender Oldcastle would be made free of taxes, tallages, tenths, fifteenths and all public imposts for ever.

Despite this amazing offer Oldcastle was not given up. The Lollard faith must have been strong indeed to resist such inducements.

While the King was seeking Oldcastle he undertook to pay a pious debt. Richard II had always been kind to Henry and there was some affection between the two; now Henry decided to carry out the wishes set forth in Richard's will.

That unfortunate King had asked to be buried next to his wife, Anne, in Westminster Abbey, in the tomb which himself had designed.

On December 4, 1413, Henry brought the remains of Richard from Langley and had the body taken from its leaden covering and laid in a new elm coffin. The great cortège, crawling at the snail's pace requested by Richard, came with the light of one hundred and twenty torches, with priests singing dolefully around the black velvet-draped hearse.

Henry attended the service at Westminster, distributed largesse, and arranged for large tapers to burn without dying beside the tomb.

I pause here for a note of tragedy. In *Archæologia*

for 1880 there is a description of Dean Stanley's opening of King Richard's tomb. When the marble slabs were lifted the watchers saw "the broken and rotten boards of coffins, and bones, apparently in great disorder, especially two skulls which lay towards the foot of the grave."

When the tomb had been built, by some extraordinary carelessness it was not made airtight, and when five metal shields on its side were dislodged five holes were exposed. Nobody seems to have bothered about filling up these holes and sightseers used to poke their hands inside and play with the bones. They also used to put stupid articles inside. These were all found when the tomb was opened, together with a fifteenth-century plumber's shears left behind, evidently by accident. Not only did these wretched people play with the bones, they also stole them. One schoolboy from Westminster filched poor Richard's jawbone. It has at last been recovered and put in its rightful place, back into the tomb.

This tomb, built with such love by Richard himself, reverenced so deeply by Henry V, rotted in the Abbey until the restorer did his best to defile whatever remained; it is with a feeling of sick horror that one reads the name of Mr. G. Richmond, R.A., who "kindly took in hand the restoration of these paintings." To such vandalism, to the grubby hands of schoolboys stealing jawbones, to the brush of an R.A. smearing over lovely if faded fifteenth-century paintings, does the pomp and magnificence of Kings descend. Yet somehow it is an end fitting for Richard. His life had been purposeless and confused, and now his bones are muddled inextricably with the bones of the woman who had been his dearest, most loving comrade.

Forgive this excursus, but that paper read before the Society of Antiquaries fills me with a sense of horror impossible to suppress.

Archbishop Arundel died on February 16, 1414. He was now sixty-two and for some days before his end he was unable to swallow, having a stricture in the throat.

He had been a sincere ruthless and yet kind-hearted man. If his sincerity carried him to cruelty, stifling the gentleness of his heart—yet he wept for Oldcastle and pleaded for Badby—he cannot be blamed, and posterity, I feel, has often damned him more than he deserves. In a way, there is something pathetic in this man who was so driven by his faith that he resisted his own humanity. The forces he unleashed were too strong for his weak hands; they must have horrified him while he admitted their necessity. Even his contemporaries thought him a little harsh because of his attempts to stop free-preaching, but he was carrying out the logic of his beliefs. In a way, he was a great man.

The tragedy is that he saw only the beginning of his own movement, and died so quickly after Oldcastle's condemnation.

Parliament met on April 30, 1414, and the anti-Lollard battle continued in the passing of a statute that placed the civil powers wholly in the hands of the Church; this decreed that every official from the chancellor to a village constable must swear to destroy all forms of Lollardy in his power; also, seculars were to have the right to inquire into any suspicion of heresy and to behave as if they were acting for the Church. The only protest to this edict seems to have come from Cambridge, but it was soon quelled.

We will go no further into the persecution of the Lollards; it is not a pretty episode in English history, and to continue with trials and recantations and burnings would but weary the reader, each trial and burning being so like the other.

Enough has been given to show Henry's strict orthodoxy. And Henry's attitude towards life is our main problem. I am liable to forget, so distracting are the varied interests of the fifteenth century, that this is not a history of England but of Henry V.

Nevertheless I find it difficult to leave this Leicester Parliament. Some of the statutes are of genuine interest, particularly the efforts to stop piracy at sea and lawlessness on land; but we must hurry on to reach what is the crowning magnificence, if chief futility, of Henry's reign—the reconquest of France.

# CHAPTER EIGHT

## *To France*

WHAT right had Henry V to the throne of France? So hazy a right that he himself did not claim it at first. It descended to him from his great-grandfather, Edward III. Edward's mother Isabel had been the daughter of King Philip IV; Philip's three sons—Louis X, Philip V and Charles IV—all reigned for a brief while, and the crown then went to Philip VI, son of Charles of Valois, brother of Philip IV. He obviously had a better right than Edward, who could only claim through the female side, and that was in direct contradiction to the Salic Law, which banned females from reigning. Actually Henry V had little right to claim any inheritance through Edward; the Earl of March was the rightful claimant—if there was a rightful claimant to so preposterous a demand.

Edward III himself had not used the title "King of France" until the war had been running for about two years. His invasion was decided on because the French King sent aid to Scotland. The English had always controlled a large slice of France in the south, the heritage of Eleanor of Aquitaine. This was held as a fief with the French King as the over-lord; Edward and his splendid son, whom to-day we call the Black Prince, invaded and conquered most of France, but their greatest success was the capture of King John, who was locked in the Tower of London. Peace was signed at Brétigny near Chartres on May 8, 1360. According to this Edward surrendered his title of King of France in exchange for the duchy of Aquitaine—not as a fief, but as an English colony, with which King John could not interfere,—and for Poitou, the Limousin, Quercy, Rouergue, Marche, Angoumois and Calais; the French had also to pay 4,000,000 gold crowns ransom for King John.

Aquitaine rebelled in 1369 because of the heavy taxes imposed by the Black Prince, and it proclaimed King Charles V as its rightful King. For eleven years there was further fighting, in which the English were gradually pushed out of France, until they were left with only Calais and Guienne. This victory must be placed to the credit of that heroic ugly little man Bertrand du Guesclin, one of the greatest of medieval soldiers, and also to the weakness of John of Gaunt. England in France was doomed when the Black Prince died. Then Richard II at the Peace of Paris signed a truce with King Charles VI by which he surrendered all lands except Calais and Bordeaux and Bayonne and the Gascon territory between them.

I do not for one moment believe that Henry V doubted his right to France when the dream began to take shape. At first he was not really aware of his own intentions but when France lay open to him he actually began to deceive himself into the fixed belief that he was the rightful King coming to claim a heritage.

On his death-bed Henry confessed to the dream of a crusade, of the rebuilding of Jerusalem's walls.

He also remarked that he did not believe that he had ever harmed any man unjustly. It is the righteousness of Henry that is his main characteristic. One can see the gigantic ambition towards which he strove, an ambition doomed at birth—not only did he wish to heal the Great Schism, in which he succeeded, and to unite England and France, but also to hold a Catholic empire against the infidel with himself on the throne. He did not begin with this ambition; it is the kind of Alexandrian dream that follows conquest, not precedes it. But in studying Henry's character there is one point that persists in one's mind and which colours all one's estimates. That was his utter belief in himself and in his own triumphant destiny. This arrogance, this sublime faith, protected him from ever realising the futility of his conquests which were indirectly to lose his own son the throne of England. He became wholly the instrument of God, and in his way—a cold, sane way—was as inspired as the Maid of Orleans who did so much to smash what he had built. But the Maid was not a soldier, she was not even a leader; she was an angel, a symbol to the troops. Henry was more than this, for he was a great soldier. His own destiny never blinded him to the present, it did not hamper his actions or muddle the decisiveness of his thoughts.

Later writers have suggested that the invasion of France was forced on Henry by the Church, because it feared that Henry intended to take some of its lands; other writers insist that it was a diplomatic move against the Lollards, an effort to unite all England by a common enemy.

I cannot believe that Henry himself had any such

motives. He followed his star with unfaltering
belief and courage.

France was still broken by civil war. To discuss
in detail the quarrels would only be monotonous:
it is a see-saw of the Armagnacs in power, then
the Burgundians; of the Burgundians, then the
Armagnacs. King Charles VI still suffered his
periods of lunacy, and his son Louis, if not insane,
was equally as useless. He preferred sleeping,
eating, drinking and lechery to fighting.

Henry listened to proposals from both sides:
the Burgundians offered help in war—always
with the proviso that Henry wished only to reconquer his grandfather's lands conceded at the
Peace of Brétigny, and not to steal the throne of
France—and the Armagnacs offered the King's
daughter, slices of territory and an enormous
dowry. Henry, only too eager to pounce, preferred
the Burgundians; his brothers, Clarence and
Gloucester, preferred the Armagnacs, Clarence
having fought with them. Despite this, however,
there is no suggestion of any quarrel between the
brothers.

Ambassadors passed from country to country,
arguing, pleading. It was quite obvious, although
he pretended to be pained by the constant re-
fusals, that Henry did not want peace, he wanted
war, and he only carried on negotiations to gain
the necessary time for arranging an army.

There is a story told that the Dauphin in a
moment of bravado insolently offered to send
Henry "little balls to play with, and soft cushions
to rest until what time he should grow to a man's
strength." Henry is reported to have answered,

"If God so wills and my life lasts, I will within a few months play such a game of ball in the Frenchman's streets that they shall lose their jest, and gain but grief for their game."

It is with real regret that I discard this story immortalised by Shakespeare, but it does not fit into the accepted facts. If this had really happened, negotiations would never have dragged on as they did, it would have meant instant war.

At the same time it is a nearly contemporary story and may have been spread for propaganda purposes to stir up the people.

Henry was quietly preparing for his embarkation all the while that he pretended to negotiate with both Burgundian and Armagnac. Arrows and bows were being cut at top speed in London; barrels of brimstone were being stowed in Poultney's Inn, Henry's old town-house; in the Tower, the smiths were casting cannon; cannon were coming from distant towns. Every possible kind of steel instrument with which to murder, every kind of ram, tower, pontoon and engine was being made. Ships were being repaired and built, oaks were chopped down, nails and rigging prepared; foreign ships were stolen, impressed. It was forbidden to export gunpowder from England.

A great council was held in Westminster Palace on April 16, 1415, and the lords and bishops were asked to help in the great invasion. Arrangements were made to protect the coast, the Scottish Border and the Welsh marches; and Henry's brother, John, Duke of Bedford, was appointed lieutenant of England during the King's absence, with a council of nine, headed by the Archbishop of Canterbury, Henry Chichele.

War was now a costly business, for the old days of feudal military service were gone. If Henry called out his feudal tenants who held their land by military tenure he could not force them to serve for longer than forty days, an impossibly brief period for a war that was estimated to last a year. Henry had to raise his men by indentures; in other words he had to pay them wages. Not only this, but he had to bear all cost of sea-transport for man and beast.

Henry did not deal with the actual soldiers but with the leader of each troop, with the noble or the knight. This officer pledged himself to produce a certain number of men, the King was responsible only for their transport. The wages were paid to the officer who then paid his soldiers. The range of prices shifted according to the status of the men. A duke was given 13s. 4d. per day, an earl 6s. 8d., a knight banneret 4s., a knight 2s.; men-at-arms and archers had a sliding scale of 4s., 2s., 1s., and 6d. (A skilled artisan in those days drew a daily wage of 5d., a labourer 3d.)

On the day appointed for embarkation the officer reported to an exchequer official who verified the number of men brought and who estimated the wages. The wages began from this day, the day of *monstratio* or muster. The indentures would be filed at the Westminster exchequer, evidently being kept in pouches that were hung on the wall. According to Dr. Wylie, 632 of these pouches were bought in 1416, and to-day we can only find eighteen.

In return for this enormous cost, the King had

certain rights. One-third of all booty was his, and any of the royal family who might be caught were his to ransom. Besides, he would have little expense beyond wages and transport: provisions were mainly taken from the conquered country, and according to old statutes every man in England was compelled to have a certain amount of harness always ready: a jack—a quilted coat of steel or bone and wadding—, a helmet, gloves—to protect the hand when firing a bow—, a sword, a dagger, a pole-axe—axe-heads on five-feet poles, with a spear-tip on top and at back, suitable for thrusting or slashing, the most popular weapon—, a number of arrows and a bow.

Henry made frantic efforts to borrow money and did manage to raise a large sum, the exact amount of which is uncertain. The clergy voted double its usual amount, and the whole country was equally as generous, all being eager for conquests.

It seems that, before embarking, Henry went off on a pilgrimage. This is typical of his new attitude and his belief in the justness of his cause. Not for one moment did he realise that his claim was worthless and that he was taking unfair advantage of a country broken by years of civil strife.

After the pilgrimage, on June 16, Henry took farewell of his stepmother, Queen Joan, and then went to service at St. Paul's. From St. Paul's he rode through the City attended by his nobles, and blessed the mayor, aldermen and citizens, saying, "Christ save London!"

The expedition had at last set out.

But first there were French ambassadors to

meet at Winchester and to be rid of, and meanwhile, when everything seemed so clear and safe in
England, there was a threat of treason.

The Earl of March, the rightful heir, was a weak
man, who was evidently afraid of Henry. As the
troops were preparing to embark he came to the
King to tell of a dangerous plot.

Many writers have defended the earl, speaking
of him as a simple man involved accidentally in
something he abhorred. This cannot be accepted.
Obviously March was thick in the plot and grew
afraid at the last moment; for some days he had
been freely discussing the matter with other
conspirators.

Henry was at Porchester when March confessed.
He acted at once, summoning all his nobles as if
to discuss the campaign. Then he told them of the
treason he had heard. Three of the most important
traitors, seeing that all was hopeless, confessed
instantly. These were the Earl of Cambridge, and
Henry Lord Scrope, and Thomas Grey.

This is a peculiar conspiracy, almost motiveless.
Cambridge seems to have been the actual in-
stigator of it. He had married Anne Mortimer,
the elder sister of the Earl of March; that gave him
his link in the chain, for if the false Richard could
not be made King after Henry's assassination,
the Earl of March was to be crowned; then on
Anne's death he had married Maud Clifford,
whose brother had married Hotspur's daughter:
that forged a second link. Hotspur's son, Henry
Percy, was a prisoner in Scotland, and a part of
the conspiracy was, by a process of exchange, to
free both Percy and the false mummet.

The second conspirator was Thomas Grey, a Northumberland knight, Hotspur's cousin. The third conspirator was Henry Lord Scrope, and he is the most peculiar of them all, for he was well-beloved by Henry. He was one of Henry's chief advisers, had treated constantly with French ambassadors, had slept in the King's bed, and had been named as one of the trustees in the King's will in case Henry died abroad. Matrimonial alliances had probably drawn him into the chain too, for he was married to Joan Holland, second wife of the late Duke of York and therefore step-mother to the Earl of Cambridge. It was Scrope's part in the conspiracy that shocked not only the King but all England. It was inexplicable. The simplest knot to unravel in his character is the explanation given by many of his contemporaries—during one of his recent embassies he had been bribed by the French.

There were too many people mixed in the plot. Oldcastle was included (he was hiding near Malvern and bobbed up for a moment, only to disappear almost immediately), and his inclusion seems to have broken Scrope who was a good Churchman. The day had been fixed for the rising and the assassination when Scrope heard that Lollards were in the conspiracy. He rushed at once to the Earl of March and warned him that if the Lollards were involved the attempt was doomed. So terrified was the earl by Scrope's fury that he went immediately to Henry and revealed everything.

Grey being a mere knight was condemned on his confession, but Cambridge and Scrope were judged by their peers; and amongst those peers we find to our amazement the name of the Earl of March!

Thomas Duke of Clarence, the King's eldest brother, presided, and both men were sentenced to be drawn, hanged and beheaded. Only on Scrope did the full penalty fall, for Henry was unable to forgive him. Cambridge and Grey were merely to be beheaded and were saved from the disgrace of being drawn on a hurdle to the place of execution and of being hanged, a humiliation which most men feared more than death itself.

The traitors had died and the conspiracy had ended before it had begun; now with a free mind Henry could leave England, and the process of embarkation began.

It is impossible to be sure of Henry's exact force; apart from non-combatants—priests and his household men, Henry did not permit the usual female camp-followers—he must have had about 2500 men-at-arms and 8000 archers.

Before leaving, Henry signed his will which had been already drawn up in London. It is unnecessary to quote this here, but it is remarkable for its extreme piety, by the amount of saints it calls upon and the exact amount of Masses it requires in the event of Henry's death. There is one point of interest which cannot be explained: amongst the legatees his brother the Duke of Clarence is not mentioned.

His rebels defeated, his will signed, on Wednesday, August 7, 1415, King Henry left Porchester, and in a boat was taken to his ship, *The Trinity*, anchored in Southampton Water. She was the greatest English ship afloat and was called "The King's Chamber," for it was the ship in which he lived; attendant ships were known as "The Wardrobe," "The Kitchen" and so on. The Trinity banner was broken at her mast-head; and streamers and getons, brilliantly decorated with figures of the Trinity, of the Blessed Virgin, and of the arms of St. George, St. Edward and England, fluttered from the rigging. At her beak-head crouched a painted wooden leopard wearing a crown.

The sail yard was hoisted half-mast as a signal for the fleet to gather, but it took three days for the fifteen hundred craft to reach the flagship. As each ship arrived she struck her flag in honour of the Trinity, and fell-to astern. Each ship came sailing to *The Trinity*, to Henry's Chamber—beautiful ships, high-arched, with poop and prow almost seeming to meet, with men saluting in the fighting-tops above the great sails, under the pennons. The blue waters were crowded with these bird-like vessels, their painted sails rich with the signs of heraldry; stiff pennons flew from the masts, and painted pavasses were stretched along the bulwarks, above the red hulls.

The great fleet of England sailed or rowed into Southampton Water, falling always behind *The Trinity* in which their King sat watching.

One ship caught fire, the flames spread to another, and to another, and all three vessels had to be pushed off and left to burn down to the water's rim. Evidently this was started by some traitor, and it seemed an omen to many of the soldiers; but the King would not listen to their cowardly superstitious advice. He knew that God was with him. Yet a feeling as of coming doom spread around the decks of that mighty fleet, and those who had been merry, joking of the plunder, of the women and the good fighting that would soon be theirs, felt the laugh die on their lips.

No omen could affect the spirits of King Henry. He had the trumpets sounded, the sails let loose, and on Sunday, August 11, sailed with his fleet out into the narrow sea towards the hidden shores of his destiny, the land of France.

# CHAPTER NINE

## *Harfleur*

As the fleet neared the Isle of Wight a cloud of swans raced to the ships and fluttered about *The Trinity*. This was a good omen and wiped the memory of that fire from men's thoughts. The adventure took on a brighter light. Nobody knew at which point the King intended to land, and the French were frenziedly rebuilding as many of their coastal towns as they could, and in particular Boulogne, which seemed the obvious point for Henry to choose.

But calm in the knowledge of his own high destiny, Henry had chosen Harfleur as the spot into which to drive his steel wedge preparatory to the great march on Paris. Harfleur was notorious as a pirate centre and was a powerfully built although small city. In fact, it was considered impregnable from any side, being the stoutest town in all Normandy. Enclosed in a brick wall two and a half miles in circumference, and beyond the wall a great ditch, it was indeed well protected; and nature was there to help man's efforts. The Lézarde pierced the walls to the north-west, flowing through the town and into the mouth of the Seine. The city at this time was beginning to suffer from the fall of the sea; eventually the sea was to steal far away, and Harfleur was to die as our own Rye and Winchelsea have died. At this period the citizens were fighting for their existence with every form of medieval engineering, building dykes, sluices, and such. It was a hopeless battle; and in the sixteenth century Havre was to rise on the opposite bank to take the place of Harfleur.

The English fleet anchored at Chef de Caux, a great chalk headland near the suburb now known as St. Adresse, about three miles from the town. Henry flew the banner of council at half-mast, and when his officers had come aboard *The Trinity* they decided that the landing would be started on the following morning. But none must leave the ships until the King himself had landed. Henry understood the danger of letting his men loose without their King being by to watch and strike them into subordination.

In the darkness of before-dawn a pinnace crept from the shadow of the fleet and edged along the shore, seeking a landing-place. John Holland was in command. He chose a nearby ridge that was about half a mile wide and which was strewn with rocks, cut by ditches and banked with walls. Between six and seven in the morning the disembarkation began. When he landed, King Henry knelt on the sand and prayed for the grace to commit naught in the ensuing war that would not work for the honour of God and the fulfilment of justice.

Boat after boat was rowed or sailed to that perilous landing-place but not a Frenchman dared sally out of Harfleur. Without a shot being fired or a blow struck, the English landed on the soil of the country they had come to steal. But the garrison in Harfleur was very small, consisting of a mere four hundred men-at-arms, and the officers, naturally enough, preferred to take the safer course of strengthening the walls rather than risk a mêlée. But a great soldier would have staked everything on this one chance and might have succeeded before the English could become organised.

Tents were pitched on a hill, each tent topped with the owner's arms. For three days the landing continued, the slow process of bringing off men, stores, ammunition and cannon being a laborious task. The soldiers spread out and in the typical medieval fashion wandered off to gather booty, murdering, stealing and ravishing as they wished. Henry soon tried to put a stop to this. That he did not succeed completely must be placed to the reckless brutality of the English soldier, not to any laxity on the King's part. He sent all captured peasants back to work and returned them their horses, oxen, ploughs and harrows. His rules were designed to stop plundering and immorality. They forbade interference with any priest, monk, nun or church; harlots were not to come within three miles of the camp at the risk of having their left arms broken after one warning; every man at muster must wear a large red St. George's cross; children under fourteen were not to be captured; no chamber was to be used in which a woman lay in labour.

When all were landed, the siege began. By breaking down the bridges across the Lézarde the French had dammed the river, and all the valley was flooded; across the harbour-mouth great chains were drawn. The English rowed over the river and the flooded area, hoping to blockade from the east side, but that was not possible at the moment.

A council of war was called and, gazing at the

glum faces of his officers, Henry is reported to have cried: "Fellows! be of good cheer, breathe you and cool you and then come up with your ease, for with the love of God we shall have good tidings!"

Although Henry kept magnificent court in his tent as if he were in his own Westminster Palace, he nevertheless spent most of his time inspecting the lines. Dressed like an ordinary soldier, he would stroll about before the walls of the town, seeking to discover the weakest points. For it was decided that, as there was water in Harfleur and enough provisions to last for months, the garrison must be fought. This meant mining, the shooting of cannon and the hammering of rams.

Harfleur had two gates, one each side of the estuary, and every day the French would charge out of these gates, would smash into the English lines and scurry back again. Yet Henry continued with his siege as if he had all the time in the world, nothing could flurry or excite him; with the same bland air he listened to a tale of victory or disaster. No man could read the thoughts in those hazel eyes, in the mask-like face, the stern mouth. His great cannon flung stone and iron at the walls, and the noise and fire of the engines did as much damage as the missiles, for such things were more or less new in warfare and they scared the French badly. Underground, his sappers sweated their way through tunnels, striving to burrow under the walls so that they could burn down the foundations. The French also dug, and there was fighting in the torchlight amongst the stinking fumes, and in the sudden darkness when somebody trampled on a torch. Day after day the catapults flung their stones at and over the walls, the gigantic metal-nosed rams thudded on the bricks and masonry. The besieged poured over the usual amount of boiling oil, lead and pitch, and flung powdered lime into the face of any man hardy enough to scale a wall.

Seeming never to sleep day and night, King Henry watched and helped his men, always calm, never disturbed or frightened, being quite certain of his destiny.

Thomas Duke of Clarence, the King's brother, with the Earl of Salisbury, set out one evening, after the French had been reinforced, to make a detour of the flooded area. Unless Harfleur was surrounded, the siege was hopeless, for food and men could always reach the garrison. The detour was successful. Clarence found a point at which the river could be crossed, and when morning broke, the soldiers in Harfleur gazed up appalled to see English cannon pouting at them from a hill to the north-east which had always been thought unscalable.

From here, Clarence not only had a perfect target, being able to shoot straight into the town, but he could intercept all supplies. And he carried off a quantity of gunpowder, quarrels—cross-bow shafts—and cross-bows that were coming from Rouen. The French charged to the rescue but they were chased back, and the booty was Clarence's.

Now Harfleur was surrounded, for with the English fleet in the estuary it had no hope of succour coming that way. Henry offered to treat for surrender with the garrison.

When the garrison refused he set solemnly to work to blow it to fragments. His cannon were dragged up through a storm of arrows and his men battered and shot at the walls, with hides and shields held up to protect them from the deluge of boiling fats and oils that was poured down.

The French worked heroically, day and night. Fighting all day, they spent the night in repairing the gaps in the walls, in dragging up stone, sand and wood, and in preparing the quota of fats and pitch for the morrow, in cutting arrows and sharpening weapons.

Under a shield of faggots, Clarence crept close to Harfleur. Inch by inch, his men pushed their way over the ground, holding up fascines against the arrows that showered on them, and at last they managed to crawl into the eastern part of the moat.

Slowly Harfleur was being broken down.

If it was not broken soon, it would be a worthless victory. The summer was an extraordinarily fierce one, and the knights were scarcely able to bear the heat inside their armour. Food too was running short. Henry had sent to Bordeaux for supplies but none as yet had arrived. His own stores were giving out, for some had evidently been damaged by sea-water on the passage over. Besides the slackening of supplies, the usual fevers were arriving. These fevers attacked nearly all medieval armies during a prolonged siege, but they were accentuated before Harfleur because of the extreme heat and the nearby marshes. Men would stagger away from the fight and would greedily lap up cold water and were immediately

struck down; the air stank with rotting bodies—
not only with the bodies of men but of the cattle
that had been slaughtered for food. Too much
unripe fruit was eaten, too much bad water drunk,
too much stinking air was breathed. Flux and
dysentery dragged the men to their beds, dragged
down knights as well as common soldiers. Henry
served wine, beef and flour from his royal store
to the fever-stricken men, but two thousand of
them are said to have died. And amongst these
was one of the King's dearest friends, Richard
Courtenay, Bishop of Norwich, Arundel's old
enemy. With his own hands, Henry bathed the
dead man's feet and closed his staring eyes.

Both armies were growing desperate. The
French sallied out on September 16 and managed
to burn some English stores—a greater victory
than the killing of men—but they were soon
driven back. Furiously the English led assault
after assault on the walls, and managed to burn a
part of them.

Henry decided that he had delayed too long.
He would finish with Harfleur in one great finale,
and a general assault was ordered for the morning
of September 18. The night before, his guns never
ceased. They hurled their missiles at the walls, the
great rams thudded continuously.

It was too much for the besieged. They sent a
message to the Duke of Clarence, offering to
surrender if they were not relieved by noon on
Sunday, September 22. They offered peace at the
exact moment necessary to save their lives, and
Henry at first would not listen to any terms. The
assault was for dawn and he insisted that the

command must be carried out. But at length his determination wavered, kinder impulses overcame him, and he sent the Earl of Dorset, Lord Fitzhugh and Sir Thomas Erpingham to discover if the offer was genuine.

They soon discovered that it was genuine enough, and were given twenty-four hostages and an oath that the garrison would keep its word.

The town had now a few days of freedom, and anxiously citizen and soldier must have gazed towards where Rouen lay, hoping to see the glittering armour of the French knights and the standard of the Dauphin curling in the wind. But always the same unbroken view remained, no army rode to the rescue of Harfleur.

What was the Dauphin doing?

He was doing exactly nothing. France was broken into parties, Armagnac and Burgundian were at each other's throats, the King was mad, his son was a lazy lover of good things with no strength in his body or his will. Each party distrusted the other. When Burgundy offered to join the Dauphin with all his force, the offer was refused in terror. He was asked not to come but to send his son instead, and of course neither of them came.

All one's sympathy must go to the French knights writhing in shame under a cowardly leader while the enemy were smashing the walls of Harfleur. The Dauphin left Paris for Rouen on September 1, and on September 10 King Charles took up the oriflamme in St. Denis.

After that, nobody bothered to do anything, and Harfleur fell.

At noon on September 22, five hundred Englishmen stood at the gates of Harfleur to demand the keys. Out came the captain of the garrison, Lionnet de Braquemont, with his officers, each man dressed in a shirt of penitence and with a rope about his neck. Through lines of English soldiers the Frenchmen passed, until at the end of this avenue of steel-clad men they reached the silken tent at the foot of the western hill. Inside this tent, King Henry sat on a throne that was draped in linen and cloth-of-gold. Sir Gilbert Umfraville on his right hand held a pike, and on top of the pike rested the King's great tilting-helm.

To make the French still more penitent for their courageous defence of Harfleur, Henry let them remain on their knees apart from him, in different tents. Then pretending to be suddenly merciful, he forgave them, promised them their lives, and passed them into the safe-keeping of various knights.

The French standard was dragged down from the broken walls and the banner of St. George was hoisted up in its stead, its blood-red cross waving above the dead of both nations.

Next day Henry entered the conquered city. He took off his shoes and walked barefoot to the parish church of St. Martin to offer thanks to God. One of his brothers made a tour of the houses to assess the inmates' goods, and the inhabitants were roughly divided into three classes—those who would bring ransom, those strong enough to remain and work after taking the oath of allegiance to Henry, and those who were old or feeble.

It could be seen now why Henry had run counter

to his great-grandfather's advice always to avoid a siege: this was not purely a war of aggression but of conquest. Henry wanted to create in Harfleur a second Calais. And even further than this, Harfleur would make an ideal base for future forays into Normandy. Henry's kindness to his prisoners, his eagerness to keep them in their homes, was the kindness of a ruler towards his own subjects. All through the campaigns we find this attitude of his. He objects to seeing murder or wilful damage, not alone for humanitarian reasons, but because these people and this country were his, and no man likes to see his personal property ill-treated.

Those who refused to remain in Harfleur as his subjects Henry shipped to England to await the paying of their ransom (rumour said they were poisoned at Calais), all ecclesiastics were given their freedom, and the poor people were presented with a few shillings each to carry off with them. They didn't have to carry the money far, their own countrymen plundered them on the way to Rouen. The knights Henry released on condition that they surrendered to him at Calais by Martinmas.

The affair had been most orderly, surprisingly orderly for a medieval conquest.

In London, inducements were offered to Englishmen who would settle in Harfleur, but the scheme never prospered. Calais alone was expensive enough without a second foreign city to support.

While in Harfleur, Henry issued a challenge to the Dauphin. He challenged him to single combat, the winner to become King of France after the death of Charles VI. Henry gave the Dauphin eight days in which to reply; of course he never did get a reply and undoubtedly did not expect one.

This challenge is of real interest to us because it is the first sign we get of Henry's larger ambitions. Until now he had never pretended to ask more than what his great-grandfather had won at the Treaty of Brétigny. By this challenge he revealed that he wanted more than these lands, he wanted the whole of France. This is the first glimpse we get of that amazing dream of his, never stated definitely but always felt beneath Henry's actions, of welding the two nations into one and thus forming a Catholic Empire to withstand the rising flood of the infidel.

Henry no longer had the vast army with which he had left England. Over half of it had died or deserted. Some of the leaders were stricken down, including his own brother, that brave soldier the Duke of Clarence, and also the Earl of March. They pleaded to be invalided home and their plea was granted. They were shipped to England.

Apart from these losses, Henry had to place a strong garrison in Harfleur lest the French try to recapture it. He left twelve hundred men under the command of his uncle, the Earl of Dorset.

Now, Henry was in a perilous position. He had lost a great many soldiers and had spent a vast amount of money, and all that he had to show for it was the capture of one town. It was scarcely a prize worth offering a country like England that was waiting to hear of another Crécy or Poitiers, and his throne was not yet secure enough for him to risk the anger of his people. Somehow he must keep their faith, their love and their loyalty. To sail home and return again next summer would have been fatal. The first inspiration would have gone. And like all great generals, Henry realised the value of inspiration, the magic that there is in a name, in a leader. Victory begets victory, failure begets failure. He could not return to England almost empty-handed—yet with this feeble force what could he expect to do? what feats of greatness could he hope to achieve?

Altogether he could not have had more than nine hundred men-at-arms and five thousand archers. This was scarcely an army large enough to invade a foreign country, even when that country was split up into factions as France was now split up. Yet, gazing on the thinned ranks, Henry never lost courage. His belief in himself and in his destiny remained. He was only twenty-eight at the time, but he had the fortitude and stoicism of a man much older.

He would march to Calais.

His council tried to turn him from this mad purpose. When lying mortally ill during the siege, the Earl of Arundel—he died shortly after his return to England—had warned the King that if he persisted in the war, Burgundy would join with the Dauphin and he would be crushed. But nothing could deter Henry once his mind was made up. With the calm courage of one who does not understand fear, who believes himself immortal, Henry prepared to depart.

He told the council: "I have a great desire to see my lands and places that should be mine by right. Let them assemble their great armies, there is hope in God that they will hurt neither my army nor me. I will not suffer them, puffed up with pride, to rejoice in misdeeds, nor unjustly, against God, to possess my goods. They would say that through fear I had fled away, acknowledging the injustice of my cause. But I have a mind, my brave men, to encounter all dangers, rather than let them brand your King with word of ill-will. With the favour of God, we will go unhurt and inviolate, and, if they attempt to stay us, victorious and triumphant in all glory."

After that there was no argument. With his tiny force the King of England prepared to strike out into the reaches of upper Normandy, crossing the Somme and arriving in Calais in time to greet the surrender of the knights of Harfleur. It seems, looking back upon it, one of the most reckless ventures in history. With a handful of men, Henry dared to face all France and the dangers of starvation, he dared to march into unknown territory without hope of reinforcements or supplies, with enemies prepared to strike on every hand. It was madness, but an heroic and splendid madness such as only a very great man was capable of performing.

That Henry did perform it has caused his name to ring with magic down through the centuries.

# CHAPTER TEN

## *The March*

On Sunday, October 6, 1415, King Henry V set out on the splendid adventure. The distance from Harfleur to Calais was believed to be a hundred miles—it was more nearly double. The army was formed up in the customary medieval three battles: vanward, mainward and rereward, with two separate columns covering the flanks to left and right. The van was commanded by John Cornwall and Gilbert Umfraville; the King commanded the centre, supported by his brother the Duke of Gloucester, with John Holland and the Lord de Roos; the rear was under the Duke of York and the Earl of Oxford. It was not the splendid army that had sailed from Southampton Water. Disease and sudden death had thinned the ranks and even these remaining veterans must have been lean and scarred, their armour dirtied, jacks torn and decayed, helmets dinted.

Out of Harfleur they marched doggedly, behind their young King.

Henry took his baggage with him. There were jewels packed on his sumpter-mule; his crown, his sword of State, the chancery seals and a piece of the True Cross six inches long and over an inch wide, all followed him under the care of a sergeant of the pantry. Besides the army, he had with him the usual non-combatants, the chaplains and clerks and court officials. Amongst these

chaplains we are indeed fortunate that Thomas
Elmham dared the great adventure. Because of
this we have two first-hand accounts written by
him—one in verse, one in prose.

Henry had issued strict orders against pillaging,
but the French knew of his advance and had laid
waste the country, and it was hard for his men to
resist stealing what food they could. All the same,
it does appear that the march was—at least at
first—particularly orderly. Most of the towns they
tramped through gave them a little bread and
wine, being terrified by the example of Harfleur,
yet there was barely enough food to keep the
soldiers alive.

The French here and there made feeble efforts
to withstand the English. At Fécamp an army
waited under the Captain of Boulogne but it
seems to have done nothing except burn the town
and ravish the women. There was little fighting,
and Henry swerved to the right, losing only three
men, and thus avoiding the town. He reached
Arques on October 11. Arques itself was only a
small town but near it, at the meeting of two
streams, Bethune and Eaulne, was a particularly
strong castle. Henry drew up his army out of
range and asked for the right of passage. The
answer was to fire great stones which luckily fell
short. After this burst of defiance the garrison
lost its courage. Henry threatened to lay waste
the town and adjacent country unless he could
pass over the bridges, and he was immediately
given food and allowed to go where he wished.

The next day, the English approached Eu
between Dieppe and Abbeville. Here it seemed
that there was to be a battle, for they were told

that a large French army barred the way. Un-
daunted, Henry had his trumpets blown, his
banners unfurled, and strode forward with his
men. There was a short scuffle before the French
ran back behind the safety of their walls, and Henry
continued his march, after being given some
bread and wine and a few hostages.

Before him was the Somme and this was the
most difficult part of the enterprise. Already
Henry was deep in the country and could scarcely
retreat, and few doubted that the French chivalry
would not permit the passing of so small an English
force unopposed through their lands. Probably
Henry was hoping for aid from John the Fearless
of Burgundy; perhaps he relied on the civil war
to keep the French away from him. Both were
risky speculations. It was true that he had little to
fear from Burgundy but that was not Burgundy's
fault; he had offered to join the Dauphin and had
been refused. He did useful work indirectly, however, for the French were afraid of leaving Paris
unprotected lest he enter and take control of the
city. Nevertheless they were forced to make some
show, and mustered at Rouen, although they
spent their time arguing about the best policy
and who was to be captain.

When it seemed that at last the Dauphin would
make some gesture, knights and gentlemen galloped
to his standard. All the Armagnacs were there,
with the King of Sicily, and the Dukes of Orléans,
Berri, Bourbon, Alençon and Bar. Despite John
the Fearless's strict prohibitions many of his
followers were unable to resist the call of France;
his brother, the Count of Nevers, and many others
rode to the Dauphin; and his son—who was to

become Philip the Good—is said never to have forgotten the smear upon his honour because his father kept him at home.

Great as the French army was, courageous as the men were individually, it was but a disorganised mass, the leaders quarrelling with each other about precedence and refusing to obey the commands of men whom they considered their inferiors or their equals. The Dauphin, who should have been captain, was entirely useless; his efforts to drag money from the people almost led to a revolt, and many began to prefer the orderly English to their own tax-gatherers.

Meanwhile, Henry had paused in his march. He heard from a captured Gascon that a great French army was ahead and he made a detour in an effort to avoid meeting it. This changed his plans for he had hoped to cross the Somme at its mouth, over a cattle ford called the White Spot. He was only six miles from this White Spot when the Gascon told his story—as a matter of fact, a lie, but Gascons were always notorious liars— about six thousand men ahead and of great pointed stakes hammered into the ford. Henry turned to the south-east towards Airaines.

At every spot he touched on the river he found broken bridges and causeways, and the river itself swirling down impassably. News came of French armies on the opposite bank, keeping in step by step with the English, waiting for Henry to try to pass. Any attempt to build a makeshift bridge would expose Henry's men to immediate slaughter by this mythical army. Before the troops could be made to form up on the opposite side, they would be shot down. And Henry *had* to cross the Somme. He had arranged for an army to leave Calais and reinforce him. Actually this army was unable to march far, being soon driven back by the French.

Along the riverside tramped the English with growing despair. It seemed that they would have to follow the accursed Somme to its source before they could pass. Broken bridge after broken bridge, smashed causeways, wide areas of swamp and a rushing river. Food was running short, and they had only prayers to help support them on that desperate march; their stomachs rebelled against a diet of dried meat, walnuts and water.

Their hopes revived a little at Boves, for the castle was under the command of one of Burgundy's men who was away at the time. Here they were admitted and given quarters for the night, but little else. All the food obtainable consisted of but two baskets of bread, which couldn't have amounted to much more than a crumb or two per man. But there was wine. And the men fought for that wine as if they were battling with deadly enemies, struggling around the vats and barrels in a frenzy.

Henry tried to stop the uproar.

"What need?" asked some one. "The brave fellows are only filling their bottles."

"Their bottles!" cried Henry. "They are making great bottles of their bellies and getting drunk!"

Corbie was the next point. Here the garrison sallied out and in a brief skirmish managed to steal the standard of Guienne from Hugh Stafford. They did not hold it long, for John Bromley, a groom of the King's chamber, "gloriously recovered it again." The garrison was chased back to the castle and the road should now have been open; but the bridge was too well guarded to risk a passage. Even a small force of French could have done great damage to the army caught while moving over a bridge, crushing it before it could be formed on the opposite side. Henry dared not take any chances. Yet the Somme must be passed.

Wearily, the English dragged on through France.

Passing through a village, one of the soldiers entered a church and stole a pyx that contained the Host. It was a copper-gilt pyx and looked very like gold. When Henry heard of the sacrilege he halted his troops and refused to budge a step until the thief was brought to him. The poor wretch was hanged on a tree and the gold-looking pyx was given back to the church.

Red rags hung from the walls of Nesle to show that the garrison was defiant, but when Henry started to burn the countryside, the rags were pulled down. The garrison, only too eager for him to pass, explained that there were two un-guarded fords nearby. These fords were at Béthen-court and Voyennes and were approached both by a causeway over the swamp. The men of Nesle had not lied. The soldiers sent to guard these fords had decided that the English must be miles away, and the path was open. It was a tricky path, how-ever, only approached over marsh-lands into which the men sank to their armpits. Then when the marsh was crossed, the causeways were found to be broken. Henry set his men to work rebuilding them, pulling down nearby houses, chopping trees, and gradually the causeways were made firm again. It took all day to finish the task, from eight in the morning until nightfall, and even then there were parts not wide enough for two men to walk abreast. One causeway was given to the troops, the other to the baggage-mules and horses.

Two hundred archers half swam over the Voyennes ford and stationed themselves on a small hill on the opposite bank, ready to repulse any French that might dare attack. The King himself, who never disdained to work like a common man, stood guard at one ford. The crossing started at midday. First came Sir John Cornwall and Gilbert Umfraville, leading five hundred lances; then the foot-soldiers. It was a wretched dirty business, the horses and mules sank into the muck up to their bellies, the men were drenched and slimy with mud. But by sunset the whole army had crossed and stood upon the opposite bank of this river which they had cursed for days.

It must have seemed to them then that they were close to their goal, that the worst was over. Of course there would be a fight ahead, but no real English soldier ever troubled himself greatly about that, so long as there was wine and food to be had.

As the army struggled over the broken causeways, slipping in the wet and slime, detachments of the enemy watched from the distance, but few dared strike. Yet if there had been any organisation amongst the French, any leader of even average initiative, the whole of Henry's dream would have been destroyed that day on the marshes of the Somme.

The French themselves realised the opportunity they had missed, and for the first time they stopped their squabbles and began to consider the dangers ahead. Both the King and the Dauphin had wanted to push forward and battle with Henry, but the Duke of Berri persuaded them that their lives were too precious to risk. "Better to lose the battle," said he, "than to lose both the battle and the King." As a return for his consideration, evidently Berri was left to guard his royal masters at Rouen while the army marched to Amiens.

The Constable d'Albret and the Marshal Boucicaut—the famous jouster—were mainly responsible for the delay. They were veterans and knew the temper of the English, particularly when cornered, and therefore wished to avoid an open battle. At first, everybody with great optimism had believed that Henry would soon starve and be wailing for peace. When they discovered their mistake and heard of the crossing of the Somme there was something like a panic at headquarters. D'Albret and Boucicaut, considering the small numbers of the English, suggested remaining passive and thereby destroying the enemy's morale; the further Henry struggled under the constant fear of ambushes, of sudden attacks, the more desperate his soldiers would become and the easier prey. But the chivalry would not hear of such reasoning. They, French knights, to be scared by a handful of tailed Englishmen!

They decided to attack.

Now came the inevitable confusion about officers. Too many officers spoil any army, even the most efficient, and the French army was by no means efficient. Boucicaut and the Duke of Bourbon were given the van, d'Albret and the Dukes of Orléans and Alençon were to have the centre, and the rear was placed under the Duke of Bar and the Counts of Nevers and Vaudémont. The Count of Richmond and Tanneguy du Chastel were given the wings.

After crossing the Somme, Henry awoke the next morning to receive a challenge from the French army suggesting a meeting-place at which to battle. The King listened calmly to the stupid suggestion and said: "Let all things be done that are pleasing to God." When he was asked what road he intended using, he replied: "Straight to Calais. And if our adversaries attempt to stop this road, they will do so to their own hurt and great peril. We indeed do not seek them, nor will fear make us move either more quickly or more slowly. Nevertheless, we do urge them not to hinder our way, nor to seek so great an effusion of Christian blood." Then giving the heralds two hundred crowns he dismissed them, probably delighted to find some tangible force ahead after the varying rumours he had heard.

Yet as he advanced, no army barred his path, but near Péronne he saw in the mud the swirl and the twist of the feet of men and the hoofs of horses, he saw the marks of thousands, of the passing of a gigantic army, and he knew then that the heralds had spoken no empty threat.

Undeterred by this, Henry calmly continued the march, passing the Canche and eventually reaching the valley of the Ternoise. Here he mistook his lodging and rode for half a league beyond it. When told of the mistake he refused to turn back. "God would not have me go back and forage," he said merrily, "for I have my coat-armour on." The point of this rather feeble jest, explained by Elmham—who heard King Henry speak those words—is that the harbingers, the men who chose lodgings for the company, took off their blazonings before marking the houses and tents.

Actually both armies were marching very close to each other; and if the French had had a great leader, Henry could have been destroyed again and again by a surprise attack. But the French had decided in council to wait until they could find a suitable battle-ground: in other words, one in which they would have every advantage. This was sound enough, but it seemed scarcely necessary when the enemy was so terrifically outnumbered and exhausted as the English. By holding the bridges, the French could have stopped Henry from crossing the Somme or at Canche, and now again at Blangy. Henry crossed here with barely any trouble. Blangy was the last crossing of the march.

When the English were on the opposite bank and had clambered up a tall hill, they saw before them, coming from the valley to their right, great swarms of French pouring along in uncountable masses. Through the narrow neck they came, armour glinting, spear-heads shining like diamonds, Frenchman after Frenchman—cavalry, infantry, archers—and Henry must surely have felt some qualms as he gazed upon the dirty ragged group of hungry men at his back?

From the hill-top, Henry stared down at the French riding through the valley—infantry and baggage-carts, guns being dragged forward—until all the land was covered between Agincourt and Ruisseauville, and the enemy looked "like an innumerable host of locusts," says Elmham, "with only a small valley between them and us."

# CHAPTER ELEVEN

## *Agincourt*

WE must glance over the ground. There were three villages, each within a wood, and the battle-field lay between these villages. Agincourt—to-day called Azincourt—was to the north-west, Tramecourt to the north-east, Maisoncelles to the south. Between Agincourt wood and Tramecourt wood the field narrowed to about three-quarters of a mile in breadth but widened out towards Maisoncelles. The ground was therefore roughly triangular.

As they poured out of the valley, the French were making for the north, to lie in the narrow space between Agincourt and Tramecourt, and this choice of battleground was—to say the least—rather peculiar. It gave no particular advantage to either side and there was no possibility of playing tricks of any kind, ambushes, surprise-tactics, and such. It would have to be a clean fight.

We cannot be sure of the numbers of the opposing forces. Henry had no more, and probably a few less, men than when he had set out from Harfleur. The French are variously stated. Elmham, who was present, says that the English amounted to 6000, which is very likely correct, but he seems to make the French too large. They probably looked gigantic to him as he watched with horror the tiny English force and the monster gathering ahead.

He said that there were ten times as many French as English. One cannot tell what to believe when examining medieval numerals. Perhaps I am maligning poor Elmham; the French may have been ten times greater, certainly their force was very superior to the English. The lowest contemporary statement places them as three times larger, although they must have been more than that. If we say from four to five times greater we shall probably get somewhere near the actual numbers.

The disparity was certainly so enormous that even Henry faltered. He sent across the prisoners he had captured on the march, on condition that they would return to him if he won the day, and he offered to treat for peace. He said that he would give up all he had won and would pay for all damage if they would but let him pass. He added that if his request was refused he asked only that they would fight him the next day.

For the first and only time we see a weakness in Henry, for once his confidence forsook him and his destiny dwindled before that locust-army in his path. Yet he was not afraid. When his offer was curtly refused, he drew up his men in battle-array, wheeling his forces so that the van became his left and the rearguard his right. All knights were ordered to dismount, the King himself doing the same, and those who could confessed to the chaplains.

"Sire," said Sir Walter Hungerford, "I would that we had ten thousand more good English archers who would gladly be here with us to-day."

"Thou speakest as a fool!" cried Henry. "By

the God of Heaven, on Whose grace I lean, I would not have one more even if I could. This people is God's people. He has entrusted them to me to-day and He can bring down the pride of these Frenchmen who boast of their numbers and their strength!"

Then turning amongst the young autumn wheat, he spoke to his men, bidding them remember Crécy and Poitiers. And after he had spoken, all knelt and raised clasped hands to God, while the chaplains went through the ranks, confessing the men and giving them the Eucharist.

But it seemed that there would be no fighting this day. As evening came upon the two armies in that little space, Henry saw the French breaking their ranks and seeking lodgings. This was a welcome reprieve, for his men were tired. He issued strict orders that complete silence must be kept: no knight was to speak under penalty of losing horse and harness, and no soldier under penalty of losing his right ear. In the rain the men stretched themselves quietly amongst the fresh, warm-smelling wheat, or in the nearby gardens and orchards.

This strange silence worried the French who were drinking, eating and shouting and laying odds on the amount of prisoners and booty they would capture on the morrow; they feared that the English were sneaking off, and lit great fires and sent out detachments to scout in the surrounding country.

At one point between Maisoncelles and Tramecourt the opposing armies were so close that they could see each other's faces through the gloom, and the silent English lay in the mud and wet grass, listening to the riot, the drinking, the boasting, the quarrelling, a few yards off. That could have been no pleasant experience. They were hopelessly outnumbered, it would seem, and in that silence they could hear quite distinctly the rowdy French laying odds on who should capture King Henry. And not far distant, the French nobles were jesting as they painted a cart in which they were going to drag the King of England through the streets of Paris and Rouen.

Thus passed the night of Thursday, October 24, 1415.

Henry was on his feet at daybreak, dressed in full armour save for his helm, and wearing the royal jupon—three gold lilies of France on a blue ground, three gold leopards of England on a red ground.

After Mass, he formed his men into one line, for his host was too small for reserves; this line was four deep and spread out before the wood of Maisoncelles. Henry himself commanded the centre, the Duke of York held the right, and Lord Camoys the left. On either side of each division his archers were thrown forward, in formation like a split triangle; therefore, when divisions were side to side these archers met, forming a complete triangle, a series of wedges, known as a "herse" or harrow. On left and right flanks the wedges were incomplete, but were safeguarded by the woods. The tip of each wedge pointed towards the enemy and was four or five deep so that the archers could fire in every direction. The Duke of York had suggested the cutting of long stakes, and these were driven into the mushy ground before each archer, point outwards, as a protection against cavalry; these stakes stretched out knee-high. The horses and grooms were taken to the rear, horses ready saddled; chaplains, baggage and the sick were sent to the wood where the religious were commanded to celebrate Mass and to pray for grace all through the battle.

His forces disposed, Henry donned his bascinet which bore a gold crown crusted with jewels—with pearls, sapphires and a great spinel ruby. Unspurred, he mounted a grey palfrey and watched his men fall into line, under the strict command of dead silence. The banners were unfurled and the royal standard shook above the King, bearing the arms of Our Lady, the Trinity, St. Edward and St. George.

Henry asked what hour it was, and was told that it was prime—that is, six o'clock in the morning, the first Church office of the opening day.

"Now is good time," he cried, "for all England prayeth for us; let us therefore be of good cheer and go to our journey."

But the French were in no mood for attack. They had spent the night drinking and gambling and were rather weary. There seemed to them no reason for haste, as their force was vastly superior to the English. They were quarrelling most of the time on the question of precedence, each knight desiring the honour of being in the front rank, and the archers were contemptuously pushed to the rear, for they were not gentlemen. There was no leader, there was a collection of leaders, which is fatal to any army. All these leaders banded themselves together to form the front rank, and the van became the flower of the army, consisting of knights and men-at-arms carrying spears. Everything was so crowded, so muddled, that it is difficult for us to understand the exact formation. These knights and men-at-arms in the van were on foot, their spears and pikes being cut down for close-fighting, and there was a detachment of horsemen on either flank which was to swerve in and turn the English archers. Towards the rear were the cavalry and cross-bowmen.

For three hours the two armies faced each other, the English tense for the expected attack, the French apparently doing nothing. So great was the crush in the French van that many of the standards had to be furled and sent away, and there were constant arguments because the Burgundians objected to serving under the Armagnacs and the Armagnacs objected to serving under the Burgundians.

The terrible strain of waiting was beginning to tell on the silent English, who were weary and half-starved, and it must have been demoralising for so small a group to watch the gathering of that gigantic host.

Crossing himself, Henry gave the command to advance.

"Forward, banner!" he cried, "in the name of Jesus, Mary and St. George!"

Each man kneeled three times, kissing the ground to show that he would rather die than run away, and pressing earth to his lips, in the medieval manner, for a last earth-housel.

Sir Thomas Erpingham flung his warder into the air, and the cry was passed to the archers:

"Knee! Stretch!"

Then amidst the trumpets and drums, the English gave three shouts of defiance, "Hurrah! Hurrah! St. George and Merry England!" and moved forward towards that mighty enemy, on the cool morning of St. Crispin's Day.

At the English advance, the horsemen posted on the French flanks wheeled in to break the archers. But the ground was sodden with rain and the horses slipped, pawing futilely for a grip; those that drew close enough, fell upon the stakes, while the "arrowy hail" terrified the beasts, killed them or sent them flying back in hopeless disorder. They penetrated their own ranks, and the van—contrary to d'Albret's command—rushed forward with the cry of "Montjoie! Montjoie!"

In one gigantic mass of knights and men-at-arms the van swept down upon that little English host; clad in metal from toe to head, gripping their shortened lances, sliding along the wet ground, the chivalry of France swept down like a living sea of steel upon the English. And the English stood their ground. String drawn to ear, the shaft let fly; string to ear again, another shaft. . . .

The French were pulled up by that unerring fire and their ranks were broken by the fleeing mounted wings; their courage seemed to fall from them as if from men standing suddenly before an abyss from which they cannot draw back. Then the English archers rushed amongst them with mace and axe, smashing at them as at so much inanimate tin, hitting them on the bodies, in the faces; the knights in their heavy armour and in the too-great crush were unable to hit back at the swift, lightly dressed English.

For a moment, weight of numbers told and the English line fell back a spear's-length, then it stood firm, and the archers, using their bows, wiped out hundreds upon hundreds of the confused French, calmly shooting at them as if at a butt. When arrows were exhausted, these yeomen—not knights but yeomen—slung their bows on their backs and charged into that sea of steel, slaughtering enemy after enemy.

The whole battle seems incredible to us now, inexplicable. These few English murdered the French. It was little else, there was almost no real fighting. We cannot explain it except on the definite charge of cowardice, for the French ran. They were driven panic-stricken like men pursued by hornets. Much of the slaughter must also be put down to the actual numbers of the French. They had so many men that they were unable to fight, they were just "rolled up"—in the army phrase—they fell down and were trampled on. Those in the van tried to push back, those in the rear tried to push forward. All the while the English were slashing at them, beating them like metal on an anvil, stabbing into their faces with whatever came to hand—with swords, axes, maces, daggers, arrow-heads, spears.

There was no opportunity for individual exploits, although Henry, we are told, did prodigies of heroism, and he actually rescued the Duke of Gloucester, his brother, by standing astride his fallen body until help came. He had a bodyguard of archers who shot or clubbed a path for him; then he would dart forward with his men and work great havoc. And there was a group of French knights, eighteen of them, who pledged themselves to capture Henry's crown or die, "which they did." One of them knocked a fleuron off, but that was all the damage done.

It was said that many of the French surrendered ten times over, but there was no chance of taking prisoners at the moment. The fighting was too hot, and the men were carried exultantly off their feet by the amazing victory. The dead mounted higher and higher, and the English used them, jumping on to the bodies, and stabbing, clubbing. . . . In their stifling armour the French were helpless. Once down they could not rise again, while the lightly armed English archers—some with wicker bascinets faced with iron, some with leather hoods, most with leather or cloth jackets, all barefoot—could be anywhere, leaping in and out of the mêlée, delivering swift deadly strokes.

And all the time, the French rear stood idle, watching the slaughter, because it had received no orders.

Within half an hour, the English had pushed their way clean through the French ranks, and then they stopped to breathe and to watch the flying enemy. It was the moment for plunder, for the taking of prisoners, and they wandered amongst the bodies on the ground, seeking, by jupon or helm, men of noble birth, killing those badly wounded, hitting them in the face and body.

As they wandered amongst the corpses and the wounded, somebody shouted that French reinforcements were coming, that the fugitives had conquered their fears and were returning. They heard the distant warcry of "Brabant! Brabant!"

and at the same time news came that peasants were plundering the King's baggage in the rear and had actually carried off, amongst other things, the royal crown, the sword of State and the chancery seals.

Fearing to be taken on both sides—for the prisoners must have exceeded his own army—Henry gave the command that all must be killed. His men nearly rebelled at this. What! kill so much ransom! But Henry was determined. The risk was too great to run for the sake of money, but at the same time he forbade the killing of any who had fallen to his share. He swore that he would hang those who did not obey; he called a group of archers to him ready to execute the threat, and sullenly the English murdered their prisoners in cold blood.

The poor wretches of Frenchmen were at the moment unhelmed, as their captors were stripping them of valuable armour, and now their throats were cut, their faces slashed, their heads hit and their bellies stabbed. Those who had been carried into houses to have their wounds tended were not spared: the houses were burnt down on top of them. Even when all danger was past, the prisoners were still murdered.

For the cry that had started the whole massacre, the cry of "Brabant!", had been the act of a few reckless men.

The younger son of the Duke of Burgundy, Anthony Duke of Brabant, had ridden hard with a small troop to join the battle. He galloped so fast that he got far ahead of his men, and with only a few knights behind him reached the tragic scene—too late. As his full armour was not with him, he tore the blazon from a trumpet, made a hole in it and pushed his head through the hole, using it as a jupon—a sleeveless surcoat. Then he charged on his courageous and lunatic venture.

His throat was cut by some soldier who thought him not worthy of ransom, not knowing who he was because of the trumpet-blazon he wore instead of the knightly jupon.

Henry has been damned heavily because of this ghastly slaughter, but only later historians have damned him. The French at the time vented their rage wholly on the dead Brabant who had been the cause of it. He should have known that his countrymen were beaten, they said; if he had not led that silly charge, the flower of France would still have lived. And this is what galled the French—not that their chivalry had died but that it had died at the hands of despised yeomen.

The amount of dead it is impossible to calculate. The English said that from 10,000 to 15,000 French were killed and from 16 to 40 English. These numbers may be correct. Other writers, including the French, place the English losses from 100 to 600. Monstrelet is the one exception, he gives the English dead at 16,000, an obviously false figure.

When the battle was over, Henry asked what castle it was he saw in the distance through the rain which had begun towards the end of the fight, and he was told that it was Agincourt.

"Then," said he, "let this day be called the Battle of Agincourt."

He tried to stop too much plundering for there

might still be dangers ahead. He commanded that no man take more than he could easily carry. This did not save many of the wounded; spared by the English, they were plundered and murdered by their own peasants as they crawled off into the woods.

The bodies of the English dead—those which could be recognised—were taken apart and placed in a large barn, together with whatever plunder could not be carried off, and the whole was set alight and burnt to the ground. Only the corpses of the Duke of York, the Earl of Suffolk and a few others were saved from the fire. They were parboiled until the flesh dropped off, and the bones were collected for transport to England.

That night Henry, we are told, was served at dinner by his more important prisoners—who included the Duke of Orléans—and talked friendlily with them, not forgetting to point out that the victory had been given by God to His favoured nation.

Then he lay down and slept at Maisoncelles, close to the glorious and bloody field of Agincourt.

# CHAPTER TWELVE

## *The Return*

EARLY on the morning of October 28, 1415, a royal pursuivant was calling for admittance at the gates of London. He had letters for the Mayor and must see him instantly. Alderman Nicholas Wolton had taken his oath at the Guildhall the day before, and now his mayoralty was to begin with the most joyous news possible.

London awoke that morning to the ringing of bells from every parish church, for the King was not only safe at Calais, he had won a splendid victory over the French. Day had followed day with a sense of impending doom, rumours had gone around the city telling of frightful disasters. Money and medicines were posted to Calais and the citizens waited, dreading what seemed the inevitable day when they would hear of the death or captivity of their young King.

As the truth spread through London, every bell pealed its joy, *Te Deums* were sung at each parish church, and around St. Paul's enormous mobs cluttered the streets. On foot, the newly elected Mayor with his aldermen travelled to Westminster and knelt before the jewelled tomb of St. Edward the Confessor.

England went almost insane with joy, and vast sums were given to prepare for the celebrations of Henry's home-coming, for pageants and feasts.

While England rejoiced, the King and his army were in Calais. After leaving Agincourt there was no more fighting. The troops took off their awkward harness that made walking a difficulty—for three-quarters of the men went on foot—and Calais was reached on October 19. Here, the Earl of Warwick and the clergy, to the singing of the *Te Deum*, met Henry at the gate; and through streets packed with cheering crowds the King rode to his lodgings at the castle, the troops stopping outside the walls.

The victory had certainly been glorious, but the soldiers were thirsty and hungry, and made a quick traffic of their booty. Prisoners were sold for almost nothing, some were released on the bare promise of payment. Meanwhile, Henry made arrangements to send the men home. There were not enough ships to go round at the moment, so he gave two shillings to each man and each horse, and their captains were to arrange transport.

Henry himself set sail with his prisoners on November 16, and his fleet was caught in a tempest, two of the ships foundered with all hands, and others were washed up on distant coasts. It took all day to traverse that little span of sea, and the French prisoners watched the English King with amazement, because he showed neither signs of fear nor sickness.

At nightfall, amidst swirling sleet, the King's ship dropped its anchor before Dover, where the beach was crowded with citizens. The Barons of the Cinque Ports rushed into the water as the longboat neared the shore, and gripping their King, they lifted him shoulder-high, in the heavy snow, and waded back to the cheering people and the singing clergy.

As Henry travelled north to London, he was greeted at every town with rejoicing; on Barham Down, the men of the Cinque Ports saluted their King as he passed.

"What!" cried the Duke of Orléans, seeing so military a force, "shall we go to war again!"

"Nay," answered King Henry, "these be only children of my country come to welcome me home."

The route was a series of fêtes, the Englishmen went almost insane with excitement and joy. But the excitement in the smaller towns on the way was nothing compared to what was happening in London where enormous sums of money were put to building triumphal arches and to devising pageants.

On Blackheath, as was customary, the Mayor and twenty-four aldermen welcomed the King. With them were hundreds of citizens in red livery with hoods of red and white. The Mayor and aldermen wore their furred scarlet gowns and hoods striped black and white.

The King arrived at ten o'clock on the morning of November 23, and with music the whole gathering marched or rode on London.

It is impossible to describe the full glory of London that day. The mind grows dizzied with the tale of pageants and of embroidered cloths. The magnificence, the colour, and the shouting have thinned down to a list of words, monotonous with repetition, being but the dulled reflection of what was once huge and impressive. It was the greatest festival that London had ever put on to welcome anybody, exceeding even the return of the Black Prince with King John; and only the echo of that joyous day now reaches us—weak, made rather pathetic by its swift decay—with ink alone to tell of cloths that blinded one by their warm colouring, with ink alone to express the shouting, the ecstatic tears of wenches, the drunken bellowing of artisans and apprentices. How to-day can we see those citizens in all their pride of furred robes and hoods, of dagged houppelandes rippling about them like autumn leaves, high-collared, low-necked, great heavy fluted folds above the parti-coloured hose? the hoods thrown back from the bowl-cropped skulls, or with turban-like chaperons on their heads? The magic has gone, the ink has dried quickly after the scribe's pen has scribbled out these lists upon lists of splendid-sounding words. We cannot see these people of the fifteenth century, we cannot see the women with their bald white faces—foreheads shaved, eyebrows and lashes plucked—white oval faces seeming so tiny under the great horned head-dresses or under the heart-shaped structures of wire and cloth; with their houppelandes girdled high and tight beneath the prominent breasts, great padded stomachs thrown forward with an air of insolent pride in the glory of maternity; their long sleeves fluttering down from the elbows and brushing the ground.

They have all gone now, bodies, clothes. . . . There is not even dust to tell us of that triumphant crowd which cheered a young King who seemed a god, made immortal by his victory. Only neat paintings in old books can bring to us again the pageant of those times. There we can see the beautiful narrow-waisted women, with hidden hair and with eyebrows and lashes plucked, mincing along, their eyelids lowered, hands crossed over the huge stomachs; we see the men stiffly erect, lower-lips pushed out, broad-shouldered, slim-legged. About all these painted figures there is a flavour of self-sufficiency, almost of complacence. The men are conquerors, every one of them—cruel, proud, unyielding; and the women seem as arrogant as goddesses in their heavy clothes, while they sit inside their little walled gardens, listening to poets or plucking herbs; they tread the tiled floors on minute feet, bellies out-thrust, heavy lidded slanting lashless eyes downcast under the gorgeous head-dresses.

A glory that has gone, it seems to us, gazing upon these splendid paintings, these miniatures. I know that I have fallen in love again and again with some small wench who smirked before a painter five hundred years ago—living and breathing, laughing and kissing, five hundred years ago. Yet when she lived, her world was eternal and unbreakable in its power; to her there seemed no falling away; no whisper of the din of the coming renascence sounded in her tiny ears save perhaps faintly in the rising murmur of the Lollards and the oppressed serfs. She was self-sufficient, this girl in a miniature, she was superb; the daughter and playmate of conquerors, of the tamers of nature, of those who seemed to themselves to be the ultimate flower of all living.

That is the feeling these old paintings always bring to me, a feeling of the sitters' most intense arrogance. But the figures, after all, are only limned. The quick flesh, the firm rosy bodies of young girls, the hard strong limbs of men, all these have turned to liquid in the coffins. How can we now, fumbling outside the magic, hope to recapture with soiled words the joy of those times, the fresh surprise of each morning when a victorious King with a handful of men could crush a giant army like the French at Agincourt? The words are dull, and it is difficult to see beyond them to that intoxicatingly joyous day when Londoners cheered their King through freshly gravelled flower-carpeted streets.

On to London Bridge rode King Henry and his cavalcade. Above the Stone Gate at the Southwark end there was a wall of halberds, and on each side of the Gate stood a figure as high as the Gate—one a man, one a woman. The man gripped a mighty axe in one hand, in the other hand he held the city keys on the end of a stick. The woman wore a scarlet cloak and scarlet petticoat. Between the two figures wound a painted scroll, "*Civitas Regis Justiciæ.*"

"Hail to the royal city!" cried King Henry at the sight.

He passed beneath the Gate, then through the houses, many of which met overhead, forming tunnels, until he came to the drawbridge. Here stood a wooden arch covered with cloths of white, green and jasper, with the figure of St. George on top.

At every point—statues, arches, Latin and English inscriptions. It must have cost a huge sum, but of what value was gold compared to

202

honour and glory? Over the Bridge went Henry, into London itself, up Fish Street Hill:

> *"Deo gratias Anglia redde pro Victoria,*
> *Our King went forth to Normandy,*
> *With grace and might of chivalry;*
> *The God for him wrought wondrously,*
> *Wherefore England may call and cry—*
> *Deo gratias Anglia redde pro Victoria!"*

On Cornhill at the new conduit there was a tent, and as Henry approached, old men wearing gold crowns and crimson turbans came out and let fly hosts of birds that settled about the King, roosting on his head and shoulders, fluttering around his breast.

"Hallelujah!" sang the old men. "Sing to the Lord a new song, for He hath done marvellous things!"

Coming from the Poultry the procession was momentarily held up, so vast was the crowd; sergeants and men-at-arms beat back the people, forcing them into line. It was a wonder that those houses with their heavy penthouses jutting over the street did not all topple over, so great was the mob—people in every window, on every roof, all staring at their victorious young King.

And their King showed neither pleasure nor displeasure. Without smiling, slightly taciturn, he passed through his people. With head lowered, his purple cloak wrapped tightly about him, he seemed almost ashamed of the demonstration, as if he submitted to it only to pleasure London, as men will sometimes boredly give in to playing with children. He had asked that there be no personal speeches, saying that all the honour must be given to God, not to him, and he had refused to permit "his bruised helmet and his bended sword" of Agincourt to be borne triumphantly before him.

A pasteboard castle was built around Queen Eleanor's Cross at the end of Wood Street in Chepe, with St. George on the top. From this castle a bridge ran to St. Peter's Church. A troop of white-robed most beautiful girls danced, singing, from the castle, clapping their tambourines into loud, shivering music.

"Noel!" they cried. "Welcome to the fifth Henry, King of England and France!"

And as the King passed beneath the arch, boys dressed in white scattered gold bezants into the street.

Moodily, never smiling, the King passed through the excited crowds until he reached St. Paul's Churchyard for the last of the pageants. Here the gate had been decorated and niches built around it. In each of these niches stood a tall girl who flicked and puffed gold-leaf upon the King, crying, "Noel! Noel!" Additional wenches danced and played on drums and gilt viols.

Then came rejoicing more to the heart of Henry. The bells clanged from St. Paul's when he stepped through the portals into that august gloom. Eighteen bishops censed him as he entered, and a solemn *Te Deum* rang through the cathedral.

After making his offering Henry, now accompanied by his stepmother Joan, left the city for Westminster.

Here again the bells were ringing as the abbot welcomed him and while he knelt before St. Edward's shrine.

The whole progress had taken five hours.

Rejoicings were not yet over. There was feasting that night at Westminster, and on the morrow the Mayor and aldermen offered Henry, as token of their reverence and joy, a thousand pounds in two gold basins, each basin itself being worth five hundred pounds.

Soon Parliament was to offer yet greater gifts. All England adored its young King because of this glorious victory. Yet looking back upon it now through the centuries, no longer crazed by the ecstasy of the moment, it seems to us politically a worthless thing. Henry himself was not satisfied by it. For him it was but the corner-stone on which to build a gigantic structure with himself on the top—a great Western Empire, the controlling force of Catholic Europe, the bulwark against the teeming East.

He was never to attain his dream but surely that does not lessen each individual achievement? We must forget that we can see the effects, we must look only on the splendid victory itself, isolated from the years to come; and at that moment it seemed full of promise. And it did achieve this— it made all Europe turn with new eyes upon England; it placed England definitely as one of the great powers of the Western world.

# CHAPTER THIRTEEN

## *Politics*

We have watched Henry the soldier; it is time
for us to see him at work as diplomatist. Without
doubt he intended to continue the war with
France. Lack of money and the weather had driven
him back to England. With the coming of spring
he hoped to return and finish what he had begun
at Harfleur and Agincourt. For eighteen months,
however, he was forced to wait, carefully preparing
for future conquests, testing other countries for
alliances, healing the Great Schism, building the
navy as a most essential part of his invasion—to
protect England and to carry supplies and reinforcements—and raising money. This last point
was not so difficult for Henry as it would have
been for a less popular King. It was the poverty of
the country, not lack of generosity in his subjects,
that made the collecting of loans and taxes so slow.

He wished also to leave England fully at peace
before he turned his back, and therefore opened
negotiations with Scotland. Now that there was no
hope in using the Earl of March for a leader, now
that Owen Glendower was crushed and Oldcastle
incapable of organising a large army, the dis-
affected turned towards Hotspur's son, Henry
Percy, a prisoner in Scotland. To end these hopes,
and to keep Percy safely near him, Henry exchanged Murdach, son of the Regent Albany, for
the lad.

Affairs in France were as confused as ever. After the defeat at Agincourt, John the Fearless hoped to gain control, but the Gascon Count of Armagnac, his deadly enemy, managed to entice the constable's baton from King Charles and thus become master. Armagnac was a powerful violent man, a type very necessary to France at the moment. He struggled to put an end to the murderous brawls that were taking place all around the capital, and in the streets themselves where opposing parties, Burgundian and Armagnac, met and slaughtered each other. He more or less succeeded, having a brutal Gascon army at his back. Ruthlessly he hanged and drowned the marauders, and the peasants at last were able to return to work.

Just before Armagnac was made constable, the fat Dauphin died. Nobody regretted his going, he had been a lazy lecher and drunkard who slept all day and danced and caroused all night, but his death produced difficulties. The succession fell to his next brother John, Duke of Touraine. John had been betrothed to one of Burgundy's daughters, and although the marriage never took place, he had married Jacqueline, heiress to the counties of Hainault, Zeeland and Holland, and daughter of Burgundy's sister Margaret. When Armagnac asked John to come to Paris to help control the city and govern the country, Burgundy refused to let him go and sent him off to Valenciennes in the guardianship of the Count of Holland.

Everything was remaining in France exactly as Henry wished it to—in constant turmoil. But now a strong man was in control, and but for Burgundy, Armagnac might really have hammered the country into unity.

The Emperor Sigismund was soon to come to England, and his visit is of real importance to us because it reveals Henry's efforts at diplomacy. Perhaps we should not call him Emperor of the Holy Roman Empire, because he was yet only King and would remain King until crowned by the Pope. That was one of Sigismund's main difficulties—there were three Popes at the time, and it became his ambition to break for ever this Great Schism which had torn the western world into continual fighting. In this, with Henry's help, he was to succeed.

The three Popes were Benedict XIII, the Avignon or French Pope (although Benedict was actually a Spaniard); Gregory XII, elected by the Roman cardinals in 1406 and deposed by the council of Pisa in 1409 (he refused to be deposed, however, and still called himself the Vicar of Christ); and Pope John XXIII, a Neapolitan pirate who was reputed to have ravished two hundred women, including his brother's wife—with whom he lived in incest in Rome—and various nuns, and who mocked at God, never even hearing Mass in the bad days when he was known as Baldassare Cossa. Of the other two, the Avignon Pope Benedict, was probably the greater rascal; the third, Gregory, had been elected on the death of Innocent VII. He was over seventy and had been made Pope on the strict understanding that he and Benedict would abdicate together, thereby making way for a fresh election. Gregory, however, showed no desire to abdicate, and while loudly denouncing his rival in France wrote secretly to him, and the pair agreed that before the world they would be enemies but in private each would cling to his own tiara and keep his separate power. Gregory was a dull old man who insisted upon doing everything himself, with the result that almost no public business whatever was concluded. He also, as was customary, preferred his friends and relations, and made cardinals of two nephews; two other cardinals he created were particularly low rascals, being accused of murder and of raping nuns.

Altogether, Gregory's election had made the problem more acute, and at last both Popes fled, each still insisting that he was the rightful one.

In desperation, a third Pope was elected— Alexander V, a generous old man, who at Milan, it was said, used to have forty girls dressed in appetising uniforms to wait on him at table. Alexander did not live long. Rumour whispered that his successor poisoned him with a clyster. This is probable as his successor was that debauched scoundrel of a pirate, Cossa, who became Pope John XXIII.

This is the problem that King Sigismund set himself to unravel in 1414. Sigismund was almost a great man. He was cultured, a soldier and was particularly handsome; he was also a notorious lecher. His life had been a thrilling one of victories and defeats; he had been involved in numerous battles, had once been imprisoned by his own subjects, and on another occasion only rescued from poisoning by being hung up by his heels so that the poison would run out of his mouth—he hung like that for twenty-four hours—, and from the ages of fifteen to forty, it was said that not a year had passed for him without its battle. This was the man who swore to heal the Great Schism.

The Holy Roman Empire had other problems to face. Wycliffe's doctrines had not only been effective in England, they had crept to the Continent and had had enormous effect, particularly in Bohemia. The leader of the movement here was John Hus, a goodly-living man with little originality but with the fire of the fanatic to stir his listeners. Before long the whole of Prague seems to have turned Lollard. On July 16, 1410, there was a bonfire of Wycliffe's books in Prague, and Hus was excommunicated. This did not prevent him from continuing to preach, and the excommunication had no effect on the people; he was as deeply loved as ever and was listened to with the same reverence. The secular arm was told to do its duty and burn this reformer, but the secular arm refused to do anything of the kind: it did the opposite and protected Hus against Rome. There were uproars in the streets of Prague, and two pardoners—men selling indulgences—were chased and thrown out of the city; their pardons were put in a cart containing two harlots. Papal bulls were tied around the harlots' necks, and the carts were dragged through the streets and the indulgences publicly burned. A friar with a packet of relics was nearly murdered, the mob shouting, "These are only dead bones! you are taking Christian people in!"

Prague was laid under an interdict, there were no services, no preaching, no Mass; and Hus decided to leave. With a bundle of Wycliffe's books, he strolled about the country, spreading his faith, teaching the people this new doctrine according to which not a human being but Christ alone was the true Pope.

At this time not only the Lollards but the Popes

themselves were in difficulties. It was decided that John XXIII must set a good example to Benedict and Gregory by abdicating. Instead of this, John fled, but was quickly caught, accused of the most diabolic villainies, and locked in prison.

Having dragged down John, the cardinals decided to catch the reformer Hus. Sigismund granted the heretic a safe-conduct to Rome and then sacrificed both Hus and his own honour by giving him up to the Church. As usual in these trials, the pivot of heresy was the question of transubstantiation, and Hus refused to believe that the bread became the actual body of Christ after consecration. On July 6, 1415, he was condemned and burnt.

With Hus burnt and John XXIII in prison, Sigismund turned towards the two rival Popes. Gregory was made to abdicate, and only Benedict remained.

Sigismund decided to treat personally with him, and travelled to Perpignan where Benedict was then staying. He was too wily a man to be tricked into abdicating, and the two were arguing the question while King Henry V was struggling on the walls of Harfleur. And towards this war, Sigismund—an incorrigible peace-maker—now turned his eyes. Besides, as England and France supported rival Popes, if he could get them to stop fighting he might also force them to agree on this point. Already he had spoken to Henry's envoys, headed by the Earl of Warwick, at Constance, and had offered them a most holy relic, the actual heart of St. George. Warwick, with his usual tact, refused the gift, saying that Sigismund himself had best bring it to England.

His problem now was how to make these two centuries-old enemies embrace and agree to a new Pope. Except for this, the Papal question was really settled, as it was not long before Benedict was pushed into the fortress of Peniscola, which he never left alive. All that remained was to elect a fourth and final Pope. Both England and France must agree to this election if Sigismund's dream of a complete Christian world with himself as Emperor was ever to materialise.

He reached Paris on March 1, 1416. His mission was a hopeless failure, for the French were infuriated by him because of his meanness—which might have been poverty, he had but little money—by his indecent behaviour towards some high-born ladies when drunk at a banquet, and particularly for daring to knight a Frenchman—the French King's prerogative.

Although France had always been his family's ally, Sigismund was so hurt by his rebuffs in Paris and by the contemptuous attitude of Armagnac that he decided to visit England.

Warwick received him at Calais with great honour, and Henry sent three hundred ships to escort him over the Channel. As the fleet nosed its way into Dover, the Duke of Gloucester with others rode into the water with drawn sword, and demanded to know if Sigismund claimed imperial rights over England; if he did, Gloucester swore to resist him. Sigismund instantly disclaimed any such idea and was permitted to land.

This story, for some time thought a fable but now believed to be authentic, shows Henry's attitude. He was determined to treat his visitor with all courtesy, not as his suzerain the Emperor of the Roman Empire, but as a fellow-monarch. His attitude was probably suggested by Sigismund's behaviour in Paris when he knighted a Frenchman. Henry was not going to tolerate this kind of interference in England. Having made the bold gesture in the waters at Dover, he could afford to be generous, and wherever he went Sigismund was treated with great respect. He was lodged in the King's Palace at Westminster while Henry himself stayed at the Archbishop's Palace at Lambeth, and he was made a Knight of the Garter. This honour so delighted Sigismund that on all State occasions he was to wear the collar as his most prized possession. Soon he and Henry were close friends.

There was much in these two men that was similar and which made either their friendship or their enmity inevitable. Both had the same dream, the dream of a united Christendom; Sigismund had the title, an empty title, and Henry had the strength with which to uphold the fabric. It could have been a most powerful combination.

Very foolishly, France had insulted Sigismund, and Henry set himself to heal that wound. With Sigismund's blessing, his war would take on a touch of holiness, it would be backed morally by the Roman Empire, and such things were important to medieval men. Their passion for logic and legality often drove them to the queerest tricks to justify their actions. Henry had another purpose in fondling Sigismund. As the Great Schism was being broken, the election of a genuine Pope was a matter necessary to the world. If with Sigismund's help he could have one of his friends elected, his power would be great, he would have the backing of Rome for every action.

The war with France had only simmered down; it still existed. While Sigismund was in Paris, on March 11 and 12, there was fighting around Harfleur. On the 9th the Earl of Dorset, captain of Harfleur, with his two lieutenants, Sir John Fastolf and John Blount, and a thousand men, sallied out to ravage the country. After the usual burning and stealing, they found their retreat cut off by the Duke of Armagnac himself with five thousand soldiers. Dorset could not escape, the fight was forced on him, so he formed his troops in the customary order—horses to the rear with the baggage, men on foot in three battles. The French offered terms, but Dorset would not listen, he merely answered, "Go tell your master that Englishmen never surrender!"

The boast was a proud one, and Dorset soon proved it to be genuine. The French cavalry broke the English lines again and again. One hundred and twenty were left for dead on the field, and while the victorious French plundered the bodies, Dorset crept away in the night. It was a weary march the English made on their way back to Harfleur, for Dorset was sore wounded; his broken army dragged itself along the coast for twenty miles until it reached St. Adresse and was nearing home. But morning revealed to Dorset that his enemies had followed him, had swept ahead and were now waiting on the heights above to continue the slaughter.

The French were so exultant at again cutting the English off from Harfleur and were so eager to wipe away the shame of letting them escape last night, that they charged headlong down the hill in utter disorder. The English stood firm, waiting for the shock of that advance. For a moment their line broke, then quickly it shut again; the English rallied at once. And this handful of exhausted men killed two hundred of the French, and would have killed the others had not Armagnac galloped up to the relief.

Again Dorset managed to escape, and was back in Harfleur by March 23. This might have meant the end of Harfleur if only Armagnac could have continued after his first success, but a revolution was pending in the capital. Friends of Burgundy were conspiring to deliver the city up to him, when the news reached Armagnac. He made a short truce with the English and hurried back to Paris, where five hundred men were captured and publicly executed.

Having crushed this conspiracy, Armagnac turned again to Harfleur. He realised that unless he could command the sea he would never capture the town, as Henry could always send it supplies and reinforcements. He decided to collect a heavy navy, and borrowed ships from Genoa.

In England, Sigismund and Henry were like brothers, Sigismund being enchanted by everything he saw and particularly, it seems, by English women and horses. At his invitation, William Count of Holland and Duke of Bavaria arrived to negotiate, and they drew up a three years' truce to offer France. According to this, Harfleur was to be placed in the neutral hands of the duke until French and English came to a settlement. The truce, of course, came to nothing. Henry explained that France did not give sufficient guarantees. At any rate, the whole affair was the work of Sigismund and Duke William; Henry only entered it to gain a breathing-space so that he could send supplies to Harfleur and prepare his army for the second invasion.

Then Armagnac appeared with his great navy and with the Genoese to back him. At that time, the Genoese were the greatest sailors in the world, the most expert cross-bowmen, and their ships were the stoutest and swiftest sailing. With this navy in the estuary and in the Seine, it seemed that Harfleur was doomed. Armagnac had nine Genoese carracks—the only really efficient fighting-ship, carrying two masts and a great steel beak for ramming—and eight galleys, the whole under the command of Jan Grimaldi. Each carrack held a hundred cross-bowmen, while the largest held two hundred. To this fleet were added sixty smaller Biscayan ships lent by the King of Castile. It is said that Scotland and Brittany also added their quota, and the combined allies amounted to three hundred vessels, apart from long-boats, skiffs and the French themselves. The French added a dozen royal galleys and one hundred cogs—broad ships with rounded prow and stern.

With this blockade, Harfleur was completely cut off from England, and so confident were the French that they roved up and down the Channel, capturing numerous English craft, stealing the cargoes and throwing the crews overboard. The English scraped together what ships they could, but they were as yet unable to retaliate. The Genoese appeared off the coast of Hampshire, and except for the lighting of beacons, the English seem to have done nothing. The enemy actually landed on the Isle of Portland, laid waste the countryside, and attacked the Isle of Wight. They then blockaded Southampton and Portsmouth, attempting to destroy the navy Henry was building to relieve Harfleur. Weather came to his rescue, and the allies were driven away.

Henry was working hard to relieve Harfleur, intending himself to sail, but Sigismund managed to persuade him that his presence was more important in England playing with treaties, and his brother, John Duke of Bedford, was given command.

We cannot be sure how many ships Bedford had. Foreign writers give him from two hundred to four hundred, but a German visitor who had no reason to lie says that he had but seventy.

He battled against the winds and at last, on August 14, the combined English fleet met off Beachy Head. King Henry had arranged for beacons to be built so that the news of sailing could be rushed to him at once at Westminster. He prayed there for victory and sent urgent messages to the Westminster hermit and to the Carthusian monks in London and Sheen to pray with him.

Bedford's arrival came as a great surprise to the French. They had expected relief to come from Calais and were all on shore when the English sailed into the estuary. As usual, there were troubles about the command in the allies. The Genoese objected to having Frenchmen put over them, while the Spaniards in haughty disgust turned their rudders, swung round their sails, and made for Honfleur. They were followed by eight Genoese galleys and many smaller vessels.

The allied fleet was therefore much reduced and amounted now to about one hundred craft, and the English were probably slightly superior. They may have been superior in quantity but by no means in efficiency. Their ships were smaller and the Genoese were the finer sailors.

In the darkness the English sent out small boats to reconnoitre, and when morning dawned both sides knelt on their decks and prayed, for this was August 15, the Feast of the Assumption. The English held a meeting of captains, then the command was given to attack.

The French were straight before them, blocking the Seine. Each man stood at his post, gripping his weapon, bow or sword or axe; seamanship was little used, the vessels rammed each other or grappled and boarded, while those in the fighting-tops fired bows or hurled down stones and javelins. To the shrieking of horns and trumpets, the English fleet sailed calmly on to its larger adversaries. Then when near them, the order was given, and the ships swung out into a crescent formation, hoping to outflank the enemy.

The allies kept their places while the English approached, and they remained firm as English ship after ship thudded its prow against them, hoping to ram or to get a hold for boarding. Again and again the English charged, as if trying to butt the allies aside. But the carracks towered over them, they were too high to grapple. From those castles, from the fighting-tops, arrows, javelins, stones and shot rained down. The enemy's bulwarks were a lance-height above the little English decks.

For seven hours the fight continued, the English trying to board the giants and being continually beaten back. But at last they managed to scramble into four of the carracks, and the battle was theirs.

At hand-to-hand fighting the English were invincible; and when four carracks were in their hands, the rest fled.

Bedford, who had himself fought most bravely, relieved Harfleur, but he could do nothing else. His ships were too crippled to chase the enemy.

Henry was at Smallhythe when the news reached him. He leaped upon his horse and galloped to Canterbury, first thoughts being for God from Whom all victories come. With Sigismund, he entered the great cathedral to attend the *Te Deum*. The honours went to Our Lady, not to Bedford and his men. It had been the day of her feast on which the battle had been fought, so Henry arranged that his chaplains at Westminster must sing an antiphon with versicle and collect in thanks to her every day of his life.

This victory taught Henry a very great lesson, the necessity of building a strong navy. He may not have been the creator of England's command of the sea, as some have claimed for him, but at least he was one of the first Kings to realise fully and to act upon the necessity of having strong ships to guard the treasured island. In the King's dock at Ratcliffe below London Bridge, men worked day and night, fashioning a mighty fleet, and orders were sent to Bayonne for a particularly large ship, eighty-six feet long, to be built there.

Negotiations with France had reached no

finality because neither country wanted a finality, each merely wanted a breathing-space in which to recuperate before continuing the conflict. Sigismund had fluttered between both sides but nothing of importance was arranged.

Before Armagnac's campaign against Harfleur, the Duke of Berri died. The duke had been a cultured man without particular force, but his territories now reverted to the Dauphin John, and thus unknowingly he helped to rebuild France. His death also lifted a certain restraint from the fiery Armagnac, making him the chief man at the council just at the moment when Sigismund was sending an embassy to Paris to arrange some truce.

The Duke of Holland had left England in a fit of rage because Sigismund, as head of the Roman Empire, had refused to recognise his daughter Jacqueline, as the duke's own successor. Either from stupidity or spite—probably spite—Sigismund had said that women should never rule and had asked the count if he had no brother who might be his heir instead of the daughter. It was this very brother whom the duke wished to ban from ever getting his duchy, and he left England at once, deeply offended, after telling Henry that if he ever invaded France, he—the duke—would fight against him.

Undeterred by this rupture, Sigismund sent his ambassadors to Paris. Armagnac, trying to be cunning, instructed his envoys to travel to England and temporise with Henry. But Henry was too shrewd a man to be taken in by so obvious a trick, and the attack on Harfleur—which followed shortly—proved that his suspicions were correct.

This attack also drove Sigismund frankly into Henry's arms. Already at the first signs of renewed war he drew up a formal treaty between himself and Henry, both Kings pledging their oath to support each other against France.

John the Fearless of Burgundy was intriguing with them, and on August 24, 1416, Sigismund travelled to Calais, Henry following ten days later. Then came a feeble effort at peace-making with Armagnac, but the French offers were more insulting than conciliatory, and three days after the Armagnacs had left, John the Fearless came for his agreement.

John was too cunning a man to trust anybody. Before he would enter Calais he demanded hostages, and received Humphrey Duke of Gloucester, as pledge for his safety. For a week there were conferences, but what was at last decided we unfortunately do not know. At any rate, whatever it was, it came to nothing, probably because of Burgundy's trickery. He left on October 13, and visited the Dauphin and William of Holland—whom Sigismund had insulted—and the three, ignoring England, swore to join forces against their own countrymen, the Armagnacs.

This was Sigismund's final effort. On October 16, Henry returned to England after an affecting farewell with his guest, both Kings embracing, weeping and kissing each other, and shortly afterwards Sigismund set sail for Dordrecht.

These negotiations do not seem to have gained much, and scholars still argue over the question whether Sigismund duped Henry or not. It seems, however, that Sigismund was perfectly genuine in his promises. He did intend to join Henry with three thousand men-at-arms, but his own troubles and poverty always prevented him. England had not gained very much material benefit but Sigismund had lost by angering both France and the Duke of Holland. Yet even if Henry got no material help, he did gain morally by this treaty, and he was hopeful of putting a friendly Pope into power. Spiritual things were of great importance to medieval rulers. Henry's war with France was now backed by the leader of the temporal Roman Empire and there was a possibility—a strong possibility— that it would also be backed by the spiritual leader, the new Pope. These moral points, seeming so futile to us to-day when wars are waged more or less frankly on economic and territorial grounds, were of vital importance to the medieval soldier. Henry never won a battle for which he did not quite sincerely thank God instead of the courage of his men and his own inspiring leadership. Thus, when we were at last beaten out of France, a French soldier is said to have taunted an Englishman by asking when he would return. "When your sins are greater than ours!" was the reply. The French after the defeat of Agincourt were quite certain that they had lost the battle because of the wicked behaviour of the whole country, while the English were equally certain that St. George had been fighting with them. The saints were continually fighting in medieval armies and very often the Blessed Virgin herself deigned to spur on her favourites. "On every battlefield of Europe," writes Henry Adams in his delightful *Mont Saint-Michel and Chartres*, "for at least five hundred years, Mary was present, leading both sides." We must realise how close the material part of Christianity, the actual presence of saints, the living bodies under the images, the flesh of Christ in the Eucharist, was to the average medieval man and woman—although at this date it was rapidly on the decline—to appreciate what the endorsement of the King of the Romans would mean to stiffen the strength and belief in himself of a man like Henry V.

He was now determined to return to France as soon as possible.

# CHAPTER FOURTEEN

## *Back to France*

MEDIEVAL warfare was not carried out in the winter owing to the difficulty of gathering supplies and of finding warm quarters. Henry had to delay his offensive until the spring, but he did not waste his time. Parliament granted him the best subsidies possible and he borrowed every farthing he could; he had scarcely a jewel that was not continually in and out of pawn. Early in 1417, privy seals were posted to the nobility and others requesting troops and asking that the numbers of men who could be brought would be sent not later than February 14. It was the navy, however, that absorbed most of Henry's time—the navy and the collecting of munitions, of which *The English Chronicle* gives us a weird assortment of weapons, ancient and modern: "Armour, guns, tripgets [slings for stones and arrows], sows [roofs under which the besiegers could approach a wall], bastilles [wooden towers to place against the walls of a besieged town or city], bridges of leather [pontoons], scaling-ladders, mallets, spades, shovels, picks, pavises [shields for archers and gunners; also, but obviously not here, fighting-cloths placed above the bulwarks of ships], bows and arrows, bow-strings, tuns, chests and pipes [barrels holding about half a tun] full of arrows as needed for such a worthy warrior [as Henry], that nothing was to seek when time came."

Apart from this comprehensive if indiscriminate list, we have particulars of some individual consignments. Craftsmen were brought from St. Sever to make steel cross-bows, arrow-heads were forged in England, and sheriffs were told to have six of the wing feathers taken from every goose in the land with the exception of breeders; these were for arrows, and the sheriffs were expected to send 1,290,000 feathers by Michaelmas. Later, in February 1418, John Louthe, clerk of the Ordinance, was commanded to produce 7000 stones for gunners (it was cheaper to hire sculptors to chip stone or marble than it was to cast iron), 300 pavises for the gunners, 80 blocks, 7000 tampions [to plug the mouths of the guns when not in use], 50 wooden yokes for oxen and 100 chains to go with them, 12 wains to carry the guns, 20 pipes of powder, 100 oxen and 320 horses with harness and with leather for repairs, 400 caltraps [great spiked metal balls] and 300 pickaxes.

The navy had been augmented by the ships captured in the Seine and now, just as Henry was on the point of departure, the Earl of Huntingdon took four Genoese carracks in the Channel, which were renamed and included in the fleet. The earl had not won these ships except after a stiff fight lasting three hours. The Genoese carracks had been in a fleet of twenty-six under the command of Percival, bastard of the Duke of Bourbon. At first the English had been unable to get at grips with the enemy, being held off by the rain of cross-bow shafts. When they grappled, as was usual, the victory was theirs.

Henry's fleet now numbered about 1500 vessels; we cannot be certain about the size of his army.

P

The French writers give us the wildest figures, ranging up to 50,000—from a country of about three million population! The English estimate of 16,400 seems the safest to accept.

Henry went aboard his flagship in Southampton Water, July 23, 1417, and reached Touques on August 1. Touques was a small fortified town and stood close to the modern Trouville. Henry's objective had been a subject of speculation, not only in France but also in England and amongst his own captains. The French naturally expected him to use Harfleur as an excellent base, and they had endeavoured to fortify various coastal towns. But Henry had many reasons for his choice. He did not intend to behave in the usual medieval fashion, leading his troops into the interior until he met the enemy and then staking everything on one battle. Such a campaign was really useless and explained why such great victories as Crécy, Poitiers and Agincourt actually attained almost nothing. Henry did not want a war of mere conquest; he wished to build, to recover what he sincerely believed to be his by divine right and by descent. He was the disinherited returning to claim his own.

His plan was to begin at Touques and to strike from there direct into Normandy, netting first all the lesser cities and towns, then sweeping round to concentrate on Rouen, the centre of Normandy, and—next to Paris—the largest city in France. If he could capture all the smaller places he could gradually cut Rouen off completely from the rest of the country and could march on it with Paris at his back. He knew that John the Fearless would not interfere as things stood, but had he marched direct on Paris, not only would he have lost touch with his base but the duke would probably have turned against him.

To understand this, I fear that we must pause for a few lines to examine the French situation. Otherwise the simplicity and ease of Henry's campaign will not be completely understood.

Since the death of the Dauphin Louis, all conspiracies had centred around his brother John who was in the hands of Burgundy. The Duke of Anjou, since the death of Berri, had with Armagnac complete power over the French council and he wished to get the new Dauphin to Paris. At last, after much suspicion, it was agreed that the Dauphin—who was just eighteen—should visit the capital with his wife Jacqueline, daughter of the Count of Holland. The Dauphin never did enter Paris. Negotiations were started with Queen Isabel, when sudden rumours of a conspiracy sent the negotiator, Holland, scuttling back to Compiègne to find the Dauphin seriously ill. On April 4 the lad died, and everybody agreed that the Armagnacs had poisoned him. Then a few weeks later the Count of Holland also died, and as John the Fearless had visited him at the time he was accused of murdering the Count.

Burgundy lashed out at the Armagnacs as the poisoners of the Dauphin, and soon he had most of northern France on his side. He then marched on Paris to besiege the Armagnacs, hoping also to betroth the widow Jacqueline, to his nephew, the Duke of Brabant.

This was the French situation when Henry

landed at Touques for his great invasion. The situation could not possibly have been better from his point of view. With Paris in the midst of civil war he could ravage Normandy almost undisturbed. And he wanted as little fighting as possible; his ambition was to bring the country back to English rule quietly, making it accept him as its liege-lord.

With him went two of his brothers: Thomas Duke of Clarence, a brave soldier, and the shifty Humphrey Duke of Gloucester. The other brother, John Duke of Bedford, was left as warden of England.

As has been remarked, Henry's choice of a landing-place was excellent for his plans, which were far more ambitious than his enemies realised. There was at first a small brush with five hundred French horsemen; but on the leader being killed by the English archers the rest ran away, and Henry could disembark without danger. Then, standing again on French earth, he praised God and, in honour of the day, knighted forty-eight men and appointed Clarence constable of the army. Tents were pitched, and Henry and his captains lodged in some nearby houses.

The first point to attack was the castle of Bonne-ville about a mile from Touques. This was a particularly powerful castle, one of the strongest in Normandy, but the captain surrendered almost instantly. He pleaded for the customary grace, asking for six days; if he was not relieved by then he promised to capitulate. A messenger was sent to Rouen, but he was only hanged for bringing such cowardly news, and on April 9 the garrison marched out. Henry had won his first battle without a blow being struck. Auvillars too had offered terms, and it surrendered to the Earl of Salisbury on August 14.

Henry was very strict about the morals of his soldiers and he issued stern commands against pillaging, murder and rape. Particularly he was careful that no ecclesiastics be injured, and many of the French hurriedly shaved their crowns and dressed like priests. Even that they soon found was not necessary, for Henry desired these people to be his subjects and did not want them hurt.

Leaving a garrison at Bonneville under Sir John Keighley, a Yorkshireman, Henry marched towards Caen, keeping to the coast. In September, Lisieux surrendered with little fighting. We know almost nothing about this episode, probably because it is so overshadowed by the siege of Caen, but a contemporary French chronicler tells us that it was taken after some kind of a fight. Later generation spread the story that when the English entered they discovered only one old man and an old woman in possession, which is obviously untrue, as Lisieux was a cathedral city and Henry was famed for his kindness to ecclesiastics. Very likely Keighley made this capture.

Henry was marching on Caen.

This was a large town well protected by a wall six to seven feet thick with twelve gates, thirty-two towers, and on three sides it was girdled by ditches, with the river Orne on the south. The Orne had Caen on one bank, and the Ile St. Jean, also well fortified, exactly opposite. But the city had two weak points—two famous abbeys were outside the walls, one on each side, and they were so tall that they were higher than the town: these were St. Stephen's, in which lay the body of William the Conqueror, to the west, and the Holy Trinity, in which lay the body of the Conqueror's wife, Matilda, to the east.

Henry had sent Clarence ahead with a thousand men, and he arrived just in time to rescue the suburbs which had been set alight—the common procedure, to stop the besiegers using them as shelter. The French had also intended to fire both abbeys but Clarence's sudden appearance saved the Holy Trinity, which he made his headquarters. St. Stephen's, too, was eventually saved. A monk could not bear to see his beloved abbey destroyed and he turned traitor to save it. He crept on hands and knees to the English and found Clarence asleep in the garden, dressed in full armour, lying with his head on a stone. The monk offered to reveal the points where the abbey was most weakly guarded and could be entered. Immediately, Clarence summoned a scaling party and set out. The monk had not lied. The abbey was captured without difficulty, and the defenders were let go except for one man whom Clarence hanged for sacrilege, as he had been caught pulling the bars out of the windows.

Clarence now held both abbeys and could therefore command the city, so that when Henry arrived all was ready for an immediate siege. On his march Henry had sent King Charles a letter in which he called on God to witness how he had struggled only for peace since the beginning of his reign, and for the last time he demanded the surrender of France, otherwise swift retribution would fall on Charles for his obstinacy.

Henry took up quarters in St. Stephen's, Clarence remaining in the Holy Trinity. Guns were hauled on to the roofs and towers, but the larger ones were given to Gloucester, who ranged them between St. Stephen's and the western wall. Other guns were placed by Clarence on the Holy Trinity. Henry divided his army into four, and completely surrounded the town except for the south and south-east walls, where the Orne flowed; his leather bridges, however, could be used here, if necessary.

Against this attack the garrison had no hope. Its guns were smaller and the town's streets were open to the cruel English fire; at one point, Henry was restrained from breaking through the wall for fear of injuring the Church of St. Stephen, which stood on the other side. He used the great stone and iron balls made for him in England, and also a kind of bomb—a hollow metal globe packed with straw, sulphur and other combustibles which caught alight as it fell and set fire to parts of the town. He also set his pioneers hard at work and they dug mines under the walls. The method used here was to dig until the foundations were reached; these foundations were then propped up with wood which was set on fire, and when consumed the wood fell, bringing the foundations with it. The besieged soon had a trick by which they could detect the pioneers at work. They placed brimming bowls of water on the ground: if the water quivered men were digging, and a countermine was started.

The Caen garrison was under the command of William de Montenay, who had one thousand two hundred men-at-arms under him and six thousand citizen-soldiers. These were no match for the sternly disciplined and large English army. Caen had to fall in time, but the defence was stubborn and courageous.

After a little over a fortnight of siege-work, on September 4 Henry decided to launch a mass-assault, de Montenay having refused his demand for surrender. The King was up very early on the appointed morning and heard three Masses. Then a bugle was blown from before the royal tent, and the great assault began.

From camp to camp sounded the bugles, from Clarence in the west, from Lord Talbot and Gilbert Umfraville in the north, and from Warwick, Huntingdon and Salisbury in the south. From. camp to camp—the signal for attack.

First charged the scaling-parties, gripping their ladders; the ditches had been crammed with fascines [bundles of faggots] so they were easily passed. But the besiegers were prepared, and they tipped over their pots of boiling fats and pitch and oil; they threw down large stones; and if a man set his ladder against the ramparts and scaled to the top they blew quicklime into his eyes and blinded him. Some of the ladders were too short and were flung aside into the moat. Wave after wave of English clambered over the sticks, they struggled together to mount the ladders and fought their way up into that deluge of scalding torment. But the pots could not be brought quickly enough, even the Genoese cross-bowmen— the best in the world—were unable to stay that charge.

One of the new knights—the only Englishman of rank to die that day—slipped on a ladder-rung and fell backwards with his weight of armour. The French threw burning straw on him and roasted him alive. His name was Sir Edmund Springhouse, and Henry was saddened at the news. But his death only inspired his men to stronger efforts. They scrambled up their ladders and were on the ramparts.

Clarence, that splendid fighting man, was the first on the walls. He fought his way into the Ile St. Jean, south of Caen proper. The first English-man to set foot in the street was one Harry Ingles. It was street-fighting now, close-fighting, at which the English were superb. They drove the French back, right to the bridge near the Black Friars, even in that mêlée being careful to hurt no religious.

The Earl of Warwick was first on the bridge and he battled his way to the great tower called the Little Castle. Pushing a ladder against the wall, he shouted "A Clarence! a Clarence!" and sprang up. He placed the royal banner on the wall.

In the streets that day, it was said, over eighteen hundred Frenchmen died. The slaughter was ghastly, only ecclesiastics were spared. The English looted and murdered, running like insane creatures from house to house. Even Henry's iron rule could not have stopped the plundering; but by refusing to surrender, the city had earned this fate. That was the code of the Middle Ages. If a city fought to the end, thus squandering lives which would otherwise have been saved, no mercy was shown it.

Henry has of course been blamed for the fury of his men, but he deserves no blame according to the laws of medieval warfare, and you cannot judge the past by the ethics of the present. In fact, he proved himself humane, more humane than most other leaders of that time: he commanded that no priest be harmed, no woman ravished and no church looted. It was impossible for these commands to be obeyed at every point but Henry kept what order he could amongst men momentarily crazed by the letting of blood.

Henry marched in through the gates opened by Clarence, and he went direct, as was his wont, to a church. In St. Peter's he gave thanks.

The town was reduced but the castle held out. Here Henry found little difficulty, for the garrison was badly overcrowded by about a thousand non-combatants who had to be fed. Five days after the capture of the town, the castle offered to surrender if no help came by the 19th, ten days off. Henry promised to spare their lives, to let them keep horses, armour, clothes and money up to two thousand crowns.

Rouen did not heed the cry for help, and on the 20th the governor knelt before the tent of the English king and offered him the keys. The garrison was permitted to depart unharmed, as Henry had promised. His soldiers later complained that many of the women had sneaked off with more than the stipulated sum of money, hiding the coins in leather bottles, and also that before leaving they had set fire to the rest of the booty.

Keeping to his ambition of building an empire, of reconquering only a rebellious fief, Henry sent to England for settlers to come to Caen, and most of the French appear to have sworn allegiance to him quickly enough, the clergy in particular having a natural love for him.

He took up his quarters in the palace built by William the Conqueror in the castle bailey, and detachments were sent out to suppress the countryside. Soon Creully and Villers-Bocage were his: two very useful posts protecting Caen from the west. And before long, other towns had surrendered; amongst them, Tilly-sur-Seulles and, in particular, the very important well-fortified Bayeux.

Young Gilbert Umfraville was left as captain of Caen when Henry moved on to further conquests.

The next important fortress was Argentan, which surrendered at once. Henry offered the usual terms, freedom to those who would swear allegiance to him—and most of the townsfolk did so immediately—and all others must leave property and homes. About five hundred of them left.

Further castles quickly gave in, castle after castle ; even the powerful castle of Alençon was prepared to treat even before the English appeared. From here the English struck south, and town after town, garrison after garrison, became theirs.

We cannot blame the Normans. It seems to us to-day, with our exaggerated sense of nationalism, that they were either cowards or traitors, but they were neither. They were cut off, isolated, without hope of succour. The Duke of Burgundy was besieging Paris, he was in league with Henry, and they had been misruled for years. Henry offered them peace and freedom; the only alternative was death or the life of a penniless outcast. What could you expect of the citizens, the labourers and the farmers when their lords were treating with the enemy? Even the Duke of Brittany showed signs of wanting to make an agreement with Henry.

We cannot blame these unfortunate oppressed people. France was broken under a lunatic King, both elder Princes were dead, and the new Dauphin Charles was in Paris in the control of Armagnac, while Burgundy stormed at the city's gates demanding justice on the so-called poisoner of the Dauphin John. His intention was to starve Armagnac out, but the count stuck behind his walls and refused to budge, no matter how tempting a sally appeared.

Burgundy was thinking of retiring to winter quarters when chance gave him a fresh opportunity. Charles and his Queen no longer lived together, the Queen, Isabel, being a most notorious creature. Although she was no longer in her youth, being close to fifty, she had many lovers. The King, too, had his leman—a dollish wench called Odette de Champdivers. This did not prevent him from a sudden burst of jealousy, during which he had one of the Queen's lovers, Louis Bosredon, knotted in a sack and dropped into the Seine. The Queen herself was sent to Tours where she immediately started to intrigue with her old enemy the Duke of Burgundy. Burgundy rescued her, and the pair of them started a determined assault on Paris. They expected some friends to open the gates on their arrival, but Armagnac got wind of the conspiracy and soon crushed it, so the Queen and Burgundy were forced to draw back. At Troyes, Isabel created her own court as if she ruled the country, and she appointed the Duke of Burgundy governor of the kingdom.

This has carried us far ahead of Henry who was considering the vital problem of the winter.

He should, according to medieval warfare, have gone to some town and waited for the weather to permit operations in the open. But success had fired him, and he could not contemplate the inaction of wasted months. Despite the inevitable desertions, the killed and the troops he had been forced to leave to garrison his prizes, he was confident of now capturing the almost impregnable fortress of Falaise, the birthplace of his mother.

The Earl of Salisbury was sent in advance to prevent the inhabitants escaping, and the fighting was bitter before Henry's arrival. On December 1 he pitched his camp in front of the city-gate leading towards Caen; Gloucester was to the right, Clarence to the north.

Falaise was built on a rock impossible to assault. Henry's only hope was to starve it out, a difficult task in the winter. But he was undeterred and set cheerfully to building huts for his soldiers. These huts were made of logs bound together by withies and roofed with turf. Around the camp he dug a trench and placed a pale of stakes; then with plentiful food he settled back with his men through a most abominable winter to wait for the town, or the castle under Olivier de Mauny, to surrender. He knew that Falaise could not be relieved. Paris was under the control of Armagnac and the Dauphin, and because of his brutal rule Armagnac was hated by the people who were even prepared to have Burgundy back. Burgundy was friendly with Henry and would not fight, and Henry had also signed a treaty with the Duke of Brittany which was to last until Michaelmas, 1418, on condition that the English did not attack Anjou and Maine. If he could capture Falaise and a few lesser towns, all lower Normandy would be his.

Falaise was soon in a desperate condition. Henry and his men lay snug in their huts, but inside the town the streets were frozen and the constant hail kept the besiegers indoors, where the very houses were liable to tumble on top of them under the English cannonade. The English had dragged their large guns on to the heights of Guibray, and from there could play inside the walls.

The town decided to treat. If relief did not come by January 2, it would surrender. This formula, which we come upon again and again, really means nothing. Falaise knew that it couldn't possibly be relieved, but—like all other towns—it put this clause into the agreement to save its own honour. The onus of the capitulation then rested on the French leaders who should have come to the rescue.

Henry agreed to the surrender, with the understanding that all those who had fled from captured towns and who had taken refuge in Falaise should be given to him, while the garrison could depart minus its bows and arrows and guns. The castle was not included in this, so that when Henry entered on January 2, 1418, the garrison there still held out against him.

The castle was considered impregnable, and having his quarters now in the town, Henry was in the same position as his enemies had been in before—he could be fired into. Mining was useless, for you cannot dig through solid rock; and the only thing to do was to attack the castle as Caen had been attacked. But first, the walls must be breached.

To attain this, Henry sent detachments to the very walls themselves. They worked under awnings on to which thudded stones, arrows, lead and balls; they dug at the walls with pick and hammer, pulling out the heavy stones, fighting with the besieged, until the breach was widened to forty yards, ready for the great assault. It had been a desperate task. Not only did the garrison fight the English as they worked, throw great stones and iron on to the protective sows, but they lowered stinking torches, hoping to smoke the English out.

The defence was doomed once that breach was ready. De Mauny offered the usual terms: surrender if not relieved by February 16. On the appointed day, Henry did not let the garrison go free. He kept them, presumably, to rebuild the walls, for one of the stipulations in de Mauny's surrender was that at his own cost he must carry out this task.

Soon Henry had returned to Caen, then went from Caen to Bayeux for prayer and Lenten devotion. He had another purpose besides praising God: he visited the cathedral city because it was the ideal base for his western conquests. And castles and towns were falling as rapidly as he had planned. The one reverse was an accident. Gilbert Talbot, while returning from a raid into the Cotentin, was caught in the sands by the incoming tide in the bay of Les Veys. Although he managed to beat back the French who rushed to take advantage of his predicament, he lost his baggage. Henry relieved him from his position of captain-general of the marches of Normandy shortly after this, and his failure here was undoubtedly the cause of his disgrace.

By the end of April 1418, all lower Normandy was Henry's. He did not lay waste the country, he strove always to keep the citizens at peace in the towns under his rule. He pardoned those who came to him, as a King might pardon rebellious subjects. His main problem was the apportioning of the captured estates. He naturally did not wish to return them to their rightful lords who might—and probably would—rebel against him at the first opportunity; nor did he wish to give them to the English who, having no ties with the land, would ill-treat the peasants and overtax the towns. He granted various estates to English soldiers on the understanding that they were only for life: a fatal mistake, but he had no other alternative as yet, and probably hoped to win the Normans completely to his side in time and by just rule.

His efforts were all towards calming the country. Clarence, Gloucester and his other captains continued the conquests; Henry himself attempted to rule honourably what he had taken. Many of the Normans had fled to the woods, and, under the bastard son of the late Duke of Alençon, struck at the English when they appeared in troops small enough to be attacked. They had to be subdued; and then there was the question of taxes to consider. The most important of the taxes, the one best hated by the people, was the salt-tax, which was about 50 to 70 per cent.; and no retail price was fixed, so that the merchant could charge whatever he liked—and usually did. Also everybody had to buy a certain amount of salt at whatever the price. Henry modified this. Under his law you could buy whatever quantity of salt you wished, and it became a government prerogative, being stored in garners, and retailed from there at a duty of 25 per cent.

In the summer of 1418, Henry continued his campaign. A few lesser castles had been recaptured by the bastard of Alençon, but only three really important ones remained defiant, apart from Rouen: these were Domfront, Cherbourg and Mont-St.-Michel. Domfront was the largest. It was built on top of a rock and therefore could not be assaulted, mined or bombarded. Warwick, who was in command, decided to starve the garrison out. He succeeded after sharp sallies from the castle and forays from the bastard of Alençon. The town surrendered on June 29, the castle on July 22.

While Warwick crouched before Domfront, the Duke of Gloucester was at Cherbourg. Here the task was the most difficult that the English had yet encountered, for the town was at the foot of some hills with a castle to the north, the walls were from five to six feet thick, and at every tide the ocean laved the walls; at high flood the town was almost an island, for great trenches had been cut around it to the south.

Gloucester found his task more than difficult. The bridge across the harbour had been broken and the town was therefore safe from the east; Gloucester pitched camp to the west, on sands that moved continually. Here he could be attacked by the garrison, for the suburbs were of course burnt down except for a few walls and houses. All night the English toiled at erecting palisades against the gun-fire. They would drag stones from the suburbs and faggots from the woods, and had to swim with them, propelling the stones and wood before them on rafts. Then in the day the garrison would break down what was built so painfully at night, and only by the most heroic efforts was a palisade at last erected. It was hopeless to think of assaulting. Gloucester took his men out of range, built huts and settled down to starve the garrison into surrender, bringing ships from Jersey and Guernsey to blockade the sea-front.

Attempts were made to turn the river, but in vain; the earth which the English dug in their efforts to make channels piled so high that in places it overtopped the walls. From these mounds the English tried an assault, but they could not battle through the cross-bow and gun-fire and had to retreat. They tried mining but the shifting sands defeated them. The Earl of March, with great courage, managed to creep right up to the walls and started battering at them under the usual sows. The French swarmed out, burnt his sows and bulwarks and broke his engines. They failed, however, to drive the English back, and the damage was quickly righted.

On August 22, relief being hopeless, the garrison surrendered on condition that help did not come by Michaelmas. No help coming, after five months of stubborn defiance, Cherbourg fell to the English.

To the east, the fearless Duke of Clarence was capturing town after town. The powerful castle of Harcourt with much booty was his on April 9, after a fifteen days' siege; he had fierce fighting at the Benedictine abbey at Bec but soon forced the garrison to surrender; Evreux fell next, to the Duke of Exeter.

It is here that we meet one act of Henry's that seems almost despicable, and such for which I can find no excuse save in his belief that he was God's agent and therefore as sacred as any saint or religious.

During the siege of Louviers he was standing at his tent door chatting with the Earl of Salisbury, when suddenly a stone smashed past him, hit the tent pole and broke it to splinters. When the town surrendered, Henry hanged eight of the gunners who had fired that cannon and he would have hanged a ninth if Cardinal Orsini had not pleaded for the man. Henry imprisoned the unfortunate gunner instead.

This is a savage act of revenge against men who were only doing their duty. It shows, I feel, Henry's belief in the divine right of his destiny. He did not hang these men because they had nearly struck down the King of England but because they had fired at a man marked by God for a great crusade.

Henry's troops were by now augmented by unspecified numbers of men from England under the Duke of Exeter. These probably healed some of the gaps made by desertions, by the necessity of leaving garrisons and by those killed in battle. Nevertheless, they could scarcely have brought his forces up to the amount with which he had left England.

Pont de l'Arche was the next place to be attacked.

On June 27 Henry arrived before the town and took up quarters in the Cistercian abbey of Bonport. This was to be no easy task that was before him for the town was well fortified. It was, however, a key position and had to be taken, as it was only eight miles above Rouen towards Paris. With this prize in his hands, Henry could march directly on to Rouen, cutting it off completely from help on every side.

The main part of the town was on the opposite bank of the Seine, connected to the other lesser portion by a bridge. This bridge was strongly fortified, for it passed over a little island on which was built a great tower. The town itself was on the south bank, the island being close to the north. Somehow Henry had to cross the river, reduce this tower and take the town. After desultory fighting, he sent Sir John Cornwall with a formal demand for surrender.

When the French captain, the Sire de Graville, refused, Cornwall is said to have told him: "Graville, I pledge you on my honour that to-morrow, in spite of you and your men, I will cross the water of the Seine. If I cross it, you shall give me the best charger that you have; and if I cross it not, I will give you my helm of steel which I value at five hundred nobles."

With this wager, the real battle started. The first attempt of the English was at night, with broken boats for pontoons and with the bridges of hides stretched on wicker-work that Henry had brought from England. To distract the French, some men were sent to kick and swim and splash about three miles downstream while the main force of five thousand passed over on the boats and pontoons. To redeem his oath, Cornwall was one of the first to cross. With sixty men and with a horse to carry the guns, he rowed over in eight small boats. The whole march across that river, under the eyes of a wary garrison, was attained without the loss of a single man. This is scarcely credible but we have it on the authority of Clarence himself.

Evidently Cornwall's task was to cover the troops with his little artillery which he carried on the back of a horse. One statement tells us that he landed on a small island, but there are no islands close to the southern bank at this point; we are also told that Cornwall knighted his thirteen-year-old son at the same time.

After this extraordinary feat, the reduction of the town was only a matter of time. Bridges were placed across the Seine so that Henry could keep in touch with his conquered territory, and Gilbert Umfraville pushed his way up to the fort at the bridgehead. He protected his men under the usual sows, and raised his banner in defiance. A Scotsman from inside the fort cried that he would pull the banner down that night, and sallied forth with five thousand men. With but a force of eighty, Umfraville drove the Scotsman back and even forced his way over the drawbridge before it could be lifted, firing inside through the crossbars of the portcullis.

The town surrendered on July 20, and we are told that Cornwall rated the Sire de Graville for his feeble defence, saying: "Had I been in your place with my sixty English I would have kept the passage against the power of the Kings of France and England."

We are unfortunately not told if he was paid his wager.

Now came a surprise for Henry. He discovered that the Lord of Chastellux had been fighting against him, and Chastellux was one of Burgundy's captains. On inquiring the cause of this, he discovered that his truce no longer held good and that John the Fearless was ranged against him. This was unpleasant news but it did not frighten Henry. He continued his planned moves.

The next city to be attacked, and the consummation of the campaign, was Rouen. Henry sent Exeter with heralds to demand its surrender, but at the Englishmen's approach the garrison swarmed out, only to be driven back by Exeter who " overthrew a heap of them."

When told of this, Henry swore that he would be at Rouen within three days, and marched from Pont de l'Arche on July 29. His heralds, who were immune from attack according to the code of war, had been fired on. That was an insult which must be wiped out immediately.

# CHAPTER FIFTEEN

## *Rouen*

BEFORE following Henry to Rouen, I feel that we must retrace our steps a little. We have seen that Burgundy had repudiated his treaty with Henry by permitting a captain of his to fight against him, and the reasons for this change must be examined; in England there was the capture of Oldcastle, which cannot be ignored; and lastly, something must be said about Sigismund's efforts to break the Great Schism.

The question of the rival Popes had become a political question, and now that Sigismund was backed by Henry he had France against him, and soon Italy was aligned with France. The reason for this was that Robert Hallam—the chief English representative—proposed that the Council of Constance should be divided into four nations: into Italian, French, German and English, each voting separately. This outraged the Italians, who, being vastly in the majority, had expected to have their choice elected with ease. The French argued that there were only four nations, the Italian, French, German and Spanish, and that the English must be included with the German, which thus gave the preponderance of votes to the Latin countries. The English arguments against this were involved and are not worth repeating. The whole council was now ranged behind two men—the Englishman, Robert Hallam, and the

French cardinal Pierre d'Ailly, Bishop of Cambrai. Then unfortunately Hallam died, and Sigismund had to fight alone.

We will not go into details about the conflict, but the English and Sigismund eventually won their point. Their choice was the Cardinal Odda Colonna, and at last grudgingly he was elected Pope Martin V. Martin was actually the ideal choice, a nobleman whom no scandal had ever touched, well-liked for his charm and tolerance and admired for his cunning. With his election, the Great Schism ends, and by his efforts the Roman Church returned to unity, returned almost to its old power and prestige.

But Sigismund and Henry, congratulating themselves on their success, soon began to doubt their own wisdom. Martin was concerned only with the Papacy and had no intention of becoming the tool of any country. And he struggled fiercely to regain control of England. Since the days of Innocent IV (1243–1252) the Popes had been pushing hard to have all benefices in their hands, and very soon they had managed to seize all vacant English livings—and often livings before they fell vacant—; they confiscated the first year's income from these and appointed their own " pro- visors." If there was any trouble the provisors carried the case to Rome and the question had to be settled there. It was Clement V (1305–1313) who abused this power most heavily and who drove England to retaliate; great sums of money were leaving the country and fattening Rome, and the rich livings were often controlled by foreigners, friends of the Popes, and these were usually ab- sentee bishops. To curtail the Roman power a

Statute of Provisors was enacted in 1357, which was followed by a second in 1364 and by a Statute of Præmunire in 1353. But these statutes were of no avail against the Popes' determination to control England, and a third Statute of Provisors was enacted in 1389 which demanded that the 1351 statute be adhered to " in all manner of points."

It was Martin's intention to override these statutes and to ignore the concord sworn to between Edward III and Pope Gregory XI. He tried to bribe Henry Beaufort to his party by offering him a red hat which Henry sternly forbade his accepting. Henry then sent his representative John Catrik, a very weak fellow, vastly inferior to the late Hallam, to remonstrate with Martin. Catrik pointed out that the French had been one of the most violent promoters of the Great Schism, that Henry's war was almost a crusade and that Henry had helped to heal the Schism and to put Martin himself on the papal throne. On being reminded of all these things Martin almost swooned with love for Henry. His ecstasy managed to cover him from being definite on any point that Catrik might put to him about the renewal of provisors, the freedom of English livings from papal domination. All questions were evaded with uplifted eyes and murmurs of reverence at the very name of Henry.

Within a few months Martin was back at his tricks again, exactly as if Henry had never complained, and as if he himself had never spoken with such admiration for England. We certainly cannot blame Martin. He was a highly intelligent man whose battle, quite rightly, was to rebuild a church almost wrecked by the Great Schism.

*249*

Gratitude naturally could not sway him from this great purpose.

What interests us in the negotiations is this fresh glimpse we get of King Henry. Deeply as he might revere the Catholic teachings and imagine himself as a red-cross warrior, he had no intention of surrendering his rights. Just as the Papacy came before every consideration with Martin, so did England come before every consideration—even the Papacy—with Henry.

The English situation and the capture of Oldcastle must next be examined. When the King left for France, England was ruled by his brother the Duke of Bedford, at a salary of 8000 marks a year. Bedford was a clever diplomatist and a brave soldier but he had many difficulties with which to contend. There were still grumblings from the Lollards who swore by the false Richard in Scotland, and there were Scottish forays over the Border. These were soon stopped, and Bedford was able to concentrate on the snaring of Oldcastle.

With Oldcastle the religious question had become a political one; by renouncing the Catholic Church he had renounced King Henry and sworn allegiance to Richard, whom many still believed to be living. We do not know where Oldcastle lurked during these years, but even the greatest bribes could not make his friends surrender him to the Church. We are not even certain where it was that he was arrested. Tradition states that he was caught at Broniarth in the parish of Guilsfield, Montgomeryshire, but it appears that he was actually trapped at Welshpool. He certainly put up a brave defence before he was overpowered. One story says that he could not be pulled down and was only at last thrown off his balance during the fight by a woman hitting him on the shins with a faldstool. At any rate, we do know that he was badly wounded when he was carried to the Tower on a horse-litter.

On December 14, 1417, he was arraigned before Parliament and accused of being a traitor and a heretic. Oldcastle seems to have behaved rather stupidly, answering few questions and continually calling on God, saying that no man had the right to judge him. Eventually he was cornered into stating that he owed allegiance to King Richard II, not to Henry V. He was immediately condemned to be drawn, hanged and burnt.

If Oldcastle behaved with little dignity and a touch of hysteria before Parliament, he certainly redeemed his courage in St. Giles' Field. When asked to confess, he replied that even if the apostles Peter and Paul were present he would not confess, and he called on Sir Thomas Erpingham, a re-canted Lollard, to speak when he had risen on the third day. The iron chain was locked around his body, under the armpits, and the faggots piled high. Not a murmur escaped him during that frightful death.

It has been suggested that Oldcastle was first hanged, and that this explains his magnificent stoicism. There is no contemporary evidence for this statement. The inclusion of hanging in his sentence obviously meant not death by hanging, but his hanging in chains while being burnt alive, so that he could not fall down.

As he had remarked to Erpingham, Oldcastle expected to rise on the third day, which certainly suggests that his mind had become unhinged during his privations. Crowds gathered to witness this miracle, with the subsequent disappointment. His followers rubbed his ashes on their eyes, expecting the scales to fall off immediately and the martyr to appear in all his glory. According to the Catholic statement, this merely blinded them.

And now, back to France, to the confusion there. You will recall that we left Armagnac with the Dauphin in control of Paris, and Burgundy with Queen Isabel holding regal court at Troyes.

Pope Martin V had sent two cardinals, Orsini and Fillastre, to patch up the war between England and France. Failing in this the cardinals decided to repair the civil conflict. Burgundy agreed to their overtures but Armagnac refused even to listen to them. This infuriated the Parisians who were driven desperate by his high-handed brutality and by the threat of Burgundy ever at their gates. Nine men, two of them priests, wrote to John the Fearless, telling him to assault the city at once as most of the important Armagnacs were away fighting the English. His men under Jean de Villiers, lord of l'Isle Adam, were admitted secretly on the morning of Sunday, May 29, 1418.

Reinforced by many citizens, de l'Isle Adam charged through the streets, shouting the warcry of "Our Lady and the peace!", breaking into the Armagnac homes, murdering, looting. The battle raged for days, but at last Burgundy's troops had the victory. Armagnac was killed. His naked body lay for three days, exposed to vile insults, in the palace courtyard.

On July 14, John the Fearless himself appeared

and was received in triumph. He did no harm to the King, and Charles actually thanked him for having been so kind to Isabel in her exile.

No sooner did it seem that now at last everything was settled, that France was united, than the Dauphin Charles refused to ratify any agreement that included Burgundy, denouncing him for having instigated the Paris massacre and for daring to rule with a Parlement at Troyes.

And the muddle became as great as ever. Henry was left undisturbed in his conquests.

Rouen was a great city. In Henry's own words, it was "the most notable place in France save Paris." And the citizens had had full warning of his approach. For months they had toiled at the walls and the ditches. Inside the walls, earth was banked up until at the top it was so wide that a loaded cart could be driven round it. The ditch had been deepened and heaped with caltraps, and pitfalls were dug over all the approaches. The very beautiful suburbs were levelled down until all around Rouen was "as bare as your hand," and the garrison itself had been lately reinforced. On one side of the city flowed the Seine, on the other side rose the vineyard-covered hills. These hills were useless to the besiegers, being out of range. On the landward side, Rouen had five gates, with over sixty towers between the gates. Each tower mounted three guns, and in between each tower were eight smaller guns and catapults. On the river side there were gates opening on to the wharves, and a great stone bridge ran from the centre of the town to a small islet close to the opposite bank. On this islet was a fort called the

Bridge Castle, joining the shore by a drawbridge. Three streams flowed through the city.

The commander of the garrison was a mere gentleman, Guy le Bouteiller; and he was assisted by Guillaume Houdetot; by Alain Blanchard, the captain of the cross-bowmen; Jean Jourdain, captain of the gunners; Robert de Livet, leader of the clergy, who had excommunicated Henry; and Grand Jacques, a Lombard, who headed the sallies.

For a description of the siege we are indeed lucky to have had a shrewd eye-witness in John Page. Page wrote two versions of his poem—the first one,

> *"All in rough and not in rime*
> *Because of space he had no time,*
> *And when this war is at an end,*
> *And he have life he will it mend,"*

and the revised version itself. We also have our old friend Elmham who, although not present, must have written his description from the tales of those who were.

Henry's advance-troops arrived before Rouen the evening of the day they left Pont de l'Arche, Henry himself coming shortly after them.

To attack so well fortified a city was hopeless, and a few days were spent clearing the caltraps and spears out of the ditches and in filling up the pitfalls; and on August 1 the command was given for each captain to take up his position. Henry himself lodged in the Charterhouse of Notre-Dame-de-la-Rose about a mile from the eastern wall; Clarence took his camp almost on the opposite side of the city, in the Abbey of St. Gervaise, facing the Porte Cauchoise; the other captains were distributed so as to surround the city.

John Page gives a minute description of each camp, lauding the captains, and speaking highly of Clarence in particular—

> *"Of princehood he might be called a flower,*
> *For when all princes are y-met,*
> *Next to the best let Clarence be set,"*

with which summing-up I am sure that no one who has studied these campaigns could possibly disagree.

To the east of the city, below Henry's position, on a tall hill, stood the Abbey of St. Catherine's. This abbey was connected to the town by a causeway, eight or ten feet high, stretching over a marsh. The Earl of Salisbury was placed here to intercept communication between abbey and town, but it was an impossible task owing to the marshy ground, and Henry decided that if Rouen was to be cut entirely off he must capture the abbey.

The first assault was beaten back, for the English had to fight uphill; but after that the garrison decided to surrender. It could do nothing else. Surrounded by the English, it would have been only a matter of a few days before it was captured or starved out, and the captain did the sensible thing by treating before many lives were lost. With his men he was permitted to march away, and Salisbury took command of the position.

The siege was to be a prolonged one, and food was scarce. Henry relied mainly on supplies from

England, passing through Harfleur, the estuary being patrolled by the fleet of Henry's relation, the King of Portugal. From Harfleur the goods were then shipped down the Seine in small boats. They had to pass Caudebec, and here raiding-parties were always ready to attack and capture them. Warwick was sent to take the fortress, and did so in six days; it is reported that Henry himself commanded the operations, and this may be true. With Caudebec in his hands, Henry's connections were fully open and he could continue the siege indefinitely.

To prevent relief-ships coming from the French, Henry next dragged chains from bank to bank above the bridge, twining them around posts or laying them on barrels for buoys. These chains were from a foot and a half below water to two feet above. And to guard below the bridge, ships were carried overland at the point apparently between Moulineaux and Orival where the land is but three miles wide. The Seine was now Henry's, and the French vessels fled to hide in the arsenal at Rouen where they were burnt for fear they should fall into English hands.

Slowly, carefully, with his usual thoroughness, Henry went about the preparations for the taking of Rouen. He built a bridge from Lescure to the opposite bank, raising it on a chain fastened to piles, and it was so stoutly made that horses could gallop over it. This bridge was most necessary if he wished to keep his communications open with lower Normandy where the Earl of Huntingdon was in command.

Food was now coming from England, and also reinforcements. These included a troop of Irish under Thomas Butler, prior of the Knights Hospitallers at Kilmainham near Dublin. At first these Irish only excited interest because of their outlandish dress and manners—they wore no breeches, had one foot unshod, and fought with darts and knives; they did not ride a saddle but a kind of pad—then the interest rapidly changed to fear. These Irish were excellent at foraging, being too ill-disciplined for the common tasks; but their foraging took on the air of ravaging and they often returned with even babies slung over their horses' cruppers. Henry was forced to threaten flogging if they did not quieten down and obey his orders.

In everything, Henry used the same stern discipline, himself examining all matters personally. Nothing—not rain nor snow nor wind—could hold him in his snug quarters when the hour came to make the rounds. He hanged without mercy and praised without favour; attending to the smallest matters, even to the disposition of tents and the dispatch of every raiding-party or convoy.

There was a certain amount of skirmishing, for the French were at first as assured of victory as were the English. Rouen was powerful, the garrison was large, it had food and water. There were duels between both sides: challenges were given and accepted, and the jousts and tournaments were carried through with all the customary old-fashioned formality. In one of these jousts, a Knight of the Garter, John Blount, was killed by the captain of the Porte Cauchoise—the western gate. His body was dragged into Rouen and ransomed for 400 nobles.

R

This chivalrous spirit did not last long. The citizens began to feel the grip of hunger, and the English became irritable with inaction. Both sides now began to act in a most savage manner: the English hanged their captives on the hills where they could be seen from the town. The French hanged theirs on a gallows in a ditch beneath the walls, placing dogs on their beards and round their throats, or they tied them in sacks and drowned them in the Seine like puppies.

Rouen was suffering badly, and even its water was giving out to a certain extent, for with his usual foresight, Henry had dammed the Renelle. By October the food was nearly gone, and men and women were becoming desperate.

John Page tells us:

> "*And also their bread was near hard gone,*
> *And flesh, save horseflesh, had they none:*
> *They ate also both dogs and cats,*
> *And also both mice and rats,*
> *And also an horse-quarter, lean or fat,*
> *And a hundred shillings it was worth at;*
> *And also a horse's head at half a pound,*
> *And a dog for ten shillings of money sound:*
> *For forty pence they sold a rat,*
> *And for two nobles they sold a cat:*
> *And for six pence they sold a mouse,*
> *Full few was left in any house.*
> *And for half so mickle bread as a hand*
> *Was worth a franc of that land . . .*
> *And then they eat both roots and rind,*
> *And dew of the grass that they might find . . .*
> *All love and kindness was gone aside*
> *When each from the other their meat would hide.*"

The citizens sent to Paris, pleading with Burgundy to rescue them. An old priest managed to creep through the English lines, and on reaching Paris, hired a famous university doctor, Eaustace de Pavilly, to plead for him the tragic case of Rouen.

Eaustace pleaded in beautiful style on the text, "Lord, what shall we do?" but I feel that the poor old man's words must have been far more effective than the most polished dialectics.

"My lord the King," said he, when Eaustace had finished, "I am bidden by the people of Rouen, to make before you, and before you my lord of Burgundy, their great cry for the oppression which they suffer at the hands of the English. And they will have you know by my mouth, that if of default of succour it should happen that they become the subjects of the King of England, you shall not find in all the world worse enemies than them, and they will destroy you and your generation."

Burgundy listened with extraordinary patience to this threat and gave his promise to relieve the city and to bring King Charles with him.

The tidings rang every bell in Rouen, they brought courage to the despairing and hope even to the starved and wounded. Amongst the English the news was received with equal joy. Henry was delighted to think that there might now be a decisive battle, and with "merry cheer" he called his captains to him, saying (as John Page tells us, and if his words be twisted for the sake of a rime, it does not mean that their context is not similar to what the King said):

> "*Fellows be merry now every one,*
> *For we shall fight soon anon!*"

The wild Irish were sent out to intercept any messengers and to be the first to bring news of the coming relief-forces. That night, men slept in their armour, gripping their weapons. To the north of the city, from the direction Burgundy would approach, Henry built towers, well fortified, and piled up mounds of earth.

It was but a false alarm. Henry must have known this, but like a good general he was taking no chances. At first it seemed that the weak-willed but peculiarly styled John the Fearless might actually do a courageous action. All Paris was eager to follow him, and the excommunication ban under which he had laboured was annulled; on November 17, King Charles again took the oriflamme from St. Denis, and with his Queen, travelled to Pontoise where the army was gathering.

That army never went near Rouen. The Dauphin swore to do battle with it himself if it ever dared take the road under the banner of his enemy, for he hated John the Fearless even more than he hated England. Besides this, Burgundy had little money with which to pay his troops and many of the nobles had refused to answer his call. The army wasted five weeks, eating up everything in Pontoise, and then disbanded.

Henry was in touch with both sides and therefore could not have been really deceived. Cleverly he juggled the Dauphin against Burgundy, Burgundy against the Dauphin, making each suspicious of the other. As Burgundy had turned from his English alliance when he entered Paris, the Dauphin was eager to treat with Henry, suggesting that he marry his sister Katherine, in return for aid against John. Henry's demands were

too high for even the Dauphin to swallow, and then
Burgundy offered a fresh alliance, but again Henry
asked too much. Henry handled both parties very
shrewdly, leading them on with hopes, then setting
them against each other.

We cannot doubt that if either party had
accepted his terms, the enormous territories and
money he demanded, Henry would have settled
the bargain then and there. But neither side dared
accept them, not from loyalty to France but
because they feared the people would turn against
them if they did. Henry was intelligent enough to
realise this and could scarcely have expected his
terms to be taken. Vague as these conferences
seem, leaving everything exactly as it was before,
they succeeded to the extent that they gave Henry
leisure to continue his siege of Rouen, and they
set the Dauphin and John the Fearless at each
other's throats with more fury than ever.

Rouen was falling fast. "Hunger breaketh the
hard stone wall" which the cannon could not
pierce and the English could not escalade. At
first the besieged had attempted to hide their
desperate situation, they behaved as if they were
as fresh and as well filled as ever. But men crept
out of the city, seeking bread, and were captured.
The story they told was a tragic one, the story
that I have already given as John Page heard it
and recorded it in rime. And a French chronicler,
Le Fèvre, adds the pitiful touch that girls were
eager to bargain their thin bodies for a little meat.

The first rush of joy caused by the tidings of
Burgundy's approach soon died out as the citizens
realised that it had been but an idle boast. Henry,

rather brutally—if there is brutality in the necessities of war—sent forged letters inside the town giving the poor wretches hope of relief, and he dressed some of his men with St. Andrew's cross and made them dart out of the woods as if they were Burgundy's men. The plan was to cheat the garrison into a sally and thus cut it down before it could retreat. His efforts failed: the garrison was not deceived.

Inside those walls the dead men dropped too quickly to be buried. Bedraggled men and women crawled over the cobbles of a once mighty and prosperous city; merchants and beggars grew leaner side by side, for gold was useless, it had returned to the metal it was before the lusts of the belly.

Now Rouen dropped all pretence, no longer did the soldiers on the walls act heartily as if well nourished. The truth became too obvious when the scarecrows crept to the English lines, weeping for food.

There were too many people in Rouen, too many non-combatants. It was a cruel but a necessary act—the garrison pushed all the non-combatants out of the gates:

> *"At every gate they were put out,*
> *Many a hundred in a rout,*
> *It was great pity on them for to see,*
> *How women came crawling on their knee,*
> *And their children all in their arms,*
> *For to save them from harms;*
> *And old men came kneeling them by,*
> *And there they made a doleful cry,*
> *And all they cried at once then,*
> *'Have mercy on us, ye Englishmen.'"*

But Henry would not let them pass. The rules
of war forbade such an act of mercy. The city
had held out and could hold out longer if it had
food enough; these people should never have
fought against him, and the garrison, if it wanted
to continue the battle, should have kept all its
people. Until the garrison submitted, everybody
must starve. Mercy is a most dangerous weakness
in a leader, it can create too easily a precedent
that will in time bring down destruction. By
pardoning these poor wretches Henry would have
given courage to future towns; by letting them die
he made his coming conquests easier. And if war
is to be waged it must be waged in all its horrors,
to the last corpse, to the last drop of blood in the
veins. Mercy is misguided in a soldier, it is a failing
that must not be submitted to.

Henry steeled his heart as the lean ragged
creatures struggled into the open. When they tried
to pass through the English lines they were fired
at and were forced to limp back against the
walls, cursing not the English but their own
countrymen.

The sight was too distressing, and Henry permitted enough weakness in himself not to forbid
his men giving the starving creatures some food.
They lay in the flooded ditch, covered only by the
clothes they wore, in continual rain. Some women
suffered childbirth in this hell, and the newborn
babies were hoisted up to the walls of Rouen so
that the priests might baptize them before they
were lowered again to a ghastly death. John
Page was a soldier and he must have witnessed
many cruel acts, but he speaks with horror of
the remembered sight in the ditch of Rouen,

between the walls and the well-fed English lines:

> *"There men might see a great pity,*
> *A child of two year or three*
> *Go about and bid [beg] his bread*
> *For father and mother both lay dead;*
> *And under them the water stood,*
> *And yet they lay crying after food.*
> *Some starven to the death,*
> *And some stopped both eyen and breath,*
> *And some crooked in the knees,*
> *And as lean as any trees,*
> *And women holding in their arm*
> *A dead child, and nothing warm,*
> *And children sucking on the pap*
> *Within a dead woman's lap."*

Christmas was coming, and the sight of that suffering on a feast-day was too much for Henry to bear. He offered a day of peace to the city, which was agreed to rather reluctantly. The starving people in the ditch were placed in a row, and two priests attended by three men went amongst them and gave them food. Then they rejoiced because "of tender heart is the Englishman" compared to their fellow-countrymen the French.

With no hope of relief, faced by a future of slow inevitable starvation, the garrison of Rouen decided to die bravely. They would sally out and with swords in their hands would meet a death worthy of soldiers.

Two thousand rushed through the Porte St. Hilaire upon the English; a second band charged through the Castle Gate. Here the stanchions on the bridge had been cut and it fell beneath their feet, hurling them into the moat.

This was the garrison's last fling, it was too exhausted for another sally, and on New Year's Eve, 1419, the chief citizens went to each gate in turn, but only at one gate were their cries answered. This was at the south gate commanded by Sir Gilbert Umfraville. When the men of Rouen were told his name they were delighted because of its Norman ring, and they asked him to plead with Henry to let twelve of them treat for peace. Umfraville ran to Clarence and the other captains, but Henry was not disturbed until the morning. All were delighted at the news, even Henry was pleased, and he agreed to grant the French an audience.

There were still minor points to arrange, however, and Umfraville was all day at the gate. It was not until January 3, that four knights, four clerks and four burgesses at the hour of prime— six a.m.—issued from the Porte St. Hilaire, all garbed suitably in deep black. Before escorting them to the Charterhouse, Umfraville was careful to warn the suppliants how to treat with the King: they must think carefully before they spoke and must not talk too long, and they must also be very tactful, one word out of place might cause them to "fall full hard." With this caution, Umfraville led them to Henry who was hearing Mass, and the Frenchmen were forced to wait until the service was concluded. Then Henry appeared, unsmiling, stern, while the suppliants knelt before him. Still on their knees, they offered him a bill at which he did not deign to look, passing it to the Duke of Exeter. He told them to speak, and they prayed for love of Jesus and the Blessed Virgin to have pity on the starving creatures in the ditch. Still unsmiling, still frowning at them, Henry retorted: "Fellows, who put them there? They abode in the city while they might. Let them find what they have sought." He said that the city was rightfully his and that they had kept him from his inheritance; and when they pleaded that they would be his servants if he would but permit them to ask the Duke of Burgundy's permission, he said that there was no need for that, for he had been in touch with Burgundy and to send further messages would be a superfluity. Forgetting what Umfraville had told them, the desperate Frenchmen were foolish enough to boast that Rouen and its people was a fair city to capture. Henry flared out at that. "It is mine!" he cried, "and I will have it. Let those within prepare themselves, for men shall speak of me till the day of doom!"

He turned aside and talked quietly with his brother Clarence while the men from Rouen waited on their knees. Whatever the brothers said, it must have been pleasing, for when Henry again looked at the suppliants a little of his sternness had abated. He gave them time to treat and suggested that they might yet find mercy in him. This gave them courage enough to mention again the starving people in the ditch—who were evidently on their consciences—and he promised to take advice on the question of their fate.

With that he dismissed them, and on the way back to their city the twelve Frenchmen were loud in their praises of the King, telling Umfraville how deeply impressed they were by his looks, by his mien and his wisdom.

Negotiations dragged on. Later French writers state that the garrison intended to fire the city and fight its way through the English lines, and that on hearing of this, Henry offered terms. The tale may or may not be true. Negotiations certainly continued for a long time. Two tents were raised in Gloucester's camp for the terms to be discussed in, and for days the commissioners on each side quarrelled over small points. At last the English wearied of it and pulled down the tents.

This was the final blow. Those inside Rouen threatened to burn down the gates and open to the English unless the city was surrendered on any terms whatever, and the frightful starvation ended. At that, the envoys shouted from the Porte Hilaire that they were ready to give in.

Tents were again pitched, this time the clergy on both sides managing the terms, and it was finally decided that Rouen would surrender on January 13 if help had not arrived by then; it would also pay 300,000 crowns and would surrender all war-harness and weapons, the garrison being permitted to depart except for any Norman soldiers.

Food was passed into the city, the starving men, women and children were lifted out of the ditch, and on January 19, after the streets were cleansed of many of the dead, the capitulation was finalised. Guy le Bouteiller with the more important citizens knelt at Henry's feet in the Charterhouse. The keys were offered and accepted, and were given to Exeter who had been made captain of the town.

The gates opened, and to the sound of music,

Exeter rode through the streets of the conquered city, his men crying "St. George!" and "Welcome, Rouen, our King's own right!" and feebly the citizens echoed—"Welcome."

When Henry entered on the following day, he rode a black horse and wore a robe of black damask held over his chest with a golden clasp. Behind him came a page holding aloft one of his badges, a fox's brush, on a spear. The bells rang and the people cried "Noel! Noel!" Yet Henry rode in silence, without music or insignia of war, as was his manner. Not like a victorious conqueror but like one stern and saddened by the wreck caused by his own triumph, he entered Rouen and did not linger until he reached the west door of the cathedral. Before him then went the clerks of his chapel, along the nave, chanting the antiphon. "Quis est Magnus Dominus?"—"Who is so great a lord?"

After hearing Mass and having made his offering, Henry mounted again his black horse and rode quietly to the castle where he was to sleep that night.

Rouen at last was his, and only Paris remained.

# CHAPTER SIXTEEN

## *Dauphin Charles and John the Fearless*

HENRY stayed for two months in the conquered town. It was not a time of rest however, but of administration. The starved people could not be fed at once, many were too exhausted to live, and the food only dragged out their miserable existence a little further. For fifteen days people were still dying horribly in Rouen, while the King of England's standard shook above the castle and there was peace inside the broken walls. In the agreement, Rouen had sworn to deliver to Henry's mercy nine named men. We cannot be certain of the fate of all nine, but four of them paid ransom and saved their necks; one who "spoke the foul words"—who evidently shouted insults at Henry from the battlements—disappears completely from history; an Italian also fades away; Robert de Livet, who had excommunicated Henry, was sent to England, but we find him back at his canonry in 1424; and Alain Blanchard, as one of the leaders and a brutal leader, was executed.

On Candlemas Day King Henry wore the robes of the Duke of Normandy; and when the estates of Normandy met in February many of the conquered made obeisance to their new master, but no nobles appeared. Guy le Bouteiller, who had been governor of Rouen, was the only important Norman to join the English. Because of this, French writers have denounced him as a traitor, but the country at the time was so split up into parties that we can scarcely blame any man for choosing the stronger and juster, even if a foreign, party. And it must not be thought that medieval France was the same‾as modern France, no more than medieval England was like modern England. The two nations, although dissimilar, had not swerved quite so far apart as they have to-day; particularly this must have been true in Normandy from where our great Kings came. Both nations had a common root, a common tradition and a common faith. The English might have been more stolid. the French more reckless, yet between the two there was a bond that has now entirely disappeared. French too was still the official language‾ of England. But all Europe was webbed together by the Roman Empire, there was the unity of belief, and—amongst the cultured—of the Latin tongue. Nationalisms had not grown to the vast extent which they have to-day.

According to his agreement with the city, Henry had arranged to build a ducal palace in Rouen, and he now purchased a plot of ground in the south-west corner inside the walls, close to the waterside. Here he immediately started building. Although the palace was never finished, it was for many years the strongest part of the city even in its incomplete state.

Besides erecting a palace, Henry turned his energies on to the question of weights and measures. The fluctuations in these most vital things of commerce had helped to stifle free-trading, but he now arranged for a uniform Norman rule— the Rouen standard for grain, the Arques standard for liquid, the Paris ell for cloth, and the Troyes mark for weight.

The most important problem in Rouen at the moment—at least for the citizens—was the effort to raise that monstrous ransom of 300,000 crowns. This ransom nearly destroyed the city. Heavy taxes were imposed, and because of their crippling effect many people left to live elsewhere. The sum apparently never was paid in full.

The news of the fall of Rouen shocked all France, drove it into sudden panic, for now Paris must be Henry's objective. His captains were sweeping over the country, capturing town after town. Horrified as France might be by the fall of its second largest city, the loss of Rouen did not affect the two rival parties, the Dauphinists and the Burgundians. Henry negotiated with both sides, as already stated, and he also spread his nets for larger game, in a kind of Napoleonic dream of conquest, of creating a European family. He hoped to marry his brother John Duke of Bedford, to a German princess, and his other brother Gloucester to a princess of Navarre.

These foreign negotiations of Henry reveal the flowering of his dream. He wished to net all Europe, if possible, to England's side. He made an attempt to win the throne of Naples. Naples was ruled by a Queen who, although forty-four years of age, was still famed for her debaucheries. Her debaucheries, however, could not produce her an heir when she married, and the throne was going vacant. On becoming Queen when her brother died, Queen Joan—she was Queen Joan II —could not make up her mind whether to take a Frenchman or an Englishman for husband, and finally settled on Jacques Count de la Marche. The marriage did not last long. Within a few years de la Marche was in prison, from which he managed to escape and run to France. Joan after that had had enough of husbands. She decided to adopt a son, and Henry suggested his brother John. Unfortunately the effort came to nothing, but for a while it did seem that Naples would sign an English alliance.

John had almost married a princess of Aragon and had then almost got Jacqueline of Hainault, who was eventually to marry his brother Humphrey. Henry now sent commissioners on a roving journey about the German courts, but all the women were too unattractive to accept even for political reasons, save for an eight-year-old child who unfortunately was already betrothed to René, son of the Duchess of Anjou.

Not only by adoptions and marriages but by treaties Henry was striving to bring Europe to his side. He was in touch with the Genoese, with Flanders and with the Archbishops of Treves and Mayence. Apart from these diplomatic lines, Henry was also angling with France itself, with both the Dauphin and Burgundy, while his captains were seizing town after town, castle after castle. He had also made a truce with Brittany and Anjou.

Town after town was falling to Exeter, Salisbury or Clarence—Montivilliers, Lillebonne, Fécamp, Etrepagny, Tancarville, Dieppe, Gournay, and Neufchâtel-en-Bray, Eu, Honfleur; the so-called impregnable La Roche Guyon (taken by Warwick by digging under the foundations), Ivry (by Gloucester after a fierce battle).

The Dauphin offered to treat with Henry and they decided that they should talk things over on March 26, but it appears that no actual meeting-place was arranged. Nevertheless, for some reason, the English fully expected the Dauphin to be at Evreux, and his non-appearance on that date infuriated the soldiers, although Henry himself could scarcely have believed he would be there. We find the mood of the English shown clearly in a letter written by one of them to London; he denounces the Dauphin, saying that he had "made the King a *beau mient* [a fine fool], therefore no one may hope yet for peace," and he ends pathetically, "Pray for us that we may come soon out of this unlusty soldier's life into the life of England."

Henry probably did not share this soldier's exasperation at "the double and false" dealings of the French; himself was in touch with Burgundy at the moment as well as with the Dauphin, and his commissioners headed by the Earl of Warwick —a subtle diplomatist as well as a brave soldier, and the "father of courtesy": we find him on nearly every embassy—had been arguing for days with the Burgundians at Mantes, Rouen, Vernon, Provins and Troyes. At last it was decided that Henry could confer with King Charles and John the Fearless, who would bring Katherine with them, on May 15, 1419. As the French King was insane at the time Henry agreed to postpone the meeting until the 30th.

A large field outside the west gate of Meulan was decided on for the great day of the meeting of Kings. It lay opposite the Ile Belle in the Seine, and was bounded by the river on the south and

s

by the marshes on the north. Palisades were hammered into the earth to ring in an enclosure, and two trenches were dug clean through it, thereby dividing the enclosure into three portions —one for the French, one for the English, and in the centre a neutral one on which the negotiations could be carried out. The nations were not to mix but were to be penned off like sheep—the English being separated on the neutral ground by stakes a foot high, and the French by stakes very much higher. This was in terror of the English long-bow in case of treachery. The arrangements were made with great care and formality. Neither King was to bring more than fifteen hundred armed men, and fifty soldiers were to guard each gate—there were six gates, three aside. No horseplay was permitted; brawling, wrestling or the shouting of insulting remarks was to be rewarded by instant beheading; while one English soldier who leaped over the barrier on the opening day—evidently out of stupid bravado—was hanged.

Three tents were pegged out in the neutral ground, the centre one being more of a pavilion. There was a tent for each King, and the pavilion for both Kings. This was a beautiful object, hedged in by a palisade and covered with cloth-of-gold and with hangings embroidered with the leopards and lilies of England and France.

Not only were there tents in this centre enclosure, but the soldiers themselves erected small temporary towns, with streets; each nation striving to outvie the other with magnificence.

On May 29, oaths were sworn that there would be no treachery, and on the 30th, Henry arrived at the Meulan field with his two brothers, and with Warwick and other nobles. The French King had not yet recovered from his madness, so he did not appear. Instead, the Queen arrived at two o'clock, amidst music, lolling in her litter, and attended by the Duke of Burgundy and her ladies-in-waiting.

At a given signal, Henry and Isabel stepped out of their respective tents and, preceded by their escorts marching two by two, met before a stake pitched into the earth. Henry kissed the hand of Isabel, and Burgundy half knelt on one knee. Henry caught him, embraced him, then led the Queen to the thrones in the centre pavilion. Speaking in French, Warwick explained exactly what was intended, and the remainder of the day seems to have been given up to feasting and ceremonies.

Henry was now to meet Katherine of Valois for the first time. She arrived on June 1, escorted by Burgundy's nephew, the Count of St. Pol. The French staked much on her effect on the English King, for she was reputed to be very beautiful despite that long Valois nose of hers; and the enormous sum of 3000 florins had been expended on attempts to make her look even more beautiful in rich expensive dresses. They had not misfired this time. Henry seems to have fallen in love with Katherine at once—as well he might, says a Burgundian chronicler, "for she was very handsome, of high birth and with the most delightful manners." The English were more interested to note the charming blushes that warmed her cheeks as Henry bent to kiss her hand.

He was now thirty-two and—apart from his

merry youth—had been utterly chaste in his living, according to Elmham. Perhaps Katherine had come to mean a symbol to him, and probably he was in love with her as the image of France long before they met. Otherwise, I find it difficult to reconcile that Valois nose drooping over the mouth with a great and sudden passion; but lovers are queer creatures and often find beauties where others see only disfigurements.

Henry was not to meet her again at Meulan, but that one glimpse had been sufficient. He was determined to marry her.

The negotiations dragged on their weary hours, neither side being able to strike a comfortable bargain. Henry demanded that he receive not only all Edward III's conquests but his own fresh conquest of Normandy must be his without interference from Charles: a kingdom apart. The French naturally objected, they tried to make him renounce his claims to Touraine, Anjou, Maine, Brittany, Flanders, Ponthieu and Montreuil in exchange for a goodly slice of Aquitaine to equal in size all the others put together; then it was Henry's turn to object. He objected again when they said that peace if made should include all the allies; he was not going to make peace with any Scots fighting in France. There was further wrangling over Katherine's dowry: 800,000 crowns had been agreed on as the sum, and from this the French commissioners wanted to deduct the 600,000 crowns that had not been refunded with Queen Isabel, Richard's widow. Henry retorted with the time-honoured demand for the rest of King John's ransom, King John having been captured years ago by the Black Prince and never having been fully paid for. Pushed back here, the French wanted a rebate of 400,000 crowns on account of Katherine's jewellery; Henry retorted that it wasn't worth a quarter of that sum.

Backwards and forwards went the argument. The truth seems to be that John the Fearless, with his characteristic caution, was growing afraid of his own actions. He realised—evidently for the first time—that by giving the French crown to Henry he would alienate the moderates in his party and would drive them into the arms of the Dauphin. Burgundy was an intensely suspicious man like all traitors, and was ever most wary when it came to a decisive point. He detested having to do anything and preferred to let his actions be shaped by events rather than to let events be shaped by his actions. His old fears and suspicions gripped him now as in all their nakedness he saw the pretensions of King Henry.

In his fear of making a decision he tried to put the weight on to the shoulders of others, and sought out two learned clerks in his company. The first of these advised him to agree to Henry's demands; the English were too strong to fight, he said, and the Dauphin himself was trying to strike a bargain with them; if John got in first the rest of France would soon follow his lead. The second clerk gave exactly the opposite opinion: the King of France, he said, had not the legal right to give away what was his only by descent, and Henry was a usurper on whom divine justice must fall some day.

This second opinion decided John the Fearless, for it suited his own shifty nature. He began secretly to intrigue with the Dauphin.

The same terror of what France would do if she gave her husband's crown to Henry was also affecting Queen Isabel. Some months later she was to write to Henry explaining the breakdown of the negotiations. Quite frankly, she stated that this was because she feared the consequences; she had been advised that "all the barons, knights, cities, and good towns of our lord the King would have abandoned us for our son" if she had agreed to Henry's demands.

At some period there was an actual quarrel between Henry and the duke, and it probably occurred around this date. Henry accused Burgundy of trying to evade the issue in talk. "Fair cousin," he said, "we would have you to wit that we will have your King's daughter and all we have demanded, or else we will drive him and you out of his kingdom."

To this, Burgundy replied: "Sire, you are pleased to say so; but before you can drive my lord and me out of his kingdom I make no doubt that you will be heartily weary."

This quarrel did not break the negotiations, but now it was obvious that no finality would be reached. Burgundy was more or less openly conspiring with the Dauphin; and when on July 3 Henry stepped on to the ground, he found that the French had gone.

Warwick and Archbishop Chichele he sent to Pontoise to request a further interview in which to discuss his proposed marriage with Katherine; but the duke sent them off, refusing even to see them. And all again ended in distrust.

Henry did not give up hope. He sent the fair Katherine gifts of jewellery worth 100,000 crowns.

Unfortunately they never reached her. French marauders captured the gifts and accepted them as booty.

Openly now, John the Fearless and Dauphin Charles were treating together, and Henry must have watched with apprehension, for if they joined he would have a united France against him. And it seemed that they actually would join. Negotiators passed from camp to camp and both parties swore to forget the past, to drop the party names of Burgundian and Armagnac, to fight together against their country's enemies, to repudiate all individual treaties and to rule jointly.

Henry was not idle. He had agreed with Burgundy to sign a truce until July 29, and until that date he did nothing, keeping honourably to his agreement. The moment the truce expired he struck, swiftly and terribly.

On July 30 he was in Mantes, and he commanded that the gates be shut and guarded and that no one must pass through them. Only his soldiers trooped out on a secret mission. When night came, in the darkness further troops rode from Mantes, this time carrying scaling-ladders. Their objective was Pontoise on the road to Paris, a Burgundian stronghold.

During the peace negotiations English soldiers had wandered freely through the town, noting its fortifications and its importance. Henry had not forgotten their information.

His troops, three thousand men, were placed in two companies: one under the Earl of Huntingdon, the other under Gaston de Foix, a Gascon nobleman recently created Count of Longueville.

The Pontoise garrison amounted to one thousand men-at-arms and two thousand cross-bowmen, under the Lord de l'Isle Adam. They had enough provisions to last them for two years as they had been continually expecting an Armagnac attack; for the same reason the suburbs were burnt down.

The assault was to commence at dawn, and the English troops waited in the darkness, watching anxiously for the first blur of light in the east. De Foix's men dismounted and left their horses away from the town, crawling into some ditches towards the west of the wall. Huntingdon swooped round to the east to hold the Paris road, but in the darkness he became lost and therefore was unable to give the signal for attack. It was now about four in the morning, dawn would be on them very soon and the assault made hopeless, and de Foix dared wait no longer. He decided to act on his own initiative, and gave the command. His men darted out from the trenches amongst the vineyards and raised their ladders against the walls of Pontoise. The town was almost unguarded for it was the hour of Mass; and the English were over the walls and had flung open the gates before even the alarm was properly sounded. The English outside charged through, shouting "St. George!" and "The town is ours!"

De l'Isle Adam, half-armed, leaped on his horse and tried to call his men around him. The gates were too broken for them to be shut again, and there was hand-to-hand fighting in every street. The French put up a gallant defence, but they were scattered and taken by surprise and therefore had no hope of winning.

From the distance sounded the trumpets of

Huntingdon and his troop, who had found their
way again; dirty after their night's roving they
galloped through the broken gates into the town,
and the battle was over. De l'Isle Adam realised that
further defence was useless. He cried: "All's lost!
each for himself!"—"*Tout est perdu! sauve qui peut!*"—
and soldiers and citizens grabbed their property
and tried to run for the open. Many were caught
by Huntingdon, others escaped only to be plundered
by their comrades, the Burgundians. It was a
swift and splendid victory.

The loot was enormous. One chronicler values
it at two million crowns, but that seems exorbitant.
Nevertheless it may be correct. Pontoise was undoubtedly one of the richest of Henry's conquests,
for owing to the suddenness of the attack, the French
had not had time to bury or destroy their property.

Apart from its material riches, the moral effect
of the fall of Pontoise was exceptionally valuable.
Henry was delighted when told the news, and he
had a *Te Deum* sung at once; and when writing to
England he states that in all his campaigns he
had captured nothing so useful.

When the fugitives reached St. Denis, John the
Fearless and Queen Isabel fled to Lagny, for Paris
was now open to the English, nothing remained
to bar Henry's progress. At the same time, his
success was darkened by the possibility of an
alliance between Burgundy and the Dauphin;
and behind him, the captured towns were not
settling placidly under his rule, just though it was.
There were constant insurrections, conspiracies.
Peace seemed as far off as when Henry first
landed on French soil.

Yet Paris was open. Clarence galloped to the

very walls with his troops and paraded gallantly around them, hoping to entice the garrison into a sally. In this he failed, for the Paris soldiers were mainly mercenaries who did not seek fighting for the sake of patriotism or honour. One story tells us that Clarence banged on the gates and asked to visit the shrine of St. Denis. On being refused, he cried, "What you refuse to-day I will get some other day, whether you will or no!"

This show of defiance had to satisfy the brave reckless duke, and soon he returned to Pontoise where Henry was now lodged.

Paris was suffering from an evil worse than the English knocking on its gates: Pontoise captured meant that the city's food supplies were cut off, and prices rose to five times above the normal.

Henry remained in Pontoise until August 18, and then dispatched his captains to various points that had to be subdued. In quick succession towns fell to him. Lavilleterte and Bouconvillers both were his before the end of August; Gisors—a strong castle —was his by September 23; Meulan fell by October 30; Montjoie and St. Germain before the end of November; Château-Gaillard in December.

While Henry continued his conquests, tragic events were happening amongst the French, events that threw the kingdom at last into his hands.

John the Fearless and the Dauphin were still intriguing, both rather distrusting the other. The Dauphin suggested a meeting at the junction of the Seine and the Yonne; but when he turned up on the appointed day, John the Fearless did not appear. He explained that he did not like the meeting-place, Montereau, but at last he was persuaded to take definite action, and agreed to be on the Montereau bridge on September 10, 1419.

What followed at that meeting we shall probably never know exactly. Each party told its story, Burgundian and Dauphinist, and the truth is inextricably mixed with the lie. We have many of the externals; on some points both tales agree but the exact details often conflict.

I feel, however, that the description given by Monstrelet—although a Burgundian—seems the most plausible, and it is that description which I have mainly followed.

John the Fearless arrived at Montereau on the 10th, with seven hundred fighting-men at his back. The castle was to the east of the river and the bridge was barricaded, leaving a small enclosed square in which the interview was to take place. Into this square only the Dauphin and Burgundy, each with ten followers, were permitted to enter.

John the Fearless seems for once to have conquered his usual desire to put things off. Some of his comrades, we are told, tried to dissuade him from going, but he answered, "We must risk something in the cause of peace."

As he reached the barrier he was met by Tanneguy du Chastel. The duke slapped Tanneguy on the shoulder, saying, "This is he whom I trust." The Dauphin, fully armed, was leaning on one of the barriers, and the duke bowed before him. There was some sort of a quarrel between the two, some high words passed although nothing particularly serious was said. Then when Burgundy stood again to his feet he found that his sword had got twisted behind him. He caught it by the grip to pull it straight. This was the opportunity the conspirators desired. Robert de Lairé shouted, "What! do you put your hand upon your sword in the presence of my lord the Dauphin?" and Tanneguy—in whom the duke had trusted—said, "It is time," and he struck the duke with a little battle-axe; so sure was the cut that he almost lopped the chin clean off.

Falling, Burgundy tried to drag his sword out of its sheath; but the Dauphinists hit him, stabbed him. As he lay bleeding on the ground, it is said that one man—Olivier Layet—pushed his sword up under the duke's habergeon—a sleeveless mail coat—and struck him in the belly. De Nouaille tried to rescue his captain but as he struggled with one who held a dagger, another hit him on the head with a battle-axe, "which put an end to the scuffle and his life."

While the murder was enacted, the Dauphin still leaned on the barrier, never moving. Then he suddenly grew afraid, and his friends carried him into the castle.

The other Burgundians on the bridge were all captured or killed except for one who dived into the river. The troops, drawn up outside, were attacked, but having no artillery they were forced either to fly or to surrender.

Was it a premeditated murder, as the Burgundians swore it was, or was it an accident? Did Burgundy really try to draw his sword, as the Dauphinists insisted?

These questions cannot be answered. But amongst the conflicting statements the above tale appears to me to be the most likely, for the entire unpreparedness of the Burgundians seems to exonerate them. They could have had no suspicions of treachery, for only one of the duke's attendants was quick-witted enough to take action. The others were evidently struck statuesque with horror. And if any treachery had even been thought of, surely those seven hundred men outside would have been standing to arms?

The Dauphinists struck too quickly for the thing to have been an accident, their behaviour was altogether too concerted. It was not the act of one man but of all. If de Lairé had really been so outraged by Burgundy touching his sword-grip, the others would not have all leaped so swiftly to the occasion and have known exactly what to do.

The Dauphin himself was only sixteen at the time, and therefore he cannot be blamed for the killing. He was in the hands of strong men, of men fired with the lust for revenge by the memory of Armagnac's naked body lying for three days before the gloating eyes of Paris, and of the Duke of Orléans struck down by assassins as he rode singing through the dark streets.

If the act was premeditated, as I believe, then the Dauphinists were the most stupid of conspirators. They threw the Burgundians straight into the hands of King Henry at the very moment when an alliance between both parties might have saved France.

To these men, however, personal hatreds were of greater importance than their country's needs. And by their ungovernable fury they leagued France against them, they lost moral support and were driven back from the little they owned.

# CHAPTER SEVENTEEN

## *The Treaty of Troyes*

WHEN King Henry heard the news, it was said that although he mourned the death of Burgundy, he could not help crying that now by the help of God and St. George he would have the lady Katherine even if every Frenchman said him nay!

Through the country the news spread a trail of rage and horror, and many Dauphinists were murdered in Paris. Burgundy's son Philip—later called the Good—swore to live only to revenge his father's murder. Queen Isabel seems to have been distressed particularly and she wrote at once to King Henry, while the duke's widow sent ambassadors to the Pope and Sigismund, pleaded with Philip to rouse himself from his despair, and bullied the University of Paris to seek revenge for its patron's death.

Negotiations were immediately opened between Henry and Queen Isabel. Her envoys came to Mantes on October 26, 1419, and Henry could afford to appear restrained and very stern. He knew that he was now the arbiter and that heavy throws would be made by each parties to entice him to its side. He told the envoys that he was distressed by the duke's murder and he commended Philip's desire for revenge, but he harshly told them that if Philip thought to play him as his father had done, he had best stop immediately and

England would continue with its conquest of France. The Dauphin, he reminded them, was also seeking his aid, and he would give them until Martinmas to decide what his help was worth. Another interview on the following day produced all Henry's demands: he would marry Katherine without charge to her parents; Charles VI would remain King of France with himself as governor of the country, but on Charles's death the crown must fall to him and to his heirs; and one of his brothers would marry Duke Philip's sister.

These demands were too huge for the envoys to answer, but Henry pointed out that the King or the duke could settle them quickly with a Yes or a No. He added that if Philip thought to become King of France he had best beware, for he would rather have Orléans—a prisoner in England—on the throne than Burgundy.

The envoys hurried to Arras, and a great council discussed the question. Their needs were pressing, and the terror that Henry might ally himself with the Dauphin was too strong to be denied. They decided to give in.

After that there was no further difficulty. On Christmas Day Henry signed a treaty between himself and Philip, and afterwards there was feasting, at which it was noticed that Henry was particularly merry.

The Burgundian and the English forces now worked in concert—or should have worked in concert. There was a certain rivalry between both sides at first, but Philip's lust for revenge and Henry's unflinching harshness to insubordinates eventually curbed all jealousy. After an attack on the tower of Tremblay, the English and Burgundians nearly fought together on the question of which country had done the boldest deeds.

Then came news of a disaster at sea: the English fleet off La Rochelle were badly beaten by the Castilians, losing seven hundred men.

While negotiating with Philip and Isabel, Henry still administered his conquests, and under his rule Normandy was rapidly recovering. It recovered so fast, indeed, that Henry found he could place heavier taxes on it to help support the war. Trade was improving: Breton and Flemish merchants arrived and, during the truce, important Norman towns were actually visited by the Parisians.

The negotiations were rapidly being finalised. At Troyes Henry met Duke Philip, and with the aid of seven masters from the University of Paris, a formal treaty was at last drawn up. By it Henry agreed to marry Katherine who should receive an income of 40,000 crowns a year, the customary income of a Queen of England; he would not call himself King of France while Charles VI lived, but on Charles's death he would assume the crown; all documents, etc., should be drawn up in Charles's name; the country would be governed by a French council with Henry at the head as regent; he would fight the Dauphin, and whatever he captured from him would become the property of France, and on his becoming King at Charles's death, Normandy too would revert to France; he would not interfere with the laws of France but would govern by them wisely.

It was decided that the treaty should be ratified by a personal meeting between Henry and Charles.

Many French historians have regarded this treaty as a traitorous act of the Duke of Burgundy and a German Queen cheating a lunatic King, but they are regarding it from the angle of modern France, not of the medieval one. Mr. R. B. Mowat points out that the French acceptance of an English King was not so vastly different from England's acceptance of a Welsh, a Scottish, a Dutch and a German sovereign. The difference, of course, lies in the fact that while the English chose their Kings—except for the Welsh one, but Henry Tudor was half-English—the French had theirs forced on them.

There is another point that must exonerate Philip and Isabel from treachery towards Charles VI and from forcing a foreign King on an unwilling people. On April 29, 1420, seven envoys on their way to Henry stopped in the Parlement chamber of the palace to address a fully representative gathering of the French. Being asked if they agreed to the terms of the Treaty of Troyes, the gathering unanimously cried—"Yes!"

The time was drawing near for Henry's meeting with King Charles. He left Rouen towards the end of March, his men going in fighting order, expecting an attack from the Dauphinists. They slept in the fields at night, not entering towns, in fear perhaps of being besieged.

Henry was close to the walls of Paris on May 9, and the battlements were crowded with enthusiastic mobs. Despite the famine, the citizens sent four cartloads of their best wine to the King, but Henry showed no sign of pleasure at the gift.

Behind a page bearing aloft his tilting-helm with the fox's brush, he rode quietly amongst his

T

soldiers, with neither interest or exultation in his bearing.

As he approached Troyes, on May 20, he was met by the new Duke of Burgundy. Philip came with bishops and citizens, and saluted Henry without dismounting. Then side by side, talking together, they entered the city.

Troyes had been divided into halves, the English were to take one half, the French the other, to avoid any possibility of a quarrel. The lodgings, however, were too few and many of the English had to camp in the fields. So determined was Henry that nothing should mar this day, the flower of his ambitions, that he issued strict orders forbidding his men to drink any wine unless it was mixed with water. As Dr. Wylie comments, "the fact that this order was obeyed by so drunken a set as the English troops is striking testimony to the strength of his personal control over the army."

The same day as his entry, Henry visited King Charles who was suffering from one of his attacks. The hall was crowded with courtiers, the idiot King being seated on a dais at one end. Henry bowed respectfully the moment he came into the room, and walked towards the dais. The silence must have been intense because King Charles never even moved, he made no sign of recognition, he merely sat on his chair as if there was nobody near him. When his conqueror, the Englishman, stood before him, Charles looked up, moved slightly. Henry bowed low and said words of greeting, for he understood that no insult was meant and that it was only Charles's malady that made him behave like this.

Charles said suddenly: "Oh, it's you? You're very welcome since it's you. Greet the ladies!"

Henry was only too delighted to obey. He knelt before Queen Isabel but she raised him to his feet and kissed him; then Henry bowed to Katherine the Fair and with "great joy" he kissed her.

Then all three chatted merrily together.

The next day the Treaty of Troyes was sealed in the Cathedral Church of St. Peter. Henry was present, of course, with a great gathering of nobles, but King Charles was unable to attend. Queen Isabel came in his place, with Katherine and the Duke of Burgundy.

Henry and Isabel met in the centre of the church and together walked to the great altar. The articles of the treaty were read aloud, and it was sealed with the seals of both France and England. Then King Henry took his Katherine by the hand and they plighted their troth together. From this moment, even before the official ceremony, Henry always spoke of her as "our wife" and of King Charles as "our father."

Philip and the other French nobles swore to abide by the terms of the treaty, making Henry their regent while Charles VI lived, their King after his death.

It would be tedious to take this treaty clause by clause, for it is mainly an expansion of what Henry had already demanded at Meulan, dealing with the marriage, the regency, with questions of Katherine's allowance, and her income if Henry should die. A few points, not touched on previously, are that Henry promised to recompense those lords whose estates he had taken in Normandy by giving them land out of what he might capture from the Dauphin; Charles was to style Henry "our very dear son, Henry, King of England and heir of France"; both kingdoms were to be united and yet to remain separate, neither imposing its laws on the other; Charles, Henry or Philip were not to make separate treaties with the Dauphin; and lastly, Charles was to remain in his kingdom and was to be attended only by French people.

This really amazing treaty, when one considers it, prompts the thought that if the terms could possibly have been kept, France not England would eventually have become the richer. If the two countries had been welded to one, under one King, completely united—truly an impossible dream—Paris would have become the centre of the empire. This was inevitable, not only because Paris was wealthier than London, but by its territorial situation it would necessarily demand more of the King's time. England might have degenerated into a mere appanage of France, not France of England.

After the treaty came the marriage, the marriage for which it seems that King Henry had so dearly longed. But first the treaty was promulgated in both French and English. The French accepted it with scarcely a murmur, in England there was naturally great joy.

We here glimpse fleetingly a small touch of exultation in Henry, or am I striving too rashly to pierce his armour of reserve? Am I deceiving myself, hoping to find an inch of weakness in the strong cold King? He wrote to his council that this treaty would bring "perpetual peace," and he asked to have his seals altered with the words:

"King of England, heir and regent of France, and Lord of Ireland." Does one detect a certain note of regret in his suggestion that if the seals are not large enough, the word "regent" might be dropped?

Twelve days after signing the treaty, Henry and Katherine were formally married. Those twelve days were spent in merriment, in feasting and in the giving and taking of presents. Then on Trinity Sunday, June 2, 1420, in the Church of St. Jean at Troyes, the wedding took place amidst much pomp and gallantry, the English in their splendid clothes dimming the French courtiers. Katherine was driven to the church in a coach drawn by eight snow-white English horses which Henry had given her. All were dressed in their finest, with the richest of colours, the most beautiful of textures. Only Philip, Duke of Burgundy, showed strangely amidst the merry throng, for he was completely in black, from toe to crown, in memory of his murdered father. The whole affair was glittering and splendid, Henry looking, says Monstrelet, "as if he were at that moment King of all the world."

A certain number only was allowed within the church, the ceremony being performed by Henri de Savoisy, Archbishop of Sens. The pair, now King and Queen and man and wife, offered three nobles each with the candle, and instead of the ordinary dues of thirteen pence, Henry slipped thirteen nobles on the book and presented one hundred more to the church itself. All present gave three nobles at the altar.

Then, the ritual over, there was the sip of wine to be taken from the mazer, and the day ended as such days should, in the most solemn blessing of the marriage-bed—"*Benedicat Deus corpora vestra et animas vestras*"—and the sprinkling of the bedded couple with Holy Water.

Henry had at last attained his dream: regent and heir of France; and for Queen he possessed his Katherine the Fair, the girl whom he had so greatly desired.

# CHAPTER EIGHTEEN

## *Heir of France*

THE story of King Henry V is almost too perfect; one cannot help feeling occasionally that a medieval poet has foisted his drama on to us as solemn history. It is more like poetry than truth. First we see the violent lad drinking and making merry, yet at the same time a brave soldier who can fight against a Hotspur; we see the customary conflict, the risk of disinheritance, then the abrupt change, the shedding of all sins, the rising of a St. George seeking a dragon. From now, like a red-cross knight, a Percival, a Galahad, purity is the buckler held against the world; unflinching from any danger, rarely smiling, humourless and stern and ever just, our hero rides from conquest to conquest, undefeatable. It is no Holy Grail he seeks, yet the goal is holy enough—a united western front against the pagans stealing into Europe, and a great crusade to reach the very walls of Jerusalem. He will execute his dearest friend if he sins and he will reward a brave enemy; only treason and affronts to his dignity will he not forgive. Friendship cannot turn him from the path; loyalty alone, and purity and justice and faith can lead him forward; he is not blinded by love or human passions. There is no hint of coarseness in him, no wenching, no drinking; the harlots do not dare come near his camp. Then after toil and hardships, he finds his reward in the body of the woman he desires and in the land he has fought to win.

What tale can equal this? No troubadour in his most inspired moment created one that can stand beside it. Henry of Monmouth is indeed the typical, the ideal medieval hero, more perfect even than the Black Prince. It may be true that he lived in the past, that he was building on a broken faith that would soon be swept aside by humanism and the gigantic laughter of the Renascence; but that does not dim his splendour.

He stands as the last of the medievals, and as the most perfect of them all.

When his followers, eager to celebrate the royal wedding, asked if they could arrange a tournament, we are told that King Henry turned to them grimly and said that they would have tilting enough, but that it would be tilting in earnest. He was never a man to waste his strength and his time in idle shows, particularly in shows banned by the Church as works of the devil.

Married on June 2, he marched out of Troyes on June 4, off to the wars again.

King Charles went with him and Philip of Burgundy. Also in the train were the two Queens, Isabel of France and Katherine of England. Henry had arranged Katherine's household and there was not a Frenchman in it, although he allowed three French ladies and two French maids to attend her.

The main objective was Sens, and Henry arrived to find the bridge broken and the suburbs burnt. It was a leisurely siege, for there were many who were not warriors in the gathering; but as an

English soldier tells us slyly when he writes home: "So there lay at this siege many worthy ladies and gentlewomen, both French and English; of the which, many of them began the feat of arms long ago, but of lying at sieges now they begin first."

The garrison soon capitulated, but it appears that the presence of ladies had greatly tamed these English soldiers, for when an unkempt man came to parley, Sir John Cornwall refused to discuss terms with him until he had shaved. Presumably the Frenchman shaved, for Sens surrendered on June 11.

As Henry rode through the gates beside his Queen, he turned merrily to the Archbishop of Sens who had married them.

"You have given me a wife," he said, "now I restore you yours—your church!"

The next stop was Montereau, but the ladies no longer followed the army. Probably their presence interfered with discipline, for both Queens were left at Sens with Charles VI when Henry and Philip marched off on their grim task. It was on this castle bridge that John the Fearless had been murdered, and the Burgundians were almost unable to keep their ranks when they drew near.

It was evidently the fury of these Burgundians that won the castle, for it was so strong that it was said that a handful of men could hold it against the world. But not against these Burgundians lashed on by the memory of their butchered duke. They scaled their ladders and chased the garrison through the town streets, killing without mercy, until they reached the bridge leading from the town to the castle, and here the panic-stricken Dauphinists struggled so fiercely together in their efforts to escape that many fell over and were drowned.

Having boxed the garrison in the castle, Henry and Philip made a solemn pilgrimage to the parish church where the body of John the Fearless had been hurriedly interred by a priest who had rescued it from the savage hands of the murderers. Knights and esquires lifted the coffin from its place and all wept openly as they gazed upon the gashed body, otherwise so little changed, of him who had been the Duke of Burgundy. The corpse was then laid in another coffin and was heaped with salt and spices to preserve it while being carried to the Charterhouse at Dijon.

The sight of the body infuriated the Burgundians even more than ever, and the siege of the castle was continued with great vigour. Guns were placed on the right bank of the Yonne, and a bridge was built over the Seine to join both parties of besiegers.

During the rush from the town to the castle bridge, eleven gentlemen had been captured, and Henry sent them to the castle to negotiate a surrender, warning them that if they couldn't persuade the captain to give in he would hang the eleven of them. The poor wretches knelt beside the moat, weeping and beseeching Guillaume de Chaumont, captain of the garrison, to capitulate. He refused, and the eleven doomed men asked to see their wives and children once before they died. This was permitted, and both sides stopped fighting while the women, children and relatives leaned weeping over the battlements.

Next day a gallows was built and the eleven were hanged in front of the castle.

Even at the risk of being accused of protesting

too greatly, I must again point out that Henry cannot be blamed for this action. It was within the rules of war and Henry always fought most strictly within those rules. If he had permitted these men to live after threatening them, his authority would have been lessened; and it was no precedent he set. His contemporaries never dreamed of blaming him for it, they blamed de Chaumont for not surrendering when he knew that he could not hold out against Henry.

To French and English alike, Henry shone as the ideal example of justice. He was ever just—cruel perhaps, but just. On the same gibbet where the eleven were hanged he placed one of his best-loved grooms who had committed murder. There was no favouritism in his camp, English and Burgundian would suffer alike for their actions; his own brothers would probably have suffered had they dared be disobedient.

And his contemporaries were correct in blaming de Chaumont: those eleven lives were wasted uselessly, for he surrendered on July 1, and the garrison—even the Scots—were let go free.

Melun, the next objective, was a vastly different place from Sens and Montereau. It was the Dauphin's chief castle, it was from here that his troops rushed out on their foraging expeditions, pillaging and murdering almost to Paris. Melun was a large town, cut into three by the Seine: St. Aspais, the strongest part, was on the north bank; St. Étienne was on the island, with the castle at its north; St. Ambroise was the third slice, on which stood the citadel. They were joined together by a bridge and were each enclosed by high walls.

Henry, with Clarence and Bedford—recently from England, the other brother Humphrey taking his place as governor—camped to the west and south; the Burgundians under Philip, Warwick and Huntingdon, being separated from the English, obviously to avoid quarrels between both nations.

The siege opened on July 13 by a fierce assault of the Burgundians who succeeded in placing their banner on a bulwark before the Dauphinists sallied out and captured it. Then a troop of English, supported by Burgundians and others, captured an outpost next to the moat. This was a difficult place to capture and a still more difficult one to hold. Many men died at this point, but it remained English to the conclusion of the siege. Having taken it, they could not be dislodged.

This was the first violent blow, completely out of key with Henry's usual methods, and was probably the result of Philip's influence. Henry soon reasserted himself and quietly set about his customary efficient game of starving the garrison into surrender. A bridge was built across the river to connect both parties, and palisades were placed around the camps, and ditches were dug. The gates in the palisades were well guarded, and no man was allowed to pass in or out without permission.

Henry now had reinforcements. Bedford had brought men from England, and Lewis, Count Palatine of the Rhine, had come with seven hundred soldiers. The captive King of Scotland was present, brought over mainly in the hope of inducing the Scots to forsake their alliance with the Dauphin.

Henry and Philip were not continually present at this protracted siege. Both often left camp to enjoy themselves: Henry to visit his wife, Philip to more dubious pleasures, for he was considered a rake. As the siege dragged wearily on, Henry brought Katherine to his camp, building a house specially for her. King Charles, her father, also arrived, with his Queen. During the month in which Katherine stayed before Melun, minstrels played her and her father awake and asleep every day at sunrise and sunset for an hour.

The siege continued with fierce fighting, for the garrison felt sure that the Dauphin would come to relieve it. It was by no means a large garrison, consisting of about six hundred or seven hundred men under a Gascon, Arnaud Guillaume, Lord of Barbazan. Day after day the English cannons fired at the walls, but at night the breaches were always filled up with earth, timber and whatever came to hand. There were mines dug, and counter-mines. And in the underground many a fight took place. Whenever besieged and besiegers met down there in the torchlight, trumpets would blow and bells would ring; then champions would ride into the dark tunnels as if to a joust.

Young Louis Juvenal des Ursins, amongst the Dauphinists, was about to descend, armed cap-à-pie, into one of these tunnels, when Barbazan stopped him. "Louis, where are you going?" he asked; and on being told, said, "Brother, you do not yet know what fighting in mines means; give me your axe." He chopped off most of the haft, explaining, "For mines are sloping, tortuous and narrow, wherefore short handles are very needful."

Henry and Philip both joined in these underground encounters, and one story—which appears to be authentic—tells that two English knights were once quarrelling before the mouth of a tunnel, each demanding the honour of going down first, when Henry to put a stop to this, himself strode into the darkness and there encountered Barbazan. In the dim light neither knew who the other was, yet each admired the dexterity and courage of his opponent. For some little time the duel continued, when Henry asked with whom he fought. "I am Barbazan," said the other. "Then you have fought," said Henry, "with the King of England." On learning the name of his adversary, Barbazan lowered his axe and commanded that the mine be filled up; he dared not continue against the majesty of so noble and so brave a King.

Every effort was made to force the garrison to surrender. The King of Scotland failed to bring the Scots to his side, and King Charles was produced in the hope that his presence might arouse loyalty amongst the French. They retorted that they would welcome him quickly enough, but they would bow to no English King. Henry was furious at the insult and cried that the time would come when they would be forced to obey an English King, whether they wished it or not.

The Dauphin had gathered a large force to relieve his town: 16,000 men, it was said. But spies told him that the English were too well entrenched ever to be defeated; and although they were but a few miles away, the Dauphinists remained idle except for occasional forays.

There were worse dangers than forays or sallies with which King Henry had to contend. Some of the Burgundians were deserting his standard. Their old loyalty quickened and they crept away to the Dauphin. There was also the usual plague of dysentery. But inside Melun there were worse plagues: there was hunger, and vermin were eaten —rats, mice, anything. The final touch came when a reinforcement of Picards rode to Henry, and the garrison shouted itself hoarse, thinking they were the Dauphin's troops.

Melun surrendered on November 18, but to two parties Henry would grant no terms to Scots or English. And those implicated in the murder of John the Fearless must stand their trial. The garrison agreed, and twenty Scots were tried for treason, King James being with the English (rather under compulsion), and were hanged. Those implicated in the murder at Montereau were sent to Paris, and three of them were hung. Barbazan, accused of the same crime, was acquitted, but was imprisoned first in Paris, then in the Château Gaillard, from where he was rescued in 1430.

Amongst the English was a captain, a great favourite of Henry's, Bertrand de Chaumont, who had fought under the King's standard at Agincourt. He was now accused of being bribed by the garrison to let some of the prisoners escape. This news shocked Henry deeply and he was heard to say that he would rather have given 50,000 nobles than to have such treachery happen. Philip and Clarence both pleaded on their knees for mercy, but Henry would not listen.

"By St. George," he said, "fair brother, had it been yourself we should have done the same."

De Chaumont was beheaded, Henry remarking that he would have no traitors near him if he knew it.

Henry's position was a difficult one. He was nominally regent of France but there was natural resentment amongst many of his allies, and it is by no means impossible that his relations with Philip were, if anything, rather strained. During the siege some of the Burgundians had marched calmly away—the Count of Conversen departing for his castle at Brienne, although he was captured by the Dauphin on the way; and the Prince of Orange going off without offering any explanation. And there is a story about de l'Isle Adam which by its sheer simplicity rings true.

He appeared before Henry wearing a grey riding-habit, at which the King cried in jest, "What, de l'Isle Adam! is this the costume of a marshal of France?" Staring Henry in the face, de l'Isle Adam replied, "Sire, I put it on to come by boat across the Seine." We cannot explain what caused Henry's anger, but de l'Isle Adam must have stared at him most impertinently, for Henry cried, "How dare you thus look a prince in the face when you speak to him!" "'Tis the French custom," answered de l'Isle Adam, "not to address any man, whatever his estate, with a downcast countenance." "It is not ours," said Henry, and he must have spoken with an air of menace, for de l'Isle Adam cried, "For God's sake, be not angry with me!"

This atmosphere with which he was surrounded, the unspoken resentment of his allies, must have been most galling to a man of Henry's nature who was used to instant obedience. Even in Paris, it seemed, he was not very popular, although he had relieved it of the strain of civil war in the streets.

When, however, he entered shortly after the

siege of Melun, the Parisians put on a splendid
show, creating—despite their awful poverty—
magnificent pageants, and sending wine bubbling
through fountains and conduits. Henry entered,
with Charles on his right hand, and he gazed upon
the cheering crowd with his usual restrained air
which was almost scornful in its lack of interest.
Slightly behind the two Kings, and apart from
them, rode Philip still dressed all in black.

As this was Advent Sunday, the clergy met them,
singing, and gave them relics to kiss. Henry would
never kiss them first but always, taking off his
cap, passed them to Charles.

Despite the show of rejoicings it put on, Paris
really did not love Henry, it could not accept him.
He was too stern a King—apart from the natural
resentment at having a foreign ruler—for the
Parisians to love him. He never did anything to
outrage the city's feelings, but there was no warmth
in their negotiations.

And much of their dislike of him might be put
down to the famine that followed now in his wake
—although you would think that the Parisians had
been used to poverty by this time. Prices rushed up,
owing to the extra consumers and the tricks of
profiteers, and bread was soon double its normal
rate. There were long queues in front of all the
bakers' shops, and one had to bribe merchants with
drinks at least before one could get food; the poor
existed somehow on cabbages and turnips. It was
said that the Paris dung-heaps were piled high
with the bodies of children dying of famine and the
cold.

The Parisians had another score against Henry.
After his Queen arrived, the court he held at the

Louvre was magnificent, while poor Charles lived drearily in the Hôtel de St. Pol, with little money and visited by none except a few old friends.

After Christmas, Henry decided that he must return to England, for he had been absent now for well over three years and Parliament had been pleading for him to come home. He left Paris on September 25, 1421, taking Katherine with him to be crowned at Westminster, and he first visited Normandy, staying for three weeks. While at Rouen, he appointed Clarence his lieutenant in France and Normandy, Exeter his governor of Paris, and Sir Gilbert Umfraville marshal of France.

He then continued on his way to Calais, having with him, besides Katherine, his brother John, and King James of Scotland, and the Earls of March and Warwick.

On Candlemas Day he sailed into Dover, and the Barons of the Cinque Ports, in all their splendid clothes, waded into the ocean so that they might carry their King and Queen ashore upon their shoulders.

Surely it must have been with a feeling of deep relief and with the satisfaction of a dream achieved that Henry gazed upon the white cliffs with their greenery—like the grain in marble—ribbing the chalk?

Home! home after exactly three and a half years!

# CHAPTER NINETEEN

## *England*

THIS return to England was not necessary. It is
true that Parliament in December 1420 had
petitioned Henry that "with the gracious Lady his
Companion" he "would shortly return and visit
this realm," but the petition was sent merely for
love of the King. There were no affairs for him to
settle in England. Bedford had acted most wisely
as regent, and the country was at peace and was
growing prosperous. But England wished to see
again its noble King and in particular to gaze
upon its new Queen; and Henry very likely wanted
to parade the women he had won—like any
medieval knight—by the strength of his arm alone.

The only excitement, apart from the burning of
Oldcastle, that had stirred England during his
absence was a burst of heresy- and witch-hunting.
Even this would be of no particular interest, for
such trials are monotonous, had not Henry's
stepmother Joan fallen into the net.

Here, the real attack was obviously a patriotic
resentment against foreigners; and the witchcraft
charge—although probably based on fact—was
only an excuse with which to flog the mother of the
Duke of Brittany. He was a shifty fellow, this duke,
but mother and son were not friends at the time,
so she can scarcely be blamed for his tricks.

The first attack was made against her retainers,
who were deported from England because they

were believed to be taking, not only money out of the country, but information as well. The blow next fell on Joan herself. On September 27, 1419, her dowry and belongings were seized by the Treasury and she was left with only enough money on which to live. Then, on October 1, she was actually arrested and sent to the manor-house of Rotherhithe. The charge was witchcraft, the practising of magic against the life of King Henry, and others were implicated—her confessor, John Randolf, a Franciscan friar, and two members of her household, Roger Colles and Pernel Brocart. Randolf was caught trying to escape and was locked into the Tower, in which he died some years later, being killed in a quarrel with the Tower chaplain. It was presumably on Randolf's confession that Joan was arrested and charged with having "compassed and imagined the King's death in the most horrible manner that could be devised." She was never tried; she remained under arrest until King Henry himself released her on July 13, 1422.

This was the only real problem, except for the defeat of the English navy, with which England had had to contend during Henry's absence, and his return was less a matter of statecraft than of rejoicing.

Being carried ashore on the broad backs of the Barons of the Cinque Ports, Henry and Katherine landed at Dover. Crowds had gathered to see their King and his Queen as they rode to Canterbury. Henry wanted to enter London before his bride to make certain that her reception would be worthy of her; so he galloped on ahead. He rushed back to Eltham, where Katherine then was, and together the royal pair rode to London.

The mayor and aldermen assembled on Blackheath with a horde of citizens dressed in white cloaks and with red hoods or caps, each craft being distinguished by its individual badge. To the sound of "clarions and all other loud minstrelsies" they continued to London with their concourse of citizens and with "the glorious and royal sight of strangers that came with them from overseas."

As after Agincourt, money had been poured out to make pageants and statues, and the crush of people was stifling when Henry rode beside his bride through the streets of the city. Giants, as before, guarded the gates, and great lions had been modelled, and there were armies of warriors in castles; but they all bowed before the loveliness of Katherine the Fair. Giants fell to their knees, lions rolled their eyes in ecstasy and crouched down as if before Androcles; the castles opened their gates, the knights flung aside their arms, conquered by the flash of Katherine's eyes. Apostles, martyrs, confessors, virgins, hymned her as she passed, and boys and girls sang and danced around her. The streets were thick with greenery, from every window hung cloth-of-gold and richly coloured hangings.

That night, Katherine slept in the royal apartments at the Tower of London; and in the morning, dressed all in white, seated in a splendid carriage, she was taken to Westminster by nobles, aldermen and craftsmen. They rode with music, showing the Queen the beauties of their and now her city; over streets piled with greenery they went, where the windows and roofs were hung with cloth-of-gold, with velvets and with cloth of Arras, and where cloths hung from strings that stretched from house to house.

She was crowned on Sunday, February 23, in Westminster Abbey, Archbishop Chichele officiating. After the ceremony she was led into the hall for the banquet. Henry was not present, for that would have been against the strict courtesy-rules of the period. The season being Lent, the cooks had had to expend all their art on varieties of fish, except for a collar of brawn in the first course.

Fortunately we have a detailed description of this feast, and also of the menu. The latter would be tedious to describe, for every dish would need a recipe before you could understand the horrible amount of herbs and spices that went with it. For food then was never tasted: the cook's one ambition was to deceive the palate, to stew fine English beef to rags and to destroy its delicate flavour with stinging spices carried all the way through Venice from the East; and many sweet things were eaten—not sugar itself, of course, as that was little known, but mead and honey and such; to us, everything would have been sweet and rich and sickly, with no masculine flavour about it, no roast beef of old England, no pure venison, no quarts of bitter beer. The Englishman then had the tooth of a woman, and of a particularly degraded woman. There was the Leche Lombard (let us choose this at random, for an example): It was made of pork deprived of its skin and sinews, pounded in a mortar with raw eggs, salt, raisins, cloves, currants, minced dates and pepper, all of which was then placed in a bladder, and on being dried the bladder was cut into strips; after that, raisins were ground in a mortar, mixed with red wine and milk of almonds, coloured with saffron and powdered with pepper; the whole was next boiled, powdered with canelle —a form of cinnamon—and ginger, splashed with wine, rinsed, and then (as the old book tells us) "serve it forth."

To return, after this circumlocution, to Katherine's Leche Lombard. It was built into a "subtlety"—that is to say, it was sculptured—with collars of SS—the Lancastrian symbol—and had a shield marked in gold bearing the arms of the King and Queen. Another "sotlete" at this feast was a pelican "on her nest with birds and an image of Saint Katherine with a wheel in her hand, disputing with the heathen clerks." There were long scrolls over this: one in Katherine's hand saying *madame la reine*, another issuing from the pelican's bill, and a third from the birds', all giving eulogistic phrases somewhat like the cracker-mottoes we find to-day at Christmas. These mottoes were called "reasons."

We have had enough of the food, I think. We must glance through the gathering.

On Katherine's right sat Archbishop Chichele who, with the Bishop of Winchester beside him, was served immediately after her. On her left was King James of Scotland who was served next. At Katherine's feet sat the Countess of Kent, holding a napkin to place before her when she drank or if she wished to be ill. Humphrey Duke of Gloucester, the King's youngest brother, was overseer, and he stood before the Queen bare-headed; to her right and left knelt the Earls of March and Stafford holding sceptres. The Earl of Warwick acted as steward, while the Earl of

Worcester was earl marshal, and rode a horse up and down the hall between the tables, seeing that everybody behaved, having tipstaves with him to keep order and to eject any unruly person, for which of course there was no occasion.

The Queen's coronation over, Henry set out on a progress. These progresses were essential to a medieval lord. The King showed himself to his people by wandering over the country; he adjusted disputes and he lived from manor to manor. This last point was the essential one, as food was very difficult to store, and a King with numerous retainers could not remain long in one town without starting a famine. Henry had other reasons for this progress: he wished to borrow money and also to visit many of England's holy places.

On February 27 he was at St. Albans and from there his progress continued to Bristol, from Bristol to Weobley in Herefordshire, to Shrewsbury, to Kenilworth; then with the Queen to Coventry, to Leicester for Easter, to Nottingham, to Pontefract, to York; without Katherine he continued to Bridlington and Beverley, both important shrines; here came the tragic news of Baugé which necessitated a rapid return to France, but which did not stop Henry from continuing his progress to Pontefract again; here he met his Queen and the pair went to Lincoln to instal the new bishop and to settle some chapter-disputes; from Lincoln to Lynn, to Walsingham, to Norwich, and then to London.

The tragic news of Baugé that reached Henry on the road after he had left the tomb of John, the eighth-century bishop of York, must now be told,

It is a difficult story to tell because it is one of the most confused of medieval battles, and that is saying a very great deal. Each side always lies after a fight, and the man who would try to reconstruct medieval warfare must try to reconcile both stories; but at Baugé even the allies' tales conflict. There is a reason for this: it was a fight, not of tactics or strategy, not of armies well-planned as at Agincourt, but of individual exploits, of a mêlée. Each actor in the drama therefore could not tell what was happening outside his own small area, and the whole field could not be examined.

The problem is an acute one, and quite frankly, nothing in this book has given me the same trouble as my efforts to reconstruct Baugé. After a careful study of all the tales, I find myself forced into accepting Professor Waugh's description on most points; it tallies mainly with my own decision. All other historians have slipped too far towards the Dauphinist version, the Scottish, the Burgundian, or the English. Professor Waugh has kept an amazing balance amidst a tempest of lies and exaggerations. My debt to him is very great on this and on many other details.

Henry had left Clarence in command of France during his absence, but magnificent soldier though Clarence was, he was not a leader in the sense that Henry was a leader. He was not calm enough, not dispassionate enough for that; his fearlessness made him a bad general although a splendid soldier; he was a perfect leader of what to-day we would call shock-troops. One cannot also help feeling that he was jealous of Henry's reputation, jealous of the glory of Agincourt—at which he was not present, having been shipped home sick after Harfleur—

and he wanted to achieve something equally as magnificent now that he had the power and the restraint of Henry's hand was lifted.

Clarence had a force of about four thousand, the Dauphinists had about five thousand, but in the actual battle, as we shall see, the English were hopelessly outnumbered. The Dauphinist army was almost completely Scottish, under John Stewart Earl of Buchan, and Archibald Douglas Earl of Wigtown.

After Henry's departure, the Dauphin showed signs of unexpected energy and spread his troops into conquered territory north of the Loire. Clarence, eager to show that he was Henry's equal, dashed out to halt the advance. He marched south through Maine, and into Baugé; from Baugé he continued to Angers and began to besiege it. Clarence had not the temper of Henry, sieges bored him, and after knighting some of his men— including his bastard son—he moved off to Beaufort-en-Vallée. The Dauphinists then entered Baugé and thereby cut Clarence off from his base in Normandy.

It was time for a decisive battle, and the Dauphinists drew up their men near the village of La Lande Chasles about six miles from Baugé. All this happened without Clarence knowing, which shows his bad generalship. Henry would have had scouts watching every move of the enemy.

Some Scottish captives told of the great force waiting near Baugé, and on hearing this, Clarence leaped joyously to his feet, crying, "Let us go against them, they are ours!"

For some stupid reason, Clarence did not take his archers with him, and the surmise seems correct that he wished to prove that the English did not have to rely on the long-bow for victory. We do not know the exact numbers of the men who rode with him, but they must have been vastly inferior to the French—or rather, to the Scots. The Earl of Salisbury very luckily remained to gather reinforcements.

As they rode to the fight, the Earl of Huntingdon tried to make Clarence delay until an army could be collected, but he would not listen, and when Sir Gilbert Umfraville arrived with five men-at-arms, and suggested that it would be better to wait until after Easter, Clarence retorted: "If thou art afeared, go home thy way and keep the churchyard." Umfraville, a gallant soldier, was naturally stung by this taunt, yet he answered calmly, "Nay, my lord, you have no company to fight; see, my cousin Grey and I have but ten men with us and no more; yet you shall never say that we thus left you."

They rode on, "aye chiding by the way," until scouts galloped back to tell them that the Scots were near. As a matter of fact, Buchan was not expecting the English, evidently believing that they would delay until the passing of Easter. His men were not in line, having wandered about, making merry, resting or praying. At the sight of the English standard, a body of them rushed for their arms and hurriedly formed into order.

Clarence had no archers, and now he was to learn what the French had suffered at English hands. His horses refused to budge under the winged hail, and he had to stand on his feet, with his men, and lead the beasts over the bridge across the Altrée. Dressed in full armour, a golden coronet around his helm that was bright with jewels, Clarence forced his way into the arrow-storm. Soon he evidently mounted again, and chased the Dauphinist outposts into the parish church. Buchan had now had time to collect his men, and simultaneously both forces charged.

It was a mêlée, and the English had no hope. They must have been outnumbered by about four to one, at least. Over the graveyard . the two armies struggled, hand to hand. The English were cut to pieces.

The list of names of the men who, single-handed, struck down Clarence is tedious to repeat, but I feel that the truth lies in Walsingham's statement that no one knew that he was dead until after the battle when his body was found. In that quick fight, an unknown hand—French or Scot—killed the King's brother, the impetuous courageous Thomas, Duke of Clarence.

Gilbert Umfraville also died, while Huntingdon and Somerset were captured. Amongst the Scots, scarcely an important man fell.

The Earl of Salisbury had been left to bring re-inforcements, but it is doubtful if he marched far. Some of the English, fleeing from the battle, probably told him of the disaster; and with cunning, he managed to slip through the net that Buchan cast to catch him.

Others of the English dared visit the field next day, and there they found the body of Clarence. They laid it sadly in a cart and marched off, while Clarence's bastard killed what enemies he could find and rescued some of their prisoners.

In this tragic tale there is no particular deed of heroism to remember. The only figures that shine clear are the noble Huntingdon and Umfraville who rode beside their captain although they knew that they were doomed. And a word must be said for Salisbury who conducted his retreat with extreme adroitness, escaping, although the Scots and French were alert to cut him off from Normandy.

The news was rushed to Paris and spread terror. It went through Normandy, growing as it travelled, until rumour said that King Charles VI himself was killed. Out of France, through all Europe, went the tale, until it reached Rome; and that clever fellow, Pope Martin V, is said to have remarked: "Verily are the Scots the antidote of the English!"

Horror or joy might greet the news in Europe, but in England, when Henry was informed, he said not a word and made no sign that he understood. Not one of his followers realised that he had been told anything of unusual importance. With impassive face and bearing, he continued his way to Pontefract and did not even mention the tidings until the following day. Yet behind that calm mask, surely there was sorrow and despair? If the death of his brother did not stir him, could he not feel terror lest his conquests now all slip from him? But for Salisbury's prompt actions he might have lost Normandy, but for Salisbury's rapid retreat and then his offensive charges into Maine and Anjou. Whatever Henry thought or felt he gave no sign; he rode quietly to Pontefract to greet his Queen.

This disaster probably hastened his return to France but it did not force him to return. Before leaving Paris he had arranged with Charles and Philip to be back by next midsummer, and before hearing of Clarence's death he had sent around the country, asking for urgent loans, as he would probably not have time to collect them personally if there was any delay. It is true, however, that Baugé quickened his determination, for on hearing of it he wrote immediately to France, threatening his captains with death if they lost their castles.

Money, of course, was the main problem, and Henry was tireless in his efforts to raise enough to send him oversea with a fully equipped army.

He was present in the Painted Chamber at Westminster when Parliament met on May 2, 1421. Always he was present when affairs of importance were at hand; it seems that he never rested, that never for a second did he permit his own private feelings to interfere with State matters.

The chancellor, Bishop Langley, spoke of Henry's victories, and glorified him for giving his victories to God's help, not to man's; his modesty, said Langley, was like that of Julius Cæsar and his patience in adversity was like unto Job.

For speaker, the commons elected Thomas Chaucer, son of the poet—or as some say, son of John of Gaunt—and business was started.

There is nothing particular to interest us in this Parliament except that it was the last which Henry was to attend. The Treaty of Troyes was, of course, agreed to, and an ordinance was passed to reform the gold currency. The commons then asked Henry to force the Duke of Burgundy to prohibit the importation of wool from Scotland and Spain and thereby give England a free market in his country;

they asked that the justices of the assize, which had
been suspended during the war, might be continued; and owing to pestilence and the war,
there were not enough sheriffs to go round, so
would Henry abrogate the statute that prohibited
their term of office continuing for more than one
year?

Besides presiding at Parliament and trying to
raise loans, Henry had many other matters to
which to attend: he was fishing in the diplomatic
ocean, patching up a treaty with the Genoese,
arranging for a stronger fleet, stopping the Scottish
border-raids and the sending of Scottish troops
to help the Dauphin, signing a treaty with the
Duke of Bourbon, and helping Jacqueline of
Hainault to escape from her new husband, the
Duke of Brabant. This was a risky venture, for
Brabant was a relation of Philip's. Henry succeeded, however, without a rupture with Burgundy.

Then there were Church matters that had to be
attended to, various reforms to examine.

Henry must have been a man of gigantic
vitality and with a most tenacious memory.

He had over nine hundred knights and men-at-
arms and over three thousand archers when for
the last time he sailed from Dover on June 10,
1421.

Queen Katherine did not sail with him. She
remained with her brother-in-law, the Duke of
Bedford, who was for the third time appointed
regent of England.

It was not lack of affection that separated Henry
from his Queen—she was expecting a child.

# CHAPTER TWENTY

## *Meaux*

THE moral effect of Henry's return was felt almost at once. Inspired by their success at Baugé, the Dauphinists pushed their way towards Paris, and but for the stubborn defence of Chartres would have reached the capital. Salisbury did splendid work; and in Paris, Exeter was trying to hold his own against intrigue and the despair caused by a ghastly winter, famine and a debased currency.

Henry arrived at Calais on June 11, 1421, his determination being to enter Picardy and crush Jacques d'Harcourt, one of the Dauphin's most powerful supporters. The news that reached him, however, made him change his mind at once. The Dauphin was making too much headway to be left alone, and Henry's prestige demanded that he come to the aid of Paris. Then as he sailed to Montreuil he heard of the siege of Chartres. He talked with Philip, who was ill of a fever, at Montreuil, and it was decided that Henry should march to Paris and send troops to relieve Chartres.

Henry did not remain long in Paris; he soon hurried off to lead his men to Chartres, but at news of his approach the siege was raised and the Dauphin fled. Philip now arrived but his help was no longer needed and he posted off to Picardy to fight Harcourt, while the English marched against Dreux, where the siege commenced at once. The

King himself did not superintend operations here, being lodged about a mile away, and he gave the command to Gloucester and to the King of Scotland. After severe fighting, the garrison surrendered on August 20, and from here Henry moved to Chartres, and various smaller towns were captured.

News now arrived that the Dauphin was prepared to fight and was gathering his army together on the Loire near Beaugency. Henry darted out at once, but again the Dauphin drew back—if he ever had been there. Frustrated in his hope of a battle, Henry returned to siege-work and soon reduced the town, but not the castle, of Beaugency.

Provisions were beginning to fail, and there seemed less hope than ever of getting to grips with the Dauphin. Henry marched on Orléans and captured the suburbs; he did nothing more, however, but soon retreated, probably because his men had found great quantities of wine. The whole campaign had been a failure and his men were dying in their tracks. The roads were lined with English corpses, for dysentery had broken out as it continually did in medieval armies. Yet Henry could not bear the thought of returning to Paris without fresh laurels. His prestige demanded a victory; and so far, his success had been purely negative. He must do something, he dared not return without conquests.

He marched towards the Yonne, his men dying rapidly from hunger and dysentery, but rarely, alas! from wounds. The Dauphin hovered on the outskirts, but he could not be tempted into the open, so terrible was Henry's name, even when his army was exhausted, famine-struck and plagued.

On reaching the Yonne, Henry besieged Ville-
neuve, which surrendered almost immediately;
smaller towns also gave in quickly. But now Henry
had an objective. He would attack Meaux.

Meaux was a strong town built on a peninsula
in the Marne. The peninsula had been cut, making
an island of the tip. The town was built on the
neck, and overflowed on to the south bank opposite.
This cutting of the peninsula had diverted the
river and had left the town with a distant gigantic
moat which at high tide received its quota of
water. The other part of the town, on the south
bank, was called the Market and was bounded by
the swift-rushing Marne on three sides, the fourth
side having been opened to make an island. Besides
this water barrier, both town and market were
protected by the usual high walls.

Although this was not a particularly important
town it was a notorious one. Here the worst
followers of the Dauphin lurked, and it is no exaggeration to call it a den of bandits. The garrison
at this time consisted of about a thousand men
under the command of Guichard de Chissay, with
two notorious captains under him: Pierron de
Luppé and the Bastard of Vaurus. This Bastard
was one of the worst rascals in France; there was a
tree near the town on which he loved to hang his
prisoners even before the ensuing siege, and it was
called the Vaurus tree. To give but one example
of his behaviour showing what type of ruffian he was,
there is a story given us by the chronicler known
as the Bourgeois. The Bastard had captured a
peasant and murdered him, and when the peasant's
young wife came with the ransom-money he seized

the money and stripped her half-naked. The unfortunate girl was pregnant at the time, but this did not deter the Bastard from roping her to an elm, where he left her to stay all night with the toes of hanged men brushing against the top of her head. Luckily, this diabolic torture did not continue long. There were wolves in the district and they soon killed her, saving her from probable lunacy.

Such a garrison as Meaux, led by such creatures as this, was to show the most courageous defence that Henry had yet encountered. They knew that they could expect little mercy from that just King, and they fought with the frenzy of rats in a corner.

Henry began with his usual caution, building engines, arranging his troops. The Duke of Exeter he placed between the north wall of the town and the original river-bed; the Earl of March to the east; the Earl of Warwick to the south. Around his camps, Henry built palisades and dug trenches, while a bridge of boats was placed over the river to keep communications open with Warwick. Henry himself took lodgings about a mile from Meaux, in the castle of Rutel, but he moved later to the abbey of St. Faro, nearer to Exeter.

Henry was always most careful how he disposed his troops. He never began a siege in the haphazard manner of most medieval generals who squatted down anywhere until dysentery and plague drove them away. His first care, before assaulting, was to protect his own soldiers with ditches and palisades, to erect tents and huts; and he now created special markets, like a town. This siege was really a battle between French and English, for very few Burgundians were in the army, Philip being off after Harcourt in Picardy.

The Dauphinists had captured St. Riquier, so Philip rushed to rescue it, laying siege to the town, in which Harcourt was commanding. The Dauphin sent troops to the relief and Philip swerved to intercept them. The battle which followed was unlike any of Henry's battles: it was a fight to the death, a kind of gigantic tournament, without any thought of strategy or tactics. Like most battles of this kind there was no actual victor, both sides lost heavily, although nominally Philip defeated the Dauphinists. At least, they were the first to run away; but Philip himself was too badly smashed even to continue the siege. He had some valuable prisoners, however, and these were exchanged for St. Riquier and Harcourt's Burgundian captives.

To return to Henry, waiting before the town and market of Meaux.

This was to be the most difficult siege of his career, for the garrison was made of desperate men, all brave soldiers. Henry used his engines, battering at the walls with his guns, flinging stones from his catapults. He was fighting a determined enemy, men that never seemed to sleep. No sooner were the breaches gaping than they were filled up again; no sooner did he begin digging a mine than they started a counter-mine. He could never assault them by surprise. Bloody as these battles were, Henry had nothing to show for them. His men were pushed back from the walls, their ladders hurled down; they were scalded with hot oils and fats, and crushed with molten lead and with stones and chunks of iron.

The weather came to help the besieged. The Marne overflooded its banks, sweeping into the country, cutting divisions off from each other, so that parties of English were left stranded on small islands. The boats were nearly all in the grip of the garrison, and Henry was forced to retreat a little way and build new palisades, dig new trenches. A fortnight later he was able to return to his old position, but now there was a dearth of food. His convoys were harried by the Dauphinists along the route, and Henry could not retort, as he had sent his horses away. He baked bread, but the supply was not large enough, and many of his soldiers began to despair of ever succeeding. Some deserted. Even that brave warrior, Sir John Cornwall, vowed never to fight with Christians again in his life, and left for England. Him, however, we might excuse, for he was sick and his son had been struck down before his eyes. There were others for whom there is no excuse, others who sneaked away.

Not desertions, famine, diseases, nor repeated losses by fighting could depress King Henry. He was unchanged in defeat or victory—as modest as Cæsar and as patient as Job. His iron discipline never relaxed, and a soldier whom he found stealing a pyx was tried and hanged.

It was a terrible winter, continually raining, and Christmas was no merry feast about the walls of Meaux. Philip visited his ally, but he did not stay long.

Soon the worst of the winter was passed, and as spring gradually approached, the conditions in the English camp improved enormously. Supplies were coming in in good time, the desertions had ceased and the fevers had abated. It was now but a matter of months before Meaux capitulated, since the worst of the season was over. Meaux had one hope—the hope of relief. Despairing messages were sent out, but only one leader with about forty men came to the rescue. This was Guy de Nesle, Lord of Offémont.

Somehow he managed to sneak through the English lines on the night of March 9, murdering a few sentries as he passed, until he reached the walls. The garrison had news of his coming, and ladders were prepared, being covered with bed-sheets so that they would not be seen against the white wall. Some of the band clambered over safely, and all of them would have succeeded but for an unfortunate accident. Offémont fell down, banging, in all his armour, into the ditch. One story relates that the man above dropped a sack of herrings on his head, and this seems possible; otherwise it is difficult to explain so peculiar an accident. The ditch was very deep, and the lances which his men lowered over the side could not reach him where he lay. The noise of his fall aroused the English, and with some of his troop, Offémont was captured after getting a slash across the face.

Offémont's success with so small a band could not have meant much to the garrison; his capture, however, meant a great deal. It brought on them a fit of despair, and they decided to evacuate the town and move into the market opposite. They did not intend to leave the town for the English to lurk in, they were going to burn it and murder those townspeople who were not fully on their side. Their determination was probably hastened by the knowledge that Henry was digging a mine which they couldn't locate.

The townsfolk did not want their homes burnt, and one of the citizens crept to a part of the wall—which in their haste the garrison left unguarded—and called to the English to attack at once. A ladder was placed against the wall and the man was brought before Henry. News came from a Savoyard captain that the tidings were true. He had noticed queer happenings in the town and had immediately sounded for an assault.

Henry commanded a general assault, and his troops rushed to the walls. The townspeople fled to the churches, the garrison made for the market. At the bridge, there was bloody fighting.

Master of the town, Henry proclaimed that no citizen would be harmed, all should return to their usual tasks and would not be interfered with. Himself with many of his men took quarters inside the walls.

The fight was now concentrated on the bridge, and Henry brought his most powerful guns to bear on it. A tower was built, dragged round the town—the diverted river was some distance off, leaving a wide space of earth before the walls—it had a leaf projecting from it and this leaf covered that part of the bridge which was drawn up. His men could now pass over it right to the gates of the market, and there was constant fighting. One big success fell to Henry here. Mills, as was common in those days, were built on and under the bridge so that they could be turned by the rush of the water. These mills Henry captured, thereby bringing starvation on the garrison which was unable to grind its corn. These mills had a further use, they made an excellent cover for the English who could safely pound at the gates without having stones and hot oil thrown on top of them.

The net was closing in on Meaux.

A small island near the market was taken, and guns were mounted on it. Then the Earl of Warwick in some incredible manner actually pushed his way to the very walls. Unfortunately we have no details of this hazardous episode, but it must have been done only at great risk and by cool leadership on the earl's part. He managed somehow to cross the canal and to carry a sow—a large roof—on to the wide space between the canal and the market-walls. The wall here was exceptionally broad, and had a further wall behind it. Warwick, under his sow, struggled on top of an outwork near this first wall, and bombarded the garrison furiously.

This was happening to the south. To the west also, the English were creeping near. Walter Hungerford built bridges and carried his men over in boats from the mainland to the island. Under sows, he also got very close to the walls and actually built roofs there, under which he could pound quietly away at the stone and masonry. The garrison was so infuriated by Hungerford's audacity that it assisted him by tearing out the stones from the other side, for the sheer delight of hand-to-hand fighting. In a very short time, they were toiling equally as hard to stuff up the breaches which themselves had made.

Easter was now upon them, and in honour of the sacred season Henry proclaimed a short truce. He kept the truce, but when it was over returned immediately to action. The battle started again.

Henry asked the garrison to surrender, but on

his offer being rejected he called for a general assault.

Seven or eight hours of hard fighting followed, but at last Henry was forced to draw back. The market remained unconquered.

No amount of repulses could damp Henry's spirits or slacken his energy. He decided to approach the market from a fresh direction, from the east. This had been left alone until now, for at this point the Marne flowed with particular force and the current was dangerous.

His attack was carefully planned. Taking two large boats he bound them tightly together and built a platform across both decks. In each boat he placed a tall stout mast, and between the masts raised a mighty tower of two storeys that would over-top the market-walls.

Probably the sight of this monster finished the garrison. It surrendered before the tower could be used. It is worth adding that Henry's interest in such things was so acute that, although there was no longer any need for it, he afterwards carried out experiments which proved the tower to be excellent.

At first, Henry would not listen to terms. This market had cost him more time, trouble, and lives than any other town, and he probably felt cheated by its surrender at the moment when he felt quite certain of winning. For seven months he had lain before Meaux, and that was too long a time while there was so much else for him to do in France, the Dauphin being still at large.

His first determination was to refuse to negotiate, but he relented and an agreement was signed on

May 2, according to which the garrison was to
surrender by the 10th, all their prisoners were
to be freed, and while most of the garrison were
spared there was a long list of names of those who
must place themselves under his justice. Amongst
these it is curious to discover an unnamed horn-
blower. What this horn-blower had done to deserve
being particularly noticed we shall never discover,
but it must have been some act insulting to Henry's
dignity, some impertinent noise of the horn similar
to that awful medieval insult, *Tprhurt! Tprhurt!* the
frightful meaning of which no longer affects us.
We can better appreciate Henry's anger against
those men who took an ass on to the walls and who
thrashed it until it brayed, shouting meanwhile
for the English to come and rescue their King,
as he was crying for help.

These bursts of rage on the part of Henry for
acts of petty horseplay seem rather unnecessary and
degrading. But we cannot tell the circumstances
that had caused to exasperate him. And a King
must hedge himself in with divinity, he must be
sacred, and must never lower the dignity of the
crown if he would earn respect. Those stupid
soldiers had lowered Henry's dignity, they had
made a mock of him. This was bad for discipline,
and if he let such acts pass his own men would
begin to doubt his majestic godliness.

Amongst many others, the horn-blower was beheaded, but it is not certain what justice fell upon
the ass-beaters. The Bastard of Vaurus was hanged
on his own tree.

# CHAPTER TWENTY-ONE

## *The End*

THE fall of Meaux brought little material advantage, but it had a strong moral effect. Also, Henry had now in his hands many of the Dauphin's most efficient captains, who had promised to surrender all nearby castles and fortresses in their power, and these fell to Henry's bag. Other large towns gave in without an attempt at defiance, and before the end of June 1422, Henry controlled vast territories and had nothing to fear from the Dauphin northeast of Paris. He now owned Normandy, Picardy in most part, the Isle of France, northern Champagne (more territory here was soon won by Salisbury and Suffolk), and much of Maine and Orléannais.

But despite the success of the campaign, Henry's men were in bad need of rest, and Henry himself, although he did not know it fully, was sorely stricken.

While lying before Meaux one piece of news had struck great joy in his heart. At 4 p.m. on St. Nicholas's Day—what better day for children?—December 6, 1421, Queen Katherine gave birth to a son in Windsor Castle.

Henry, we are told, was delighted by the news, which was natural enough, but he merely said that Katherine must instantly hear a Mass of the Trinity and offer the child to God.

In later years the legend took shape that Henry

had turned to Lord Fitzhugh and had said dolefully: "I, Henry, born at Monmouth, shall small
time reign and much get, and Henry born at
Windsor shall long reign and all lose; but as God
wills so be it."
This is a definite sixteenth-century invention.

While fighting, Henry never dropped the lines of
diplomacy. His efforts rarely attained anything,
he was always frustrated, but his intentions were
of the soundest. With Genoa he had made a treaty
that fell to pieces, although not through his fault;
he had corresponded with the Scots for the return
of their King, but the regent there, of course,
wanted no King in the country; he had tried to
make Sigismund keep his promises and bring help,
but Sigismund was too penniless and too busy
hunting heretics in Bohemia to do anything.
Always misfortunes seemed to dog Henry's diplomacy, except in Spain, where a lucky civil war
intervened to save him from the Castilian fleet.

It must also be recognised that, although prim-
arily a soldier, Henry always desired peace. If he
could win by a treaty he was eager to sign one; and
he was now, it appears, making efforts to come to
terms with the Dauphin. His conquered countries
he ruled most justly, never interfering with their
laws and giving official positions to the natives—
although naturally keeping the more important
posts in the hands of the English.

His dream undoubtedly was for a united western
empire, and it stretched even beyond this, reaching
to the very walls of Jerusalem. During the siege of
Melun, he and Philip had clasped hands on the
oath to recover Jerusalem together when France

became quiet. That this was no idle dream but a definite ambition we discover by the fact that, in the following year, Henry sent a Burgundian knight, Philip's chamberlain, Sir Gilbert de Lannoy, to reconnoitre the east. Sir Gilbert travelled to Alexandria through Syria, round the eastern coast of the Mediterranean, and ended at Constantinople; but he returned too late with his report, which still exists—Henry was dead

Katherine had come to France, and Henry hastened to join her at Bois de Vincennes. The Prince was not with her, having been left in England.

On May 30 the King and Queen of England entered Paris, Charles and Isabel arriving on the same day. After hearing Mass at Notre-Dame, Henry lodged at the Louvre, Charles at the Hôtel St. Pol, the French again making sad comparisons between the respective states kept by both Kings. They seemed to do little else but make comparisons, for none of them troubled to wait on the unfortunate Charles.

On June 2 and 3, Henry and Katherine were escorted to the Hôtel de Nesle to see *The Mystery of the Life of St. George* produced by some Paris citizens; and on June 11 they left for St. Denis on their way to Compiègne, which was due to capitulate within a few days. With Charles and Isabel they continued to Senlis, when Henry was hurriedly recalled to Paris. A Dauphinist plot had been discovered: an armourer, his wife, and a baker had been arrested for intriguing to surrender Paris to the Dauphin, and the woman confessed. It was not a serious matter, and after drowning the woman and a few others, Henry returned to Senlis, and from there travelled to Compiègne.

Henry was a sick man, but he refused to believe it. Rumour said that he had left Paris because of the small-pox raging there; that may be true, but it is also very likely that he left to escape to the country where he perhaps hoped to recover in the fresh air after a particularly hot summer.

It is impossible to be definite about Henry's illness, but it appears that he suffered badly from dysentery. The first time we discover that there is anything the matter with him is when an English physician was summoned during the siege of Meaux. I feel that his illness must have been dysentery, all descriptions point to this. The most direct statement comes from Waurin, who was in the Burgundian army. "I have since been truly informed," he writes, " concerning the principal disease by which the said King was brought to his death, namely, that it was by an inflammation which seized him in the fundament, and which is called the Disease of St. Antony." The only complication here is that the disease called St. Anthony's Fire was ergotism, the ghastly illness from which Henry's father died. It has long been believed that St. Anthony's Fire was a form of erysipelas, but Dr. Nelson tells me that this is impossible. There are no signs of dry gangrene in Henry's illness, and Waurin must have got his medical terms mixed. Walsingham states, however, that the physicians dared not administer internal medicines. This suggests internal ulcers, but medieval medicines were such corrosive things that they would probably be fatal to any one suffering badly from dysentery.

*334*

Whatever the disease may have been that struck so suddenly at King Henry, it was most painful. But he refused to consider it, he refused to believe that his iron will could not control his own body; and he behaved with his usual indifferent air. Nevertheless, he summoned another physician from England, one John Swanwyth, M.B., and the rumour spread that he was suffering from small-pox.

His presence was needed in the field, and he dragged his stubborn body to obey his spirit. The Dauphinists were laying siege to Cosne and he was determined to lead the relief forces. With great courage he set out, taking his last farewell of Katherine.

He was unable to sit a horse and had to lie in a horse-litter, like a woman. "Forgetful of his illness, but mindful of his compact with the Duke of Burgundy," he struggled on until his tormented body refused to carry him further. Reluctantly he had to place the English command in the hands of his brother John, and himself remained at Corbeil for about a fortnight while the Anglo-Burgundian forces relieved Cosne—the Dauphin, as usual, running away at the first approach of the enemy.

Every day Henry grew worse, and at last he was taken mournfully back to Bois de Vincennes, being rowed down the Seine, for greater comfort, as far as Charenton.

His pride was hurt by the idea of having to lie like this in a boat, and he was determined that his body would not degrade his spirit. When he landed, he called for his horse, and mounted. He sat astride for a few paces, but the pain was unbearable, jarring all his body, and he had to be lifted down and placed once more in a litter across a horse's back.

On about August 9, King Henry V came back to Vincennes, and "there, alas! he entered his bed of pain."

Even on his bed, racked with physical agony, Henry thought of nothing but his soul and his life-work. At last, on August 30, he knew that he was doomed and he called to him Bedford, Exeter, Warwick and others whom he loved. He said that he knew that he was soon to die and that if he had wronged any man—which he doubted—he asked forgiveness, and he thanked those present and all his comrades for their brave service, regretting that he could not repay them now as he had wished.

They must continue the war, he said, until the whole of France submitted to the Treaty of Troyes, adding that he had not invaded the country for worldly purposes but to regain what was his, and this France was his as many saintly men had assured him. Then he particularised the tasks he wished his friends to undertake: his brother John was to command Normandy until Prince Henry was of age, and he was to be regent of France unless Philip desired the title. With forethought, Henry distrusted his brother Humphrey and gave him as little power as by justice he might: Humphrey was to be protector of England with a council to guide him, but John presumably was to be above him, the final arbiter, while Warwick, Humphrey, and Hungerford were to have charge of the little prince who was so soon to be their King. There must be no quarrel ever with Burgundy, he impressed upon them, and the Duke of Orléans was

*336*

to be kept a close prisoner. Then he showed them his will.

He talked for a while with Hugh de Lannoy, brother of that Gilbert who had been sent to the East. We do not know what it was he said, but is it too long a shot to suggest that now, in his last moments, his thoughts winged regretfully to that dream of his of the building of Jerusalem's walls?

Turning to the physicians he asked how long he had to live, but they evaded the question, saying that "it was still in the power of God to restore him to health." Henry was not the type of man on whom to play such quibbling games. He sternly repeated his question, demanding the truth. Then after a consultation together, one of his physicians told him, saying, "Sire, think upon your case, for it seems to us that except by the favour of God, we judge not that you can survive two hours."

With his usual composure, Henry gave no sign that the death-sentence had in any way affected him. He called his confessor to him, with other religious of his household, and asked them to recite the seven Penitential Psalms.

When they had reached the verse, "Benigne fac ex benevolentia tua Sioni, aedifica muros Hierusalem," "O, be favourable and gracious unto Sion: build thou the walls of Jerusalem," Henry motioned to them to pause, and said:

"Good Lord, Thou knowest that mine intent hath been, and yet is, if I might live, to re-edify the walls of Jerusalem."

After this cry—the only cry of remorse or pity that escaped him—he let the ecclesiastics continue, and afterwards received the last communion and extreme unction.

Y

Only once again did he speak. He gave one cry, one cry of fierce horror, as of a man battling against invisible enemies that taunted him; as if on this last moment, he saw behind him, false acts, cruel acts, acts that damned him for ever. As death was on him, he shouted suddenly:

"Thou liest! Thou liest! My portion is with the Lord Jesus!" and holding firmly on the crucifix, he recited in a strong voice: "In manus tuas, Domine, ipsum terminum redemisti . . ."

Then with a weak gesture, he died quietly, a little after two o'clock on the morning of Monday, August 31, 1422.

King Henry was dead, that great conqueror, dead at the age of thirty-four.

His body was dismembered and the flesh boiled from the bones, both flesh and bones being placed in a casket, with spices; and what remained over was buried in the churchyard of St. Maur-des-Fossés.

The coffin, after resting for a night in the quire of St. Denis, was placed in a cart drawn by four great horses. On top of the coffin rested an effigy moulded from boiled leather, over life-size, wearing royal robes. This effigy lay on a bed, its face turned to heaven, with a most precious gold crown on its head; in its right hand it held the sceptre, in its left a golden globe. The bed was draped with red silk beaten with gold; and when passing through large towns a silken canopy was raised, as is done over the body of Jesus Christ on Corpus Christi Day, says Monstrelet the chronicler.

Thus King Henry returned to England.

The Archbishop of Canterbury was waiting at Dover when the fleet drew in. No Barons of the Cinque Ports leaped joyously into the sea, the coffin was carried sadly to the shore.

There was mourning all the long way to London; and the mayor and aldermen and citizens were waiting on Blackheath, not dressed in merry clothes this time but all of them in black.

The clergy were at St. Thomas Waterlng, and with the citizens followed the funeral cart to St. Paul's. The coffin was exactly as it had been in France, with figure of boiled leather above. A dirge was sung at St. Paul's, and in the morning a requiem Mass.

On the afternoon of November 6, the procession wound its way downhill to Westminster, still with the same funeral cart. A page rode upon each horse, which was led by a groom of the stable in mourning habit with a hood drawn over his face. A knight rode ahead, upholding a banner bearing the King's arms; and before him rode the heralds wearing the King's coat-armour, their horses trapped in black. And in front of the heralds rode knights and earls.

The next day King Henry was buried in the abbey church, in the chapel of St. Edward, many relics having to be moved to make way for him. He lay between the shrine of the Confessor and the Chapel of the Virgin, his tomb being built of Caen stone and Purbeck marble. Queen Katherine, at great expense, raised a monument to her husband, a monument too rich to last, for the head was of solid silver and the body of oak plated with silver-gilt. Both head and sheathing have been stolen, and if Katherine had spent less money and had built a simple alabaster monument, King Henry's effigy might still be lying entire.

Over the tomb rose the great chantry-chapel formed like the letter H. This had been designed by Henry himself and careful instructions had been given in the will he made before leaving Southampton in 1415. It took eight years to erect.

And there King Henry now lies under his headless effigy. Close to him are a saddle, a helmet and a shield still to be seen, which are accounted the harness he wore at Agincourt. But as the helm is a tilting one this is not possible, and they are probably but a part of the funeral equipment, never having even been seen by Henry.

He lies in the great chantry which himself had planned—a pious man, a brave soldier and a just King. Gazing on that broken tomb, chipped, defaced, one can but whisper the lines of Drayton:

*"Oh, when shall English men*
*With such acts fill a pen,*
*Or England breed again*
*Such a King Harry?"*

# EPILOGUE

It is a sad task that remains to us, but we will be very brief. The book would not be finished, however, unless some mention, even the smallest, was made to events after King Henry's death.

Slowly the great conquests dribbled away, slowly the stubborn English were pushed out of France. They held on to the last moment, for the English do not give in easily. As Anatole France remarks in his *Jeanne d'Arc*, "The wonder is not that the English were driven out of France, but that they were driven out so slowly."

The honours for this great achievement must go to John Duke of Bedford, a worthy brother of King Henry, a brave soldier and a subtle politician; some of the shame of our defeat—if shame it can be called—must rest upon the shoulders of Humphrey Duke of Gloucester, the good Duke Humphrey of later ages.

It is more than possible that Henry V and Philip of Burgundy were not close friends towards the end of the campaign. It is rather curious that Philip took no part in Henry's funeral. Nevertheless, in the capable hands of Bedford the alliance held good for many years, although that petulant Duke Humphrey did everything he could to damage it by his personal ambitions.

Jacqueline of Hainault, as we have seen, fled from her husband, the Duke of Brabant, and reached England. As Brabant was Philip's cousin, this threatened a rupture, but Henry calmed

Philip somehow and Jacqueline remained in England. Then Gloucester married her, not for love—he was quick enough to desert her afterwards—but for lust of her property. Already this ambitious duke had been a nuisance to the council, continually trying to steal the power from his brother; now, after his marriage, he decided to invade Hainault and capture his wife's inheritance. Outraged at this, Philip challenged the duke to meet him in single combat, and Gloucester agreed. The unfortunate Bedford strove to bring peace, but it was a difficult task, for Philip was looking forward to the combat and had gone into training; but at last, at a court of chivalry held in Paris, Bedford managed to have the joust forbidden. Then he had to rush back to England because Gloucester was starting a minor revolution in London against the Bishop of Winchester.

The tale continues depressingly: Gloucester intrigues, Bedford tries to calm things afterwards. . . .

King Charles VI had died when King Henry's funeral train was on its way to England, and the Dauphin was now Charles VII. The Anglo-Burgundians therefore had behind them no longer the moral support of royalty's sanction; they were fighting against the King of France.

Yet their successes continued; Bedford was a splendid soldier with much of his great brother's thoroughness and energy. By 1429, during the siege of Orléans, it seemed that the Dauphin, now Charles VII, was doomed, and the question was actually debated whether he should fly to Spain or to Scotland.

It is at this point that Jeanne Darc appears,

whom we have rebaptized as Joan of Arc. Her
story has been retold too often for me to repeat it
here even in the sparsest outline. It is an astound-
ing tale, fascinating by its mystery, by the mystery
of her strange appearance and of the magnetic
hold she had over the troops. By this hold, this
inspiration, she welded the scattered exhausted
French together and flung them victoriously against
the English. She did not often fight herself, she
knew little of actual soldiering; it was her genius,
that mystery which is at the core of all vital beings,
which sent her on from conquest to conquest.

Even with the burning of Joan at Rouen, the inspiration did not fade; but England was definitely
defeated when Philip broke his alliance. It was inevitable that he should break some time. The first
rage because of his father's murder had long since
thinned out into memory, and he must for years
have been awaiting the opportunity of joining
Charles. After he too was ranged against England,
we had no hope; and the council at home was
continually agitated and made mistrustful by
Gloucester's selfish intrigues.

Slowly, inevitably, England was pushed out of
France. By 1453 only Calais remained to us out of
the vast tracts which Henry had won.

I feel that we must not regret this; we should be
thankful. The conquest had been magnificent,
and our defeat was magnificent. Even if Henry had
lived, surely he must have surrendered half his
dream? He would probably have remained satisfied with Normandy, Maine, Anjou and the Isle
of France. France would then have been split
into three—French, English, Burgundian—and our

slice would have been too expensive to hold. Yet would Henry have remained satisfied with merely a part of France? Logically, it seems to us now, he would have been forced to accept this; yet I cannot imagine that stern arrogant King accepting anything less than his dream demanded. He would have died for the sake of that dream and thought it worth the dying.

But we must not blur a man's achievements by hypotheses. What Henry performed in his brief life was truly superb. Tirelessly, he fought in the open and intrigued at the council-table. No task was too menial for him to attend, no act of his was dictated by personal affection or hatred; he was always just save when his dignity was hurt. Immediately when thinking of Henry one thinks also of Alexander, and Plutarch could have made a fascinating comparison between the two; but Henry was greater than Alexander—perhaps not as a soldier but most certainly as a man.

When playing the game of *If*, there is one thought that always comes to me—If Henry V had not married Katherine of Valois.

This marriage, presumably a love-match, eventually lost the throne for Henry's own son, and it ushered in the Tudor dynasty, thereby destroying the last branch of the Plantagenet Kings with Richard III. Having the mad blood of Charles VI through the mother's veins, Henry VI, whom Katherine bore that day at Windsor, was not sane. He took after his grandfather not his father. He became the tool for his Queen's ambitions and she drew upon herself, and thus upon him, the hatred and vengeance of all England.

And after Henry V's death, Katherine secretly married—or it seems that she married, she at least had a liaison with and children by—a Welsh esquire called Owen Tudor. From this union came the branch of Kings who killed all trace of the Plantagenets.

When considering this, the tragedy that tore the realm from the Plantagenets, I can find little pity for Katherine in my heart. She did not know what she was doing when she laid herself under the embrace of Tudor, but that thoughtless liaison of hers is for me one of the tragedies of English history. The Tudors became great Kings and Queens, splendid statesmen, but they did not have the kindliness and the love of justice possessed by most of the Plantagenets, who were the true Englishmen.

Katherine's life is not an interesting one. She spent her childhood and youth in poverty with a lunatic father and a debauched mother; she spent her last days in virtual imprisonment with a lunatic son on the throne and a husband in the Tower. There is nothing strong or beautiful in her character. She seems to have been lovely to gaze upon but little else. She died in 1437, and was buried in the Lady Chapel at Westminster.

Henry VII, her grandson, had such small reverence for the bones of the Queen who placed him near the throne, that he moved them, so that he could build the chapel which now bears his name. Her corpse, wrapped carelessly in lead, lay for hundreds of years in a coarse wooden chest, and people could stare upon the features of a Queen of England. They could do more than merely stare. Pepys tells us that on a visit to Westminster Abbey he was shown her body by particular favour, "and I had the upper part of her body in my hands and I did kiss her mouth, reflecting upon that I did kiss a Queen, and that this was my birthday, thirty-six years old that I did first kiss a Queen."

The impious lips of Sam Pepys touch the mouth that King Henry had pressed with his. But one's disgust is not so strong when one recalls that those same lips, when living and warm, had pouted for the kisses of one Owen Tudor, a lowly Welsh esquire.

I will not finalise with a summary of Henry's character after the fashion of old biographies. If I have not revealed him to you already, further words would be useless. That he was a magnificent soldier nobody can doubt. As the perfect medieval hero, born perhaps out of his time, he remains one of England's greatest Kings, so great indeed that I can think of none but Henry II and Edward I worthy to stand beside him—unless we include William the Conqueror amongst our rulers.

He was just, noble and courageous; he had all virtues and no sins. . . . Again, I revert to Drayton. To express my feelings I can find no words to equal the words he spoke hundreds of years ago:

*"Oh, when shall we breed again*
*Such a King Harry?"*

# APPENDICES
# AND  ACKNOWLEDGEMENTS

# APPENDIX I

## CHILDREN OF KING HENRY IV AND MARY DE BOHUN

1. KING HENRY V. Born September 16, 130) died August 31, 1422.
2. THOMAS, Duke of Clarence. Born 1388; killed at Baugé, March 22, 1421.
3. JOHN, Duke of Bedford. Born 1389; died September 15, 1435.
4. HUMPHREY, Duke of Gloucester. Born 1390–1; died February 23, 1447. It is sometimes asserted that he was murdered at the command of his political enemy William de la Pole, Duke of Suffolk. There seems little actual proof of this beyond the suspicious coincidence that Gloucester died within a few days of being arrested by Suffolk, and while in his power. He very likely died of apoplexy.
5. BLANCHE. Born 1392. Married the "Red Duke" Ludwig of Bavaria. Died May 22, 1409.
6. PHILIPPA. Born (?) 1393. Married Eric IX of Denmark, October 26, 1406; died January 5, 1430.

---

By his second wife, Joan of Navarre, daughter of Charles the Bad, and widow of John, Duke of Brittany, King Henry IV had no issue. Joan died, July 9, 1437.

# APPENDIX II. HENRY V'S CLAIM TO THE THRONE OF FRANCE

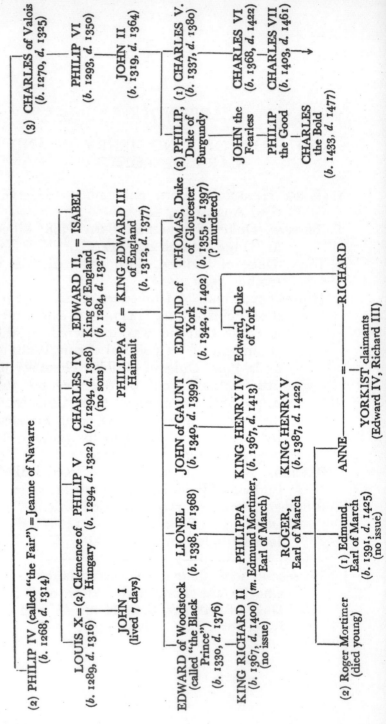

# APPENDIX IV

## THE COLOUR OF THE FIFTEENTH CENTURY

I FEEL that the background against which Henry lived should be sketched in, at least roughly. In so small a space as this I necessarily cannot go into details, but might broadly paint a backcloth of the "colour" of this period, of its essentials, its place in history.

The fifteenth century was the last of the Middle Ages and the birth of the Renascence. In the Burgundian court, under the patronage of Philip the Good and Charles the Bold, the great painters like van Eyck—Hubert, it appears, was a myth: there was only Jan—were to give us a school of genius unsurpassed by the Italians of the coming era. Yet even the Italians—although their women are flushed, like Botticelli's Venus, with the self-consciousness of the Renascence—retain a little of the proud earthliness of the medieval days. In Botticelli's paintings goddesses are still women—they are girls not yet sure whether they should disclose their full nakedness, for they know only too painfully that they are naked; the garments given them by Christianity still cling to their bodies, and they feel that the painter is duping them with his sweet lies of feminine divinity. There is something very beautiful in these soft fragile creatures, so eager to face the light, so bashful lest the light bruise or destroy their childlike souls.

The fifteenth century had not this self-consciousness. The women here are all mothers or prospective mothers, human and unafraid. The charming wife in Jan van Eyck's " Jean Arnolfini and Jeanne Cenani"—as the catalogue titles it, for it now appears that this is a self-portrait—in London's National Gallery stands with her head bowed prettily under the lace head-dress, the mistress of the magnificent bed in the background, of the round mirror and the tiny slippers; this is her home and the painter is limning it for her. Beyond that she has little knowledge, and cares for none. The rich things of earth are sufficient for her, proud little wife. She wears the great padded stomach of the period—that symbol of teeming life, of gigantic fecundity, of humanity's pride in its miraculous powers of gestation.

I love the fifteenth century as I can love no other period, and these great padded stomachs, to me, symbolise that period. The women were all mothers, the men were merchants or warriors—builders or destroyers. How tragic it seems to us who can see ahead the dawn of the Renascence! Yet they had their problems in those days. The people felt the quickening of wings below the skyline and clung tenaciously to what they held; they fought to remain medieval. And Henry was dominated by this desire; he wanted retrogression, not progress; all the world wanted retrogression. The merchant was pushing the workers back, the Church was burning heretics, the lords were trying to retain the already doomed feudal system. It is the last, most splendid flowering. In architecture, the human spiralling Gothic, that blossoming tree, had developed into the Perpendicular with its lacy stonework. This has a beauty all its own, but to my mind it lacks the glory of pure Gothic.

In my remarks on Henry's return from Agincourt I spoke of the costumes, of the women's habit of shaving all hair from the face (sometimes they left thin eyebrows in the fashion of modern film-stars), but a word might be given on the men's armour. Yet my words are unnecessary because of the illustrations in this book: the two plates from the *Warwick Pageant* will bring the scene vividly to you, far more vividly than could a list of technical terms.

This century has often been damned as one of literary dearth. Even so sensitive a critic as Miss Rose Macaulay can write that "the fifteenth century lay on poetry like a stiff blanket." This is entirely unfair, and the illusion is created because Chaucer flourished in the fourteenth century and his genius tends to dim his followers. I make no strong plea for Lydgate, Hawes, Hoccleve, etc., although they give me great pleasure, but how can the ballad-writers and the lyric-writers be ignored? I would bargain much of the Renascence, and a great deal of Miss Macaulay's Milton, for that glorious *Nut-Brown Maid,* not to speak of the *Robin Hood* ballads. And what of Malory's *Morte Darthur?* Surely that is one of the great prose-works of the world, and in its romantic splendour reaching close to poetry? Scotland was creating masterpieces of lyric-verse. In France, Villon must not be forgotten. And Froissart is not so very far back; he did not die until after 1404. In Froissart, there is colour and joy, there is a glint of poetical magic that cannot be resisted. No, no, this was no dead era, no blanketed killing of poetry. You must remember that Englishmen were still dwarfed by Chaucer, they were still imitating him, trying to break away, trying to use the splendour he threw them with such largesse. The English tongue was being discovered, it was not time yet for Surrey and Wyatt to appear with their exquisite rhythms.

It was the dim light of dawn, the awakening. Can we blame the people for clinging with such tenacity to a past that was falling from their hands? Are we not to-day doing exactly what they were doing in the fifteenth century, turning our backs to a dawn that as yet we do not understand but which frightens us?

# ACKNOWLEDGEMENTS

As this book is intended for the general reader only, it would be unnecessary for me to list here the contemporary chronicles and papers, the parliamentary, the patent and foreign rolls, etc., to which I referred in writing this chronicle. Such a list would only be tedious to the reader and unnecessary for any scholar who might chance on these pages. If a detailed list should be required I refer you to the late C. L. Kingsford's excellent volume, *Historical Literature in the Fifteenth Century* (Oxford, 1913), where contemporary sources are thoroughly dealt with. For the same reason, I modernised the spelling throughout and did not bother with footnotes. It is a queer truth that footnotes terrify the average reader, and I would like only to state here that, to my knowledge, this chronicle is exact and I have distorted nothing.

It would be vile ingratitude if I did not speak a little of those modern works that have been invaluable. And first amongst these must stand—

(1) *The Reign of Henry V*, by James Hamilton Wylie and William Templeton Waugh (Cambridge University Press, 3 vols., 1914–1929). Dr. Wylie, to my mind, is the greatest of English historians, and his references are exhaustive. After completing the first volume, Dr. Wylie by terrible misfortune did not live to see the second volume through the press or to complete the third. Here we were indeed lucky to have Professor Waugh to come to the rescue and finish the life in a manner worthy

of Dr. Wylie himself. Of these three volumes it is literally impossible to speak too highly, and any reader who has been interested enough by my chronicle should consult them if he wishes a detailed knowledge of Henry's reign.

(2) *A History of England under Henry the Fourth*, by James Hamilton Wylie (Longmans, 4 vols., 1884–1898). This is almost equal to Dr. Wylie's *Henry V*, with magnificent references. If only Dr. Wylie had been immortal and could have covered all English history in such a style!

(3) *Henry V. The Typical Medieval Hero*, by Charles Lethbridge Kingsford ("Heroes of the Nations" Series, G. P. Putnam's Sons, 1901). A splendid little volume by one of the finest historians of the fifteenth century. Mr. Kingsford's article in *The Dictionary of National Biography* (1885), vol. xxvi., is also, in its brief way, excellent.

(4) *Henry V*, by R. B. Mowat ("Kings and Queens of England" Series, Constable, 1919), covers the ground perfectly.

(5) *Henry the Fifth*, by the Rev. A. J. Church ("English Men of Action" Series, Macmillan, 1891), is the least interesting of all, being written with a strong Protestant bias.

(6) *The History of the Reign of Henry the Fifth*, by T. Goodwin, 1704, is useful even if it is rather out-of-date. Its references are most valuable.

(7) *Henry of Monmouth*, by J. Endell Tyler (R. Bentley, 2 vols., 1838), is still interesting for Henry's early life.

(8) For books of particular episodes, N. H. Nicolas's *History of the Battle of Agincourt* (2 vols., 1832) is excellent; and for Agincourt reference should also be made to the *English Historical Review*,

vol. x., for E. M. Lloyd's "The Herse of Archers at Crécy"; also to vol. xxv., 134–5.

(9) *The Council of Constance to the Death of John Hus*, by J. H. Wylie (Longmans, 1900); also Dr. Wylie's essay on "Notes on the Agincourt Roll" in *Transactions of the Royal Historical Society*, ser. iii., vol v., 1911, although the information here was incorporated into his *Henry V*.

When speaking of the *Royal Historical Society Transactions*, I must mention—

(10) *The Story of Prince Henry and Judge Gascoigne*, by F. Solly Flood, new series, vol. iii.

(11) *Prince Henry of Monmouth—His Letters and Dispatches during the War in Wales*, by F. Solly Flood, new ser., vol. iv.

(12) *The Two Sir John Falstolfs*, by L. W. Vernon Harcourt, 3rd ser., vol. iv.

Other periodicals—

(13) *The Funeral, Monument, and Chantry Chapel of King Henry the Fifth*, by W. H. St. John Hope, *Archæologia*, 2nd ser., vol. xv.; vol. lxv. full series.

Books of particularised interest—

(14) *Humphrey, Duke of Gloucester*, by Kenneth H. Vickers (Constable, 1907), and also Mr. Vickers' *England in the Later Middle Ages*, vol. iii. of *A History of England*, ed. by Charles Oman (Methuen, 1913).

(15) *John of Gaunt*, by Sydney Armitage-Smith (Constable, 1904).

(16) *Owen Glyn Dŵr*, by J. D. Griffith Davies (Scholartis, 1934), is a handy little volume for those who cannot obtain Professor J. E. Lloyd's great work.

Works of general interest—

(17) *Lancaster and York*, by Sir James H. Ramsay (Oxford, vol. i., 1892.)

(18) *The Genesis of Lancaster*, by Sir James H. Ramsay (Oxford, vol. ii., 1913).

(19) *Political History of England*: vol. iv., *The History of England from the Accession of Richard II to the Death of Richard III*, by C. Oman (Longmans, 1906).

These books have by no means covered my complete debt, but if I compiled a full list I would not be finished for days. These at least are the ones to whom I owe the greatest debt.

After mentioning the books that have helped me greatly, I must not forget the libraries and museums—in particular, the British Museum (both reading and manuscript rooms), the Guildhall and the London Library. It would be most ungracious of me if I did not add the name of Mr. G. E. Manwaring, of the London Library, who helped me again and again with his deep historical knowledge.

For reading through the proofs—although any inaccuracies are entirely mine—and for numerous valuable suggestions, with real gratitude I thank Mr. Aymer Vallance, F.S.A., Dr. Philip Nelson, F.S.A., Mr. Philip Owens and Mr. J. D. Griffith Davies.

# INDEX

# INDEX

ABBEVILLE (Somme), 176
Abbot's Palace (Westminster), 113
Aberystwyth, 86, 93
Adams, Henry, author, 222
Agincourt, 13, 87, 185–96, 202, 204, 206, 207, 222, 226, 303, 309, 313, 340, 359
Ailly, Pierre d', Bishop of Cambrai, 248
Airaines (Somme), 178
Albany, Murdach, Duke of, 206
Albany, Robert, Duke of, brother of Robert III, father of preceding, 206
Albemarle, Duke of. *See* York, Edward, Duke of
Albret, Charles, Sire d', Constable of France, 182, 191
Alençon (Orne), 235
Alençon, Jean, Duke of, 177, 182
Alençon, Bastard of, 240, 241
Alexander the Great, 115, 344
Alexander V, Pope, 209
Alexandria, 333
Altrée, river, 315
Amiens (Somme), 182
Angers (Maine-et-Loire), 314
Angoumois, 151
Anjou, 237, 272, 276, 317, 343
Anjou, Louis, Duke of, 55, 227
Anne of Bohemia, Queen of Richard II, 16, 20, 24, 60, 146–8
*Antiquaries' Journal*, 90

Antiquaries, Society of (London), 148
Aquitaine, 51, 56, 108, 151, 276
Arc, Joan of. *See* Joan of Arc
*Archæologia*, 146, 353. *See* Acknowledgements
Argentan (Orne), 235
Armagnac, Bernard, Count of, Constable of France, 105, 207, 212, 214–5, 216, 220, 221, 227, 236, 237, 252, 285
Arques (Seine-Inf.), 176
Arras (Pas-de-Calais), 287
Arundel, Richard FitzAlan, Earl of, 16, 23, 24, 26, 27–8, 29, 42, 54, 63
Arundel, Thomas, Archbishop of Canterbury, 43, 46, 94–5, 99–100, 101–2, 103, 106, 109, 112, 131, 133, 135, 136, 137–40, 143, 148, 168
Arundel, Thomas, Earl of, son of Richard above, 42, 68, 106, 107, 131, 173
Auvillars (Calvados), 229
Avignon, 97, 208
Azincourt. *See* Agincourt

BADBY, JOHN, 101–3, 134, 137, 139, 148
Bagot, Sir William, 54
Baltic, the, 34
Bapaume (Pas-de-Calais), 93
Bar, Edouard, Duke of, 177, 182

# INDEX

# INDEX

Herefordshire, 312
Hertfordshire, 60
Hoccleve, Thomas, poet, 103, 116, 127, 359
Holinshed, Raphael, chronicler, 119
Holland, Jacqueline of, 207, 220, 227, 272, 319, 341–2
Holland, John. *See* Duke of Exeter
Holland, William, Count of, 207, 215–6, 220, 221, 222, 227
Holy Trinity, abbey (Caen), 230, 231
Homildon Hill, 69, 70
Honfleur, 218, 272
Hungary, King of, 35
Hungerford, Sir Walter, 186, 328, 336
Huntingdon, John Holland I, Earl of, previously Duke of Exeter, 41, 53, 54, 55, 59, 104
Huntingdon, John Holland II, Earl of, son of the preceding, 225, 232, 256, 279, 280, 281, 315, 316, 317
Hus, John, 96, 210, 211

ILE BELLE (Seine), 273
Ile de France, 331, 343
Ile St. Jean (Orne), 229, 233
Ingles, Harry, 233
Innocent IV, Pope, 248
Innocent VII, Pope, 208
Ireland, 37, 38, 39, 40, 70, 94, 132
Isabel of Bavaria, Queen of Charles VI, 92, 227, 236, 252–3, 260, 275, 278, 281, 286, 288, 289, 291, 296, 301, 305, 333, 355
Isabel of France, Queen of Edward II, 150

Isabel of France, Queen of Richard II, 20, 55, 58, 65, 78, 276
Isle Adam, Jean de Villiers, Lord of l', 252, 280–1, 304
Ivry (Eure), 272

JAMES I, King of Scotland, son of Robert III, 68, 91, 300, 302, 303, 306, 311, 321
*Jeanne D'Arc*, 341
Jersey, 242
Jerusalem, 33, 35, 151, 295, 332, 337
Jerusalem Chamber (Westminster), 113
Joan of Arc, 152, 342–3
Joan of Navarre, Queen of Henry IV, 34, 79, 156, 204, 307–8, 349, 353
Joan II, Queen of Naples, 271–2
Joan Holland, Duchess of Brittany, 79
Joan, Henry V's nurse. *See* Waryn, Joan
John, King of France, 79, 150, 151, 200, 276
John, Dauphin of France, son of Charles VI, 207, 220, 221, 227, 236
John I, King of Portugal, 256
John IV, Duke of Brittany, 34, 79, 349
John V, Duke of Brittany, son of preceding, 105, 235, 237, 272, 307
John the Fearless, Duke of Burgundy. *See* Burgundy, John, Duke of
John XXIII, Pope, 208, 209, 211
Jourdain, Jean, 254

KATHERINE OF FRANCE, daughter of Charles VI,

*369*

# INDEX

# INDEX

# INDEX

**375**

# INDEX